Bernard Le Bargy lives in Norfolk. A career in Personnel Management culminated in his final role: Personnel Director of a large engineering company.

Sharing a passion for travel with his wife, Rosemary, they have spent their retirement roaming the World, in the past fifteen years visiting well over one hundred countries, including all those in Central and South America.

Jubilado is Bernard's second book. *Back to the Bush*, published in 2008, tells of a visit to Botswana, during which he recalls his time as a volunteer worker in that country in the 1960s.

Jubilado

RETIRED COUPLE TRAVEL
THROUGH LATIN AMERICA

Bernard Le Bargy

Matador
9 Priory Business Park,
Wistow Road, Kibworth Beauchamp,
Leicestershire. LE8 0RX
Tel: 0116 279 2299
Email: books@troubador.co.uk
Web: www.troubador.co.uk/matador
Twitter: @matadorbooks

ISBN 978 1800464 261

British Library Cataloguing in Publication Data.
A catalogue record for this book is available from the British Library.

Printed and bound in the UK by TJ Books Limited, Padstow, Cornwall
Typeset in 11pt Sabon MT by Troubador Publishing Ltd, Leicester, UK

Matador is an imprint of Troubador Publishing Ltd

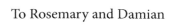

To Rosemary and Damian

Contents

Acknowledgements

In my book, I pay tribute to the many guides who have aided us on our travels. Ramiro in Ecuador, Gustavo in Colombia, Benjamin in El Salvador, Harry in Nicaragua and many more. Each one has given us a personal insight into the culture and history of their country. They have come quite literally in different shapes and sizes, all with their personal quirks, ideas and interests, but without them, our experiences would have been much diminished.

Closer to home, thanks go to our various Spanish teachers, particularly Gemma in Colchester and Rosa in Ipswich, for their efforts to teach two older novice language students, in my case with limited success. Thankfully, Rosemary proving a more adept learner.

As ever, thanks to my wife, Rosemary, who has shared all the events related in the book, for her support and companionship during both the inevitable highs and lows we experienced along the way. Particularly her patience over my failed attempts at conjugating verbs in Spanish.

Thanks also to my son, Damian, for the design of the book cover.

Travelling as a student rather than an expert, I have tried to reflect some of what I have learned on my travels but, as the pupil rather than the teacher, I acknowledge that on occasion some facts in my book may be incorrect. Where any factual errors occur, my sincere apologies. Equally, the opinions expressed are entirely mine and may not always be shared by the reader.

Introduction

I am sitting in the waiting room of a clinic in Cartagena, Colombia. A typical hospital scene with rows of seats and apprehension on every face. Today, as I look around, almost every one of the other patients are heavily pregnant women, most of which are accompanied by sheepish-looking young men. I am not in such good shape myself, arm in a sling and a rough dressing covering a wound to my chin. It is strange that after fifteen years of notetaking and very occasional writing, at this moment I decide that I must in some haste finish penning this book.

I consider myself fortunate to have had both the inclination and the financial wherewithal to retire from work at the age of sixty and together with my wife, Rosemary (hereinafter referred to as Rosie), indulge in our passion for travel. Over subsequent years as we have traversed the globe, I have made notes and collected memorabilia, and I think time is more than overdue to make use of that collection of writings and memories. Whilst we have travelled widely, perhaps our favourite region has been the countries of Latin America, and the musings that follow relate, with a few concessions, to that part of the world.

Our first encounter with Latin America came when Rosie and I travelled to Argentina twenty something years ago. We took in Buenos Aires and then journeyed south to the Argentinian Lake District and from there through the Andes into Chile. Rosie had been apprehensive about this trip, a combination of unfamiliarity with the culture and fear of anti-British sentiment following the Falklands War. However, within two days of landing in Buenos Aires, those concerns had completely dissipated. BA, as the city is popularly known, we found an exciting and vibrant place, the equal of and very similar to many of the great European capitals yet with its own distinctive character, not just some second-rate copy of cities elsewhere. It was the start of a love affair with Latin America.

Rosie had been much taken with the film *Evita* and although much of the film had actually been shot in Budapest, it was nevertheless fascinating to visit the sights depicted in the film, like Casa Rosada, the presidential palace in the Plaza de Mayo. It was easy to visualise the adoring crowds chanting for the Peróns in those heady early days of the regime. Such was our interest that for the first time in my life I found myself spending part of my holiday wandering around an urban cemetery. Our purpose: a search for the final resting place of Evita herself, Eva Perón.

We had been surprised on arriving at BA's Ezeiza Airport to be met, having anticipated organising our own taxi into the city. Maria was at the door from Arrivals and introduced herself as our travel company representative. She was a lady in her early seventies, short and plump but elegantly dressed. Her first task was to get us into the city and settled into our hotel. During the journey from the airport, we quizzed her about this and that, not least our interest in Evita. She reacted quite negatively to the idea that any visitors to the city would be interested in finding Evita's resting place. Maria was very much "old money" and she made it abundantly clear that she disapproved of Perón and the modern incarnation of the Perónistas in the form of the then President Menem. Later, when we found the cemetery in Recoleta, it was clearer why she and her family would truly believe it inappropriate that Evita, even as First Lady and internationally famed icon, be buried here amongst the upper echelons of Argentinian society. I was pretty certain that deceased members of Maria's family were to be found somewhere in Recoleta. The message was clear and we avoided the subject again, although I knew Rosie was clearly determined to find Evita's final resting place. We stayed in a small hotel close to the incredible Avenida 9 de Julio, the broad highway that runs through the centre of the city. If I recall correctly, it is fourteen lanes wide and is not to be crossed by the infirm or faint-hearted, Argentinean drivers bearing a close resemblance in driving style to the Italians. Although Spanish-speaking, and of course with strong links to Spain, Argentina has also welcomed immigrants from other

European countries; France, Germany and Britain, and most particularly Italy. The colourful La Boca area, for example, was originally home to many thousands of Italians and has a lively Latin feel.

On our first day in the city, we took a cab down to La Boca, passing La Bombonera, the stadium home of Boca Juniors where Diego Maradona first strutted his stuff, to Caminito the pedestrian street in the artists' quarter that is now very much a tourist trap. Although not far from the tourist hordes, in truth, La Boca remains a working-class area as it has been historically and Caminito with its brightly coloured houses and artists' colony a tourist oasis in an altogether grittier part of the city. It was nevertheless a fun experience strolling past the tango dancers giving exhibitions on the pavement for a few *pesos* tossed into a hat, and the artists selling their wares. I recall buying a couple of pictures of the street scenes from one young artist, all yellows, blues and reds capturing this interesting and not-to-be-missed part of the city.

Teatro Colon, the Opera House, was a couple of blocks from our hotel but at the time closed for refurbishment; however, Maria, with her connections, secured for us a behind-the-scenes visit not only into the auditorium but also to view the magnificent and historically significant wardrobe collection from productions past, costumes worn by some of the great names from the world of opera. Not being opera aficionados, the list of performers at the theatre is so complete that even we had heard of sopranos like Callas and Sutherland, tenors such as Caruso and Pavarotti and composers who have conducted at the theatre like Richard Strauss, Stravinsky and Copeland, not to mention stars of the ballet like Pavlova, Fonteyn and Nijinsky.

Although Maria was in close attendance during our time in the city, whilst visiting the tourist sights, on our final afternoon we had some free time and set out to find Recoleta. Our route from the hotel took us through the plush quarter along Avenida Alvear where Maria had an apartment, and we could easily have been strolling in the upmarket parts of Paris or Madrid. The Cementario de la Recoleta is an amazing necropolis, housing the great and the good from Argentina's past in mausoleums so grand and ostentatious, clearly demonstrating that the families who effectively ruled this country directly or indirectly for over a hundred years were still, even in death, each trying to outdo the others.

The surprising thing was that finding Evita's tomb was not an easy task. There were no signs, and after walking up and down rows and rows of wide avenues filled with, in many cases, impressive edifices to Argentina's past, we eventually came upon a gardener tending a flower bed somewhere in the middle of this "city of the dead".

At the time, we had about zero capability in the Spanish language but somehow managed to communicate what we were doing and, with the gardener's instructions, eventually located the tomb of the Family Duarte and the modest brass plaque denoting the last resting place of the former First Lady of Argentina, Eva Perón.

Times change. Some twenty years later, on a recent visit to Buenos Aires, we find ourselves once again in the Recoleta area. Rosie suggests we visit the cemetery again. A new façade is the first perceptible difference from all those years ago. Now tourist buses are parked on the roadside spewing out large numbers of visitors, and in the entrance vestibule, a map clearly identifies where to locate Evita's last resting place.

Back to that first visit, and after three days in Buenos Aires, it was time to head south into the unknown with an internal flight to the alpine town of Bariloche. Once again, Argentina did not disappoint. We emerged from a bumpy approach to our landing through impenetrably thick low cloud to views of the distant magnificence of the Andes. We were driven from the airport through the centre of Bariloche, a town with a distinctly Austrian feel, although our glimpse of it was but brief; we were not staying in the town but at a hotel some miles away at Llao Llao. This proved to be another superb choice; set on a small hill, few hotels in the world can match its panoramic views of lakes and mountains. Three relaxing days later, we set out ourselves to cross those mountains, by boat.

Llao Llao is on a promontory protruding out into the Lago Nahuel Huapi. It has as a backdrop the Cathedral Hills at around 7,500 feet and in the distance the imposing Mount Tronador at well over 10,000 feet. It was March; very late summer in these parts and only a handful of passengers joined us on the well-appointed launch in which we began our journey west towards the Chilean border. After about an hour and a half gliding, it seemed effortlessly, through the silent and still waters of the lake with just a low hum from the engines, the waterway narrowed between the dark and imposing mountains and we landed at Puerto Blest. This was followed by a short trip on a bus down an unmade road through a heavily forested area to the shores of a second lake. At the time, this was all a great mystery to us, not appreciating the complexities of the journey upon which we had embarked. Writing now with the benefit of a map, it is all so much clearer. We alighted our bus to be shepherded onto another boat for a short trip across a small and inky black lake to Puerto Frias. We later discovered that once across the lake, we were still in Argentina but close now to the border.

We had left Llao Llao on a warm, sunny day dressed appropriately in short-sleeved shirts. By now, the temperature had plummeted, and although it was still only mid-afternoon, the sun had already disappeared behind the surrounding mountains. Puerto Frias proved to be a very small community, a waiting room and refreshment bar and little else to even justify this location having a name. Here, we clambered aboard another bus, this time with Chilean number plates. Although we had not knowingly crossed any border, we wondered whether in fact we were now in Chile. The answer was no. After we had slowly climbed through the forest for perhaps another thirty minutes, the bus stopped. Here, a few solid stone buildings formally indicated the border between Argentina and Chile. We were in a narrow pass between the now towering mountains at around 3,000 feet above sea level. We got out and took some photographs. It was freezing. There were no border formalities at this the highest part of the pass, but a small roadside sign indicated we were now in Chile.

The bus began to slowly descend to the town of Peulla, where we were to stay for the night. The Peulla Hotel bore no comparison with the luxury of Llao Llao Hotel, clean but spartan comes to mind and memorable only for the sound of mice scampering across the void in the roof above our bed. Rosie confided that she wasn't so sure that she was going to like Chile as much as she had Argentina. We took an early-evening walk and found that we were close to water, but it was not until the following morning that we realised we were at the head of a very large lake: Lago Todos Los Santos, the emerald lake. Three lakes we had travelled across, all with completely different colour water: the turquoise of Nahuel Huapi, the black Frias and now the green of Todos Los Santos.

Later that morning, we continued our journey. The scenery on the 20-mile trip across the lake was truly magnificent. We sat on the deck of the boat gulping in the fresh mountain air and looked around in awe. I am sure that we were unusually blessed with the weather, the sky deep blue and totally cloudless with Tronador still in view but now behind us, beginning to recede into the distance; to the right, Puntiagudo and to the front, not the highest but undoubtedly the most impressive of the three peaks, Volcano Osorno, a perfect conical shape capped even now in late summer with a topping of virgin white snow. On this Sunday morning, we were joined by a host of late-summer holidaymakers suggesting that we were getting back to civilisation, this obviously being a popular holiday area for the Chileans. Once across the lake, we boarded yet another bus for the one-hour journey from Petrohue to Puerto Varas where we were scheduled to stay for another night. Puerto Varas is a pleasant provincial town, a sleepy resort, I guess, at the best of times. Here at the end of the holiday season, it reminded me of those small English resorts like Cromer or Deal in late September. The small hotel where we stayed only reinforced the feeling that the time machine had transported us back to '50s England. Next day, we were collected by minibus to be taken to the airport at Puerto Montt for the flight north to Chile's capital, Santiago.

Santiago is a large and busy city but it somehow didn't match Buenos Aires, so it was good to end our trip by returning across the Andes, this time by plane, to spend the final two days of our visit back in Buenos Aires. We were due to fly out of Santiago on a Sunday morning but, on arrival at the airport, we discovered our Aerolineas Argentinas flight had been cancelled. The only alternative was a Lan Chile flight leaving within the next ten minutes. Words were exchanged between staff of the airlines. Being in Spanish, we had no idea what was going on, and then suddenly we were ushered down a walkway and onto a plane. No sooner had we been seated than the doors were closed and we were on our way. Given the suddenness and speed of our departure, it was with low expectations that an hour or so later we waited in the baggage hall for our cases. However, passengers and bags were to our relief quickly reunited. Our first visit to South America was coming to a close.

However, before I go on to relate more of our travels, it would be remiss not to introduce myself and my wife and travelling companion, who by now you will have deduced is Rosemary, more affectionately known as Rosie. I say this with the certainty of the spouse who uses his wife's proper name only in formal situations by way of introduction or to admonish her for misdeeds, regrettably usually mine.

In some thirty-odd years together, Rosie and I have enjoyed our mutual interest in travel, at first during vacations from our busy jobs in industry and more recently as an increasingly significant part of our lives as we have moved towards and ultimately into retirement. As a matter of interest, just before I sat down to write this introduction, I conducted a quick count of the countries we have visited together, and the total is well in excess of one hundred. I mention this not for effect but simply to illustrate the breadth if not the depth of our travels. Almost without exception, we would have liked to spend much longer in places that we have visited, most cursorily for a few days or even a few hours. So rather than claim a hundred plus countries visited as some kind of splendid achievement, I apologise now for the inevitable superficiality of my observations and reflections.

I travel to learn not as learned. I write as the student not the teacher. For my own part, all I can say is that for us, travel is a passion, maybe an obsession. More of that anon, but back to this book, describing our travels in just some of those one hundred countries, those in what I have loosely described as Latin America.

One

Argentina: Foothills of the Andes to the Land of Fire

Argentine Republic: World's eighth largest country by area with a population of 45 million. Best known for its beef and wine. Continues to claim sovereignty over the Falkland Islands, which it calls the Malvinas. Language – Spanish.

Since the first visit, recounted in my introduction, we have returned several times to Argentina, and it remains one of our favourite countries in South America and its vibrant capital Buenos Aires one of our favourite cities, despite noticeably losing some of its lustre on our more recent visits.

On our second trip to Argentina, we had first travelled on a small ship through the Chilean fjords, our journey ending in the southern Argentine town of Ushuaia, deep into Patagonia. Here in the harbour we were fascinated to find our tiny vessel tied up alongside some of the former Russian-built icebreakers that had opened up the new tourist frontier of Antarctica. Suddenly we became aware of new travel possibilities, an encounter which would be a spark leading us to a number of subsequent visits to the Polar regions, both north and south.

Now back in Argentina for a third time and this provides a classic example of how one of our trips provides the genus for another. We are in

Ushuaia, ready to embark upon our own journey to the "White Continent". On this journey, we pass a few days in Buenos Aires before flying down to Ushuaia. Here we spend a couple of days acclimatising before our journey south, and hire a local guide to take us on a tour of the local sights. This includes a ride on the "Tren del Fin del Mundo" or "Train to the End of the World". Diego, our guide, we discover, actually hails from Salta, an Argentine city a staggering 2,500 miles to the north. We quiz him as to whether our next visit to Argentina should include Mendoza or Cordoba; instead, he extols the virtues of visiting his own native city, and we add Salta to our list of places to visit.

The Tren del Fin del Mundo reminds us of the heritage line in Sheringham, the small town where we live in Norfolk. A modest 7km-long ride on old carriages pulled by aged steam locomotives. In this instance, though, the scenery is a little different as we travel through part of the Tierra del Fuego National Park. Tierra del Fuego: the "Land of Fire".

The comparison becomes a little more tenuous when we discover that this line originally ran from the prison in Ushuaia into the Park, where prisoners serving hard labour sentences spent their days collecting timber and other construction materials, before loading the rail trucks and taking them back to the city. Although the prisoners probably didn't appreciate them, particularly during the harsh winters, the views are spectacular as the train meanders alongside the Pipo River until it reaches the station at the foot of Mount Susana. So there on a train trip in Patagonia, Salta is pencilled in as a possible place to visit sometime in the future.

Returning from an amazing trip to Antarctica for which we feel privileged to have been able to afford, we fly back from Ushuaia to Buenos Aires. To pass the time, I flick through the pages of the in-flight magazine and come to an article about the Valdes Peninsula where a special microclimate and naturally protected bays annually attract hundreds of Southern Right whales to mate and later to return to give birth. I show the article to Rosie, who becomes quite animated. At that moment, Valdes is added to the list along with Salta, and another future journey is beginning to take shape.

Our trip to Antarctica had begun in less than auspicious circumstances. Our travel company had booked us into a so-called "boutique" hotel in a supposedly "up-and-coming" part of Buenos Aires. The gentrification process had in reality barely begun; the surrounding streets had a menacing air and after one night we moved hotels to a more salubrious part of the city.

This proved a portent of things to come. The same company had arranged our transport and accommodation in Ushuaia. Landing at the airport, we collected our luggage and went in search of our transport. No sign. Our fellow travellers quickly dispersed via taxis and cars, and soon we stood alone at the terminal entrance. Ours was one of only two daily flights at that time and the airport was soon deserted. It took us an hour to find someone who could understand our dilemma and find us a taxi. Less than impressed, we were eventually dropped at the B&B recommended and booked by the travel company.

The taxi driver kindly pointed skywards to the property, situated high on a steep hill overlooking the town. A set of wooden steps built into the hillside led up to the timber construction to be our home for the next three days. I was breathing heavily as we hauled our suitcases up the steps, partly from the effort and partly fuming at the travel company's failure to select accommodation to suit our tastes, not to mention our advancing years. The cabin-like building was deserted. Even higher, up more steps, was another building. I was sent to recce and eventually, after knocking several times on his door, I managed to rouse our host. He proves to be a man of around my age sporting a heavy grey beard. We begin with some chit-chat and he proves to be a bluff retired naval captain making what I thought was an unlikely career change. After this exchange of pleasantries, including his potted life history, he grabs a set of keys and leads me back down the steps to where Rosie is patiently waiting with our bags. The cabin is, to say the least, spartan, no doubt comfortable for an old sea dog but definitely not what we are expecting. When the Captain reveals that breakfast is "rations" he will leave for us on a daily basis, Rosie's reaction is, to say the least, underwhelming.

Ushuaia is a pleasant enough frontier-style town now rapidly growing with little grace, thanks to the flourishing tourist industry, both as a gateway to wild Patagonia and to increasing numbers of vessels transporting tourists like ourselves across the notorious Drake's Passage to the Antarctic Peninsula. It has the feel of an Alpine ski resort, with endless shops selling cold-weather clothing and equipment and locally made knitwear, not to mention eateries of all descriptions. Increasingly, though, we have noted that since our first visit, there is now a proliferation of fast-food joints, and the equipment stores are increasingly selling the branded goods you can pretty well find anywhere in the world these days, but at inflated prices. In this regard, bring what clothing you need with you. Not in the scope of this tome but thankfully I can report the subsequent trip to Antarctica proved a great success.

With Salta and the Valdes Peninsula now in mind, we return home to set about planning our next visit to Argentina. In the end, this involves an elaborate itinerary with us travelling to Salta and from there taking a flight on an obscure, and certainly unknown to our travel company, airline to Santa Cruz in Bolivia and embarking on a journey around that country, which is elaborated elsewhere in this book. We then plan to return to Argentina and head south and east to Valdes. Our journey is to conclude when we take the ferry from Buenos Aires across the River Plate to enjoy a few days' much-needed relaxation in a luxury hotel in Carmelo in Uruguay.

The journey begins. We have arrived in Salta. Deciding not to overnight in Buenos Aires after our flight from London, we are pretty well exhausted by the time we reach the city; what with early airport check-ins and the hanging around between flights, it had been nearly forty hours since we left home. Fortunately, the Solar de la Plaza proves to be an elegant and comfortable hotel housed in a fine colonial building in the attractive Guemes Square, close to the centre of this well-preserved old city.

Checking out the portfolio of Visitor Information left in our hotel room under the heading *Museums*, I am amused to read:

Museum for Contemporary Arts	2 *pesos* contribution
History Museum	3 *pesos* entrance fee
Museum for High Mountain Archaeology	Outlandish 30 *pesos*,
	Argentinos 10 *pesos*,
	Retirees free

We naturally hope we are Retirees, not wishing, at 30 *pesos* a time, to be labelled as Outlandish.

The following morning and we meet Christian, the young man who is to be our guide for the next three days. After polite introductions in the hotel lobby, he leads us outside to our vehicle, a smart 4x4. First impressions are of someone rather overweight for a young man in his mid-twenties, with a chubby face and rosy cheeks. His spectacles have small round lenses, and Rosie thinks he resembles Billy Bunter, a comic book character from the last century popularised in a television series in the 1950s. For the uninitiated, Bunter was an overweight and short-sighted schoolboy at Greyfriars

Boarding School. His character was played by Gerald Campion, who oddly secured the role when he was actually in his thirties. The series helped spawn the careers of better-known actors like Michael Crawford, Kenneth Cope and Melvyn Hayes, who in contrast were at the time all schoolboys playing the parts of schoolboys.

I later deduce that Christian is probably of German extraction, certainly not a typical swarthy Latino. Christian proves somewhat of an enigma, a man-boy. He has a penchant for watching Hollywood action movies and speaks with a distinctly American accent. We have travelled only a short distance before we stop for him to collect what proves to be his daily breakfast, a double coke: a Coca-Cola drink and coca leaves.

The chewing of coca leaves is common in parts of South America amongst the native peoples, particularly in the high-altitude regions of Bolivia and Peru. It is banned in Argentina except in this northern province, being the only part of the country with an indigenous population. Its use here is frowned upon but tolerated. Christian, described as certainly not being indigenous, would not be a typical user. When we question him on this habit, Christian claims that it helps him keep calm with the stress of driving, and free from headaches, which can be troubling when working at higher altitudes.

Today, we are heading south towards the winemaking area of Cafayate. Our first stop is Alemania, a small near ghost town set a short distance from the main highway. Although the word Alemania is Germany in the Spanish language, how it got its name is uncertain. The obvious reason would be that it was a settlement of German immigrants; however, there doesn't seem to be much evidence to support this supposition, and another theory is that this was the site of a native village, the name of which in the local language was a similar-sounding word to Alemania and was subsequently written down by the Spanish in a way they could understand. The town itself really only existed because it was a station on the train line from Salta to Cafayate, built in the 1920s. A funding crisis meant that work on the line beyond here to Cafayate was never completed, and when the line finally closed in 1971, any reason for the town to exist at all disappeared. A few families have stoically remained in residence selling basic necessities and trinkets to passing travellers, but the buildings are largely disused and slowly falling apart. The whole place has the feel of a Western film set and has become exactly that on several occasions over the years. Beyond here, we enter the

Quebrada de la Cochas. Purple, pink and orange rock formations on a mega scale, the largest or more extraordinarily shaped have been attributed with a name. Usually, some imagined face or animal form. Most impressive is the "Coliseum", entered through the narrow "Devil's throat", which rather reminded me of the "Siq" in Petra, Jordan, which featured heavily in an early Indiana Jones movie. The Coliseum is a circle surrounded by perpendicular rock faces towering so high that you have to crane your neck to see the sky above. We naturally do as most visitors: whisper some words and wait to hear them reverberate eerily around the canyon. We are rather upstaged by a guitar-playing and singing young man, who could pass as a '60s hippie, who seems to have taken up residence in the Coliseum.

We travel on reaching the charming little town of Cafayate in the midst of Argentina's second most important wine-producing area. Here taking lunch and sampling the local vino at a small family winery before making our way back to Salta. It has been an altogether pleasant day, perfect weather, less than arduous driving and stunning scenery.

The next morning bright and early, and Christian is waiting for us in the hotel lobby. The same ritual, collecting his Coca-Cola and coca leaves before setting out on our journey on what he describes as a day with an uncharacteristic weather pattern, clear and sunny, Salta by reputation being prone to low cloud and fog. Consecutive sunny days a rarity.

Today, we are heading north-west on a two-day sojourn. After some 20 miles, we reach Quisano, described on billboards we pass as a "holiday village", although it does not seem an obvious place to take a holiday, just some low-level buildings set in an arid boulder-strewn valley. From here, the hitherto excellent road quickly deteriorates.

We had hoped to take the famed "El Tren de la Nubes" or Train in the Clouds, but it is not operating at this time; however, near a small town called Tastil, we come across the railway line at a point where it crosses a river on a rickety-looking wooden bridge. We ask Christian to stop the car and we use the opportunity for photos of ageing tourists balancing precariously on the bridge many feet above a fast-flowing river below. The surrounding hills are covered white, not by snow but from a heavy frost. Although we are still in the Tropics with the high altitude and cold Andean winds, the temperature here is consistently lower than I had anticipated.

Messing about concluded, Christian drives up a narrow road above the town to the site of a pre-Hispanic settlement, a gem for any archaeologist, with much residual evidence of a civilisation living here long ago, even before the Incas; stone walls, walkways and plazas all clearly visible.

Onwards and upwards. We are climbing steadily through a dry and hilly landscape, the colours now browns and orange. At one point, we emerge from a narrow ravine to find ourselves looking across to a community away in the distance; it is the town of San Antonio de las Cobres. By now, we have travelled more than 100 miles from Salta and are ready for our lunch. San Antonio is set at around 3,800 metres and we are descending down towards the town! As we approach, we can see a mine and, close by, rows of tidy but tiny miners' houses. Distances in this empty landscape can be deceptive, and it seems an age before we finally reach the town.

This is in fact a former mining community, named after the nearby Copper Mountain but now very quiet and rundown. Typical small whitewashed adobe houses and little else of note. Christian leads us to what we assume to be the best eatery in town. It is more *cantina* than restaurant. A long bar with a few gnarled old men sitting disconsolately staring into their glasses of beer. Eating is at a series of long bare wooden tables and benches set at right angles to the bar. For the second day running, we have entered a scene from a Western movie.

We take a seat at the end of one of these long tables whilst Christian goes off to order some food. When it arrives, we are presented with bowls of a tasty vegetable soup and a large plate of assorted *empanadas* and *tamales*. Food I might have expected to have been served in Central America rather than here in Argentina. When it comes to pay, Christian once again surprises us by showing his charitable side. At the far end of our long table are an old couple, really old, small, and from their dress I would more likely have expected to come across them later on our trip when we cross the border into Bolivia. They are sitting supping from bowls of *locro*, a local stew into which they are dipping chunks of bread. Christian insists on paying for their food, a gesture they clearly much appreciate. In this extreme north of Argentina, there are, unlike in the rest of the country, indigenous people. The old couple fall into this category, being small of stature, swarthy, and wearing ponchos and heavy but loose-fitting garments. Argentina of all the countries in Latin America is the one most European in culture, architecture and fundamental way of life. A country where the indigenous peoples constitute less than two percent of the population. Many indigenous tribes inhabiting this country were wiped off the face of the earth by the arrival of the Europeans. A combination of diseases introduced by the white man, wars, destruction of their natural habitat and frankly genocide. I recall a small museum in Ushuaia dedicated to the Yamani, a tribe living in Patagonia in near caveman conditions, unclothed, in a hostile climate but a tribe that had nevertheless survived until the Europeans arrived.

After lunch, we head out of San Antonio, now in a northerly direction. Again we begin to climb, stopping at Abra Blanca where a sign indicates that we are at 4,060 metres. Significant enough for a photo stop and sharp intake of breath in the thinning air. Beyond: an apparently never-ending plateau. Here, there is an interminable nothingness save for some small groups of *vicuna* and *guanaco* grazing on the very sparse vegetation. We are now on the *altiplano*, the vast high plain at an elevation of between seven and thirteen thousand feet that stretches through much of Peru and Bolivia, reaching down into the top part of Chile and here in Northern Argentina.

The animals on view are camelids, related to the llama family. The smallest in this animal grouping are the *vicuna*, the source of a fine wool, very expensive, as the animal produces only small quantities and can be shorn once every three years. The *guanaco* is larger with a coarse hair. Even in such a barren landscape, the trained eye can always uncover the secret lives of plants and creatures that reside there. Anxious to prove this point, Christian stops the vehicle for us to inhale the intoxicating smell of the *tola* plant, endemic to and widely spread across the *altiplano*. A member of the daisy family but unrecognisable as such to the untrained eye.

The distances being long and the terrain free of any trees or bushes, Rosie is by now beginning to feel the strain induced by the lack of toilet facilities when relief comes from an unexpected source. We drive into a small depression in the vast and empty landscape and surprisingly come across another vehicle: a large bus which has clearly been specially converted for travel on rough terrain. Amazingly, it is owned by the company that employs Christian, so whilst he exchanges pleasantries with his work colleagues, Rosie avails herself of the on-board "facilities".

Later that evening after a long day on the road, we find ourselves descending towards the pretty village of Purmamurca, but not before reaching another high point, Altos del Murado at 4,170 metres. Gazing down, the winding road below looks hair-raising, but Christian says that only five years before, it was just a rough track, so we consider ourselves fortunate. Despite the tiring drive, after checking in at a small *hosteria*, we decide to stretch our legs and take a walk into the hills at the back of the village. Even without a great interest in geology, it is still possible to marvel at the multi-coloured rock strata that form *Cerro de los Siete Colores*, the Hill of Seven Colours that dominates this small community.

Next morning, we head further north to another attractive little town, Humahuaca. It is festival time and the streets are busy with worshippers visiting the Candelaria Church set on a hill at the back of the town, whilst in the streets below, musicians play, and we find ourselves in an almost unique experience for Argentina; that of mingling with indigenous people like the old couple in Los Cobres. It is a colourful sight, with the women favouring a headcovering, usually something similar to a trilby hat. They typically wear the combination of a blouse and around their shoulders a colourful shawl, known as a manta, and a voluminous skirt, subject to some local variations very similar to what we are to see more commonly in subsequent visits to Bolivia and Peru.

Humahuaca has many craft and artisan shops and as is customary we buy a memento, on this occasion a woven wall hanging. The big attraction though is to be found in the town centre: the clock tower adjacent to the Church of San Francisco Solano. We are spot-on with our timing, as approaching noon we come across a large and excited crowd gathered around the foot of the tower. As the clock strikes the hour, a small statue of the Saint emerges from a door halfway up the tower and makes the sign of the cross. Today, the simple scenario is greeted with great applause, even though most of the crowd gathered below must have seen this scene enacted many times.

Equally not to be missed but demanding a climb up a broad staircase is the Monument to the Heroes of Independence. Here in the north, an army of indigenous people fought many battles against the Spanish in the Wars of Independence. At the top of the monument a large bronze statue. In most Argentine cities you will find a plaza containing a statue of the hero of the Independence struggle, General José de San Martin but, for once, this is definitely not San Martin. The statue is of an indigenous native figure; it is believed to be a representation of a *chasqui*, one of the famed Inca messengers. *Chasqui* were runners rather like those in Ancient Greece, the most famous being Pheidippides, who famously ran from Marathon to Athens with news of a great Greek victory in battle and of course whose feat is celebrated today in the event we call a marathon. The Inca represented in the statue is named Pedro Socompa, who also ran a great distance bringing news of independence to the people of this region. The climb rewards those who make the effort by providing good views not only of the monument but looking back down over the town.

Our final stop today is at Tilcara. Here, we visit the impressive pre-Colombian ruins of another past civilisation. The city dates back to around the tenth century, although it is believed that later it may have been one of the most southerly points of influence reached by the Incas. This is an exposed and windswept place where ancient ruins lie surrounded by huge cacti. A typical Inca dwelling has been reconstructed; the doorway so tiny that the people that lived here must have been extremely diminutive by our standards.

From here, we return to Salta through the Quebrada de Humahuaca, the road twisting through a deep canyon; on either side, enormous and amazing colourful rockfaces and outcrops predominantly in hues of orange and brown, yellow and ochre. A few miles south of Tilcara, Christian stops the car for us to enjoy the views. We are near the village of Maimara, where the mountains above the village are particularly colourful and the scene has been dubbed the "Painter's palette". An additional feature seen from our viewpoint is an unusually large necropolis set on a small hill in front of the village, with many elaborate tombs, crosses and vaults.

Our final day in Salta is spent exploring the city, first taking the cable car to the top of San Bernardo Hill behind the city. It is possible to climb a thousand steps to the summit, but on this occasion we opt for the easy option in deference to Christian's waistline. There is a statue to Guemes, a local hero who led a band of gauchos during the War of Independence, but the true value of the exercise is to enjoy the magnificent panorama of the city below.

The old city is a relatively small but well-preserved area around the Plaza 9 de Julio. In one corner of the square is MAAM, the Museum of the High Mountains, containing a most interesting exhibit. The Children of Llullaillaco are three Inca children whose totally preserved bodies were discovered near the top of the mountain of that name in 1999. Preserved in the ice and low temperatures, the bodies and all their organs remain completely intact as they were on the day, perhaps 500 years ago, when they were ritually slaughtered as part of some religious ceremony. Although it sounds a trifle ghoulish, the exhibit, together with the many artefacts buried with the children to accompany them in the afterlife, is quite a fascinating insight into this ancient barbaric, but in many other ways sophisticated, society. This part of our trip is reaching a conclusion, but on this same journey, we will travel to a far distant part of Argentina.

The Valdes Peninsula lies 1,500 miles to the south of Salta, stretching out into the Atlantic Ocean and joined to the mainland by the narrow Ameghino Isthmus. As you leave the mainland and travel east, the peninsula opens up left and right. The effect is to create two bays either side of the isthmus, both almost totally protected from the ocean. To the north the Golfo San José, to the south the Golfo Nuevo. This geological quirk of nature provides the ideal breeding ground for the Southern Right Whale. On the peninsula a few hacienda and farmhouses, most now offering tourist accommodation. The only town on the peninsula is Puerto Piramides on the western approaches on the road from the largest town of any note in this region, Puerto Madryn.

We have decided to stay not on the peninsula itself but on the mainland to the south, still overlooking the Golfo Nuevo, at a place called Punta Ninfas. We fly into Trelew. The Welsh-sounding name is no coincidence. Welsh sheep farmers began settling in the area as early as 1865 and founded the town in 1884, naming it after one of the pioneers, Lewis Jones. Although Puerto Madryn is called the gateway to Valdes, the slightly larger and more industrial Trelew is marginally closer to our lodgings on Punta Ninfas. After the adventures in Bolivia from where we have just travelled, it is a relief to be met at the small airport, by Juan. Swarthy, handsome and wearing clothes straight out of a Western movie – check shirt and knee-length boots – he slings our bags into the back of his pick-up truck, and before we have had a chance to absorb the scene, we are off heading out on a dusty track towards the east. In the event, we are to see little of Trelew and its heritage.

El Pedral is an old hacienda built in 1923 by Felix Arbeleche, a notable figure amongst the early settlers in the area. Set close to the beach, it is an ideal location for those like us, interested in some whale watching at close quarters.

The hacienda proves to be comfortable. The only other guests are another British couple, and we spend the next day in their company, together with Wendt. We are introduced to him immediately following our hearty breakfast. A large, lugubrious man, he has little English. He leads us along the beach and his first task is to launch our craft, a well-proportioned inflatable. Soon we are out into the bay. There is a strongish wind whipping across the water, creating quite a swell. I have to confess that as a non-swimmer I always feel a little vulnerable in this type of craft, perched on the side just holding on to a rope for safety. We have been taught the "zodiac position", legs slightly apart, weight forward towards the centre of the vessel. Today, I am very much inclined towards putting into practice what we have been taught. My aversion to total immersion comes from a near-death experience in Brixham Harbour at the age of six, and as the floor of the inflatable is already under an inch or so of water, I am torn. On one hand the desire to capture the moment on camera, on the other self-preservation.

Wendt turns up the revs a few notches and within a couple of minutes, whales abound; whales to the left of us, whales to the right and then whales precariously close, diving into the waters on one side of the boat and emerging seconds later on the opposite side.

When we arrived at El Pedral the previous evening, we had taken a pre-dinner stroll to stretch our legs after the journey and had seen clearly that the property was built in a well-protected little cove beyond which was a line of cliffs running south towards a point, Punta Tombo. Now from the boat, the cliffs along the coastline are to be seen clearly, but only for a few seconds at a time. Camera in hand, I am clicking away, knowing that most frames will be devoid of whale pictures; the sky or a wave may be discernible, but thank God for the miracle of digital photography. Maybe just one frame will capture the scene. Rosie, camcorder in hand, has adopted a pose, slipping down onto the floor of the boat and leaning on the ribbing. Good move. It is at times like this I recall the advice given to me many years ago: *Enjoy the moment not only through the lens of a camera.* One whale pays us particular attention, I am trusting in a playful mood, and I later discover that I have captured to my mind that one satisfactory still photograph.

We should not complain; we have travelled thousands of miles to enjoy this sight. Seeing wildlife this close is exhilarating and despite the discomfort, we are more than pleased with the morning's excursion.

A couple of hours later and Wendt turns for shore. Once the inflatable has been secured, he leads us a short distance along the beach to where we encounter the comings and goings of a small but apparently thriving colony of Magellanic penguins. Of the seventeen species of penguin in the world, these are of medium size and native to the southern regions of South America.

Back to El Pedral for a welcome bowl of hot broth served with chunks of bread and cheese, revivers for an afternoon jaunt with Wendt in a 4x4, taking a rough track climbing along the coastline to a high cliff from where, looking down on the beach, below we have the opportunity to view a colony of elephant seals basking upon the rocks. The group contains a harem of females and some cubs, all presided over by a huge bull elephant seal. He seems to be in a bad mood. As one of the cubs playfully approaches, he shows his annoyance and sets off after it in angry pursuit, the youngster finding refuge by hiding behind its mother.

The clifftop plateau is home to hundreds of sheep, and our next stop is at a nearby farmstead where a team of highly skilled itinerant sheep shearers from Australia are hard at work. It is work of production line proportions. A large paddock full of unshorn sheep, a narrow fenced run leading to a barn where the dozen or so shearers are at work. Watching from a safe distance, we roughly time how long it takes to shear one sheep. A little shy of three minutes. Finally making our way out of the shed, another paddock where the noisy, slightly shell-shocked shorn animals are milling around.

The next day, the other couple leave for the airport whilst Juan returns to take us on a day trip down the coast. We head for Punta Tombo, which we viewed the previous day from out in the bay. Here we come across a huge colony of Magellanic penguins. Yesterday penguins in modest family groups, today the numbers are staggering, probably the biggest colony to be found outside of Antarctica, some half a million. Unlike the King penguins that we have come across in Antarctica that stand in enormously large groups on a beach, these are less visible, despite the numbers, being partly hidden along the cliffs in nooks and crevices, bushes and burrows.

That in-flight magazine article had not overstated the virtues of the Valdes Peninsula, a magical time for us both, but all good things must come to an end. It is the following day and we are scheduled to take a midday flight to Buenos Aires, but Juan arrives at the hacienda with news that the flight has been delayed until the evening. Unfazed, he provides us with another full day exploring the area.

First, we drive to Puerto Madryn, then on to the peninsula itself. In Puerto Piramides, Juan thoughtfully stops at a local *panaderia* to buy us some cakes for our lunch and then takes us down to the harbour, where a tourist boat waits for an afternoon out in the bay to do some more whale watching.

This has been an epic journey, not only here in Valdes, but to northern Argentina and to Bolivia. From here, we head for some well-earned rest in a luxury hotel in Uruguay, on the banks of the River Plate.

Fast forward several years and a more recent trip to Argentina finds us back in Patagonia with the main objective being to visit one of the final locations on Rosie's by now much-shrunken bucket list of must-see places, the Perito Moreno Glacier. We have been quite close in the past across the nearby border with Chile, visiting the Torres del Paine National Park and Grey Glacier, a case of so near yet so far. The town of El Calafate some 50 miles away from the glacier is our base. A fairly nondescript provincial town on the banks of Lago Argentino now heavily dependent on tourists like us.

After checking into our hotel, which is set upon a hill overlooking the town, we take a stroll. Attracted by the sound of music, we walk across a park and shortly come across the source: a local festival of traditional dance and music in an open-air amphitheatre that frankly looks too grand for a town of this size. After taking some time sitting on the grass banking to absorb the scene and enjoy the music, we continue on our way down to the main street, where we find the Visitor Centre and out front a life-sized model of a man with a packhorse. It is Perito Moreno. The plaque says Francisco Pascasio Moreno 1852–1919. Who then is Perito?

The next day and we will find some answers, as we are on a guided tour to the glacier. We join an assorted group of various nationalities for the one-and-a-half-hour journey by mini-bus through the outskirts of El Calafate along the banks of the lake, past open and barren terrain dotted with cattle. Our guide explains that it takes about 4,000 hectares to sustain just one cow in this harsh environment.

After about half an hour, the bus pulls over for us to step outside to take in our first serious view of the snow-capped Andean mountains in the distance. Soon, after recommencing our journey, at a fork in the road we turn left, away from the lake, and the landscape changes as we enter a forested area on an undulating and winding road. Shortly, we arrive at a small landing stage from where we are to transfer to a boat for a short trip up to the very face of the Perito Moreno glacier. Some impressive close-up photo opportunities follow before we return to shore and resume our bus journey for another fifteen minutes or so to the well-appointed Visitor Centre and, close by, the Pasaralas, a labyrinth of solid walkways constructed to offer further views across to the glacier.

Perito Moreno is unusual for glaciers in this age of global warming. It is actually growing. This is caused by a freak of nature. The snow and rain falling high up in the Andes feed glaciers. By some quirk, maybe a rockfall at some strategic location has meant that the distribution of melting ice and rain to feed Perito Moreno has actually increased in recent years, whilst other nearby glaciers, notably the larger but near inaccessible Uppsala Glacier, have in relative terms been starved. The effect is that the head of Perito Moreno has been stretching out across Lago Argentino at the very point we are now viewing. It has breached a gap of some 400 metres, effectively dividing Lago Argentino into two. The front of the glacier now spreads out in a V-shape. Uppsala in contrast is retreating at an alarming rate with huge calvings. As a consequence, it is now forbidden to approach closer than 2 kilometres, the glacier only being accessible by boat.

At Perito Moreno, an extraordinary natural phenomenon occurs at this time of the year, late summer. An archway forms down at the level of the lake at the very front of the glacier as melting occurs, and waters from the southern and northern sides of Lago Argentino once again mingle. Day by day, the arch increases in size, eventually collapsing under the weight of ice above.

As the likely day approaches, locals gather in their hundreds in the hope of seeing what must be a dramatic event. A sign says that no less than thirty-two have perished over the years from flying chunks of ice at the time of the collapse. The walkways where we are walking have been built in recent times to help manage people so that they no longer get too close, in the hope of eliminating further fatalities. A dramatic collapse apparently occurs on average once every four years and this looks certain to be one of those years, given the enormous volume of ice at the front of the glacier. Our guide says the collapse is imminent but despite watching intently, it is clearly not going to happen today. Instead, given a wide choice, we take the longest walk along the Pasaralas to get a full view back towards the glacier in all its splendour. It is the least I can do, given Rosie has waited so long to see this sight.

Two days later and we are heading back to Perito Moreno. As a wedding anniversary present to ourselves, we have purchased tickets for a boat trip to the glacier, including a champagne lunch. The cruise departs from the private port at La Soledad and first heads across Lago Argentino to view an inaccessible-by-road glacier called Speggazini. As we cross the lake, we are also able to see Uppsala from a safe distance. Speggazini is relatively small compared to Perito Moreno but is located at the head of a pretty fjord, offering some excellent chances to take photographs.

There is a chance to go ashore and stretch our legs at Las Vacas. This now near-deserted location is where a Finnish man set up his farm some fifty years ago. It is a stunningly beautiful location with natural pastures, steep slopes heading up towards the mountains and fast-running streams running down to the lake. Petrified trees lay strewn about, adding to the mystique of the place. When the Argentinian Government decided to designate this as a national park, the farmer was required to up sticks, and now in his eighties apparently still lives in El Calafate, rather bitter about his treatment and still dreaming that one day he may be allowed to return. His deserted farmhouse has a rather forlorn air, particularly poignant when his story is related. In the distance we see some horses and further away a ramshackle hut. Apparently two gauchos have been hired to round up the farmer's cattle that have gone wild and now represent a threat to the pristine natural environment that the Government is trying to restore.

Back on board and heading towards Perito Moreno, we learn a little more from our guide about the man himself after whom the glacier is named. Perito it seems is not as we thought a Christian name but a title, in Spanish, "expert". Francisco was a naturalist and explorer and by the beginning of the twentieth century the acknowledged expert on all things Patagonian. The wild and inhospitable land at the bottom of Argentina, even by the late nineteenth century, a land which lay largely unexplored and uninhabited. Francisco Moreno conducted a number of expeditions to this still-remote region, the first of which in 1875–76 took him as far south as Lake Nahuel Huapi, which had been our introduction to South America some twenty years ago and which lies several hundred miles further to the north. Testimony to the vast expanse that is Patagonia.

Francisco came from good middle-class parents and his father had a keen interest in discovering fossils, an interest that the young Francisco embraced. Later expeditions during the 1870s and '80s saw Francisco exploring more of the Andes from the border with Bolivia down deep into Patagonia. Francisco was largely responsible for mapping the region and bringing to bear his diplomatic skills in resolving numerous territorial disputes in the region between Argentina and its neighbour Chile. In this respect, he challenged Chilean claims to much of the most southerly part of the continent by proving that many rivers draining from Patagonian lakes into the Pacific were actually part of the Atlantic Ocean basin.

Despite this successful technical argument, Francisco realised that the best way to support territorial claims was by populating the region with Argentinian citizens, and he encouraged the Argentine Government to pursue a policy of granting land rights to settlers for free, or at nominal rates of payment.

In gratitude for his public service, he himself was granted rights over large tracts of land. He subsequently handed some of this back to the Government to be used to found what is now the Nahuel Huapi National Park, the concept of a national park, land preserved in its natural state, being an idea he had picked up from his travels in the United States. This connection to the US has a strange symmetry insofar as Francisco's last visit to Patagonia took place in 1912 when he accompanied former US President Theodore Roosevelt on a tour of the region around Nahuel Huapi.

By now, a welcome lunch and a few glasses of wine later, we are approaching the face of Perito Moreno Glacier, today from the north and just in time to see a significant calving, ice falling from the face of the glacier into the waters below.

Once again, the archway remains intact. Our trip is coming to an end but about two weeks later, we read a newspaper report that the collapse had occurred, but in the early hours of a morning when the national park was closed.

Two

Chile: Extremes

Chile: Long, narrow country with a 6,000km coastline stretching from the Atacama Desert (driest in the world) in the north to Cape Horn in the south and dominated by the Andes mountain range which stretches the length of the country. Population 20 million. Spanish speaking.

It wasn't a case of love at first sight, yet Chile with all its contrasts seems to have a mesmeric quality that draws you back again and again. That first-time arrival across the Andes from Argentina put into stark relief the two countries. One, Argentina, as sophisticated and affluent as its Latin counterparts in Europe: Spain and Italy. Chile: the poor relation, just adjusting to a democratic system after a generation under a military dictatorship.

On that first visit, we had flown north from Puerto Varas to the capital, Santiago. I was interested in seeing where Salvador Allende had perished when Pinochet and his henchmen in the military decided to move against him. It didn't take long. The main thoroughfare from the airport into the city centre is the Alameda Libertador Bernardo O'Higgins, named after an earlier revolutionary leader. And there very soon on your left, set back from the main road, is La Moneda, so-called because it was once the country's Mint, although for more than a century the presidential palace. Here it was that on 11th September 1973, the British-built Hawker Hunter jets of the Chilean Air Force screamed low overhead, dropping their deadly cargo and toppling the world's only genuinely democratic Communist head of state. Although the building has been restored, bullet holes remain visible in the walls. Allende is reputed to have declined the chance of escape into exile but instead took his own life, although the truth about his last moments remains shrouded in mystery. The Palace has been restored, but evidence remains across the low façade of the true nature of that attack.

For us, Santiago remained just a large, bustling city still; one that lacked the charm and sophistication of its neighbouring capital Buenos Aires across the Andes. We decided to take a trip out of the city, and being rather partial to wineries, having enjoyed such days out in Australia and New Zealand, we booked a tour. A mini-bus collects us from our hotel the following morning and we head west out of the city. The only other passenger is a heavily accented Irishman, a true traveller. Henry had visited over 150 countries and prior to his recent arrival in Chile he had been to North Korea. He claimed to be the first Western tourist to gain an entry visa for over two years, thanks to his persistence with the embassy in Beijing. Henry looked like a man who enjoyed a tipple, and this must have been a rather more enjoyable experience than being holed up in a hotel in China for all those weeks.

The trip took us down towards Santiago's seaport at Valparaíso before heading south into a winemaking area. After a tour of the winery and sampling the local product, we headed back into Valparaíso and then to the nearby seaside resort town of Vina del Mar. The town is the epitome of the upmarket Mediterranean resort, with wide tree-lined avenues and clusters of designer shops. However, instead of stopping here for lunch, our driver insisted on taking us to "somewhere very special". After about fifteen minutes we arrived outside a very ordinary-looking restaurant on the northern outskirts of the town, owned no doubt by a close personal friend of our driver. Rosie was a bit dubious but I enjoyed a pleasant lunch of local fish grilled washed down with another glass or two of Chilean wine. Henry, our garrulous travelling companion, enjoyed an equally hearty lunch and even larger quantities of wine and on the journey back to the city fell into a deep if noisy sleep.

A number of years have passed since that first visit, and we are back in Chile. Almost as far north as you can get before entering neighbouring

Peru. The town of Arica, population 185,000. A pleasant enough place but for the pervasive smells of its exports: fish, guano and fishmeal. From our cruise ship docked in the port, we watch as vast quantities of tuna are unloaded by crane from trawlers into huge open-backed trailers. Little wonder a permanent odour hangs heavy in the air, and we wonder whether you become inured and oblivious to the stench over time if you live here. That said, Arica appears at first glance to be a town with some charm, the dominant El Morro, a high cliff immediately behind the port, offering some natural protection from the elements and with some interesting-looking old buildings around the port area.

Despite having only a day in the port to explore, we have decided to take a tour and discover something of the interior. Our journey begins with our bus leaving town and almost immediately climbing away towards the east, where the coastal plain on which the town is located soon gives way to the foothills of the Andes. The road rises imperceptibly at first, there being no sign yet of the high peaks beyond.

The first sight of interest is the huge geoglyphs carved into the now barren hillside, each depicting animals of the Andes. Later, we stop at a small village called Poconchile for a comfort break. A couple of cafés serve the thirsty traveller, and close by the historic whitewashed parish church founded by a Spanish priest way back in 1580. We wander through the churchyard, which seems far too full of graves for such a small community, only for the gravestones to tell the story of a malaria epidemic years before. The graves are set as if in the desert with an unusual feature: elaborate shades constructed above the tombs, protection from the fierce unrelenting rays of the sun.

The bus continues on its journey ever upwards. Now there is no vegetation save for the very occasional cactus standing out from the brown hues of rock and sand, the sun so high in the sky that they barely cast a shadow. We stop again at Pukara, site of an ancient Inca fortification strategically placed with clear views over two converging valleys way below.

A pass takes us through 3,530 metres and from here we begin our descent to the small town of Putre. We halt once more to take our first look down onto the town below but more impressively beyond and our first sight of the snow-capped mountains of the high Andes.

Some local women have set up stalls here selling refreshments and handmade crafts, dolls and ponchos. They themselves are wearing the colourful dresses and wide-brimmed hats so common in this part of South America.

Putre itself proves to be an impoverished place, having little reason to exist beyond that it lies on the road between the Chilean coast and the border with Peru. The large open plaza at the centre of the town comprises the customary church, a modest statue of some local dignitary and rather incongruously a table football stand on which two young lads are energetically trying to outscore each other, totally oblivious to us.

We take lunch in a small *cantina* at the side of the plaza and then amble through several of the artisan shops dotted around the edges of the square, each selling the same goods, mainly knitwear, ponchos and sweaters belying the high ambient temperature of the day.

Late afternoon and we have returned to Arica. Beyond the port where our ship is moored, a wide-open plaza stretches back to the raised site of the pretty Church of St Marcos, built improbably in far distant Europe to be assembled here to a design by Gustave Eiffel no less. We have arrived in the middle of a fiesta and the main thoroughfare and plaza are teeming with people, the square full of stalls selling homemade crafts and sweets and other local delicacies, with groups of dancers practising in readiness for an evening procession.

As another author has observed, Sara Wheeler *"Travels in a thin country"*, Chile is indeed a long, narrow country, and it takes a further day and a half for our cruise ship to travel down the coast before we reach our next destination, Iquique. The town has an elegant, albeit faded look reflecting better times. A hundred years ago, Iquique grew affluent off the back of a burgeoning nitrate industry, which generated fortunes for a few and employment for many. The town now relies on a declining fishmeal industry and has a distinctly down-at-heel look behind the splendid façades in the old quarter. However, our interest is not in the town itself but the prospect of a trip into the nearby Atacama Desert. The big surprise is how near.

Iquique is set on a narrow strip of land against the coast. Having left by road, you immediately climb up a steep sandstone escarpment, past a huge sand dune onto a plateau some 2,000 feet above the city. The desert literally starts here. Low rolling hills, sand dunes and a total absence of vegetation. We are heading due east towards Humberstone.

The nitrate industry began in these parts in the middle of the nineteenth century, peaking in the years from 1890 to the outbreak of World War I.

Demand was disrupted by the War in Europe and this was followed by economic recession and then the invention of artificial fertilisers. All of this led to a slow and terminal decline for Chile's once prosperous north. The last mine closing in the 1960s.

The mines, or Offices as they are known locally, being set in the middle of the desert, in their heyday, had to draw labour from other parts of Chile. Given their location, the Offices became not just the place where the nitrate was removed from the ground but a totally self-sufficient community with shops and bars and other amenities. Humberstone was a very typical example. Now it is a ghost town. Whilst most of the Offices have long since been closed and the remains ransacked, some ingenious local had the idea of making this particular old mining town a tourist attraction. Humberstone is conveniently placed on the road from Iquique to Pozo Almonte and just a few kilometres from the junction with the great north-south Pan-American Highway.

Arriving at Humberstone is like being transported onto the set of a Western movie, and apparently the town has been used on more than one occasion for this purpose. Something of a recurring theme on our travels. The thing to remember is that this was a company town with a very clear pecking order. Top management in the form of the owners at one end and low-skilled labourers, recruited in many cases from hundreds of miles away, at the other end of the spectrum. In this pecking order, only management and white-collar workers could use the hotel and swimming pool, whilst the labourers working long hours for low wages were confined to bunkhouses and communal facilities. This region has traditionally been a breeding ground for the political left in Chile, with a long record of labour discontent. Back in 1908 the workers from Humberstone famously marched from the Office down into Iquique to protest against their conditions, only to be cut down by the guns of the Chilean Army. In the massacre, 3,800 workers died in the bloodiest industrial dispute in the history of the world.

Although by no means a "*Marie Celeste*" scene with uneaten food on the tables, there is nevertheless an eerie sense of a live and active community having quite suddenly departed. The mine was closed in 1960 but most of the infrastructure remains in place, from the theatre with faded posters of '50s film stars still adorning the walls to the swimming pool reserved for the white-collar workers, the pool itself ingeniously built using the hull of an abandoned ship brought up to the plateau from the notoriously dangerous coast below.

From Humberstone we travel some 50 kilometres further into the desert. Initially west to the small town of Pozo Almonte at the junction with the Pan-American Highway and then south along a stretch of this famed road through the natural and absurdly out-of-place Tamuragel Forest. Here, trees not only survive but flourish by drawing water through their roots which grow down 300 feet into the desert to find sustenance from underground streams. Beyond the forest and to our right, we see a range of low sandstone hills running parallel and perhaps 3 miles to the west of the highway. We turn off and head in their direction. It is not until we are relatively close that we began to see the amazing petroglyphs set on the sides of the hills. These huge drawings have been dated back to between five and six hundred years ago, and their purpose is subject to much speculation. The "artists" were almost certainly travellers moving from the Andes west towards the coast. With figures of people and animals and clear geometric shapes, my own theory would be that they tell a story, maybe recording the history of a family or tribe perhaps added to each year as the travellers made an annual trek to the coast to find food or engage in trade. Anyway, the sheer size, extent and clarity of the drawings adds to the intriguing questions about their source and purpose and makes them a fascinating sight for visitors to the Atacama.

Overnight, our ship has carried us further south. Still sitting high above the Pacific coastline, the Atacama Desert, where, it is claimed, there are places that have seen no rain for 400 years.

Imagine our surprise when rising this morning, we pull back the curtains of our cabin to look out upon a dreary scene: heavily clouded skies hanging over the jumble of houses and shacks that is the port town of Coquimbo.

On deck, the temperature matches the greyness of the morning and only a few hardy souls have bothered to venture out. We go below and dress accordingly in a rather downbeat mood, it has to be said. This is far from the weather we have been expecting.

On shore, we board a coach, and Miguel introduces himself as our guide for the day. I whisper to Rosie that notwithstanding his name, he looks distinctly English. A receding pate and what remains of his hair is distinctly red. Add a freckly complexion and he looks totally at odds with the typical inhabitant of this, what we had assumed to be, hot, sunny climate. He bears a strong resemblance to a younger version of actor Steve McFadden who plays Phil Mitchell in TV's *EastEnders*; although it didn't take us long to appreciate that he was temperamentally quite different from the soap opera character. He is engaging and friendly with a nice ironic sense of humour that is largely lost on the Americans who on this trip form the majority of our fellow travellers.

Our analysis of his English appearance proves well founded. When later we question him, he confides that his surname is Knuckey and that his great grandfather, an English sailor, had travelled around Cape Horn once too often and had decided to settle in this part of Chile in the early 1900s. One can easily imagine those four-masted schooners being tossed around in a Southern Ocean storm. Once ashore in a warm and sunny climate and faced with the prospect of ten to twelve more weeks at sea in a ship laden with nitrates returning to Europe it must have made many a sailor prepared to take his chance on starting a new life in this, at the time, increasingly prosperous land.

Coquimbo with its higgledy-piggledy development appears at first glance to have little to offer, and Miguel tends to support that opinion. Miguel comes from Arica, as I have described, some way to the north, and he rather disparagingly describes his fellow countrymen in this part of Chile as lazy, pointing out that it is approaching nine in the morning and the streets are deserted. Apparently, Coquimbo's sister town of La Serena just a few miles to the north is more attractive and is a popular resort town. However, our journey this morning is to take us in the opposite direction through the unprepossessing suburbs of Coquimbo to once again briefly join the Pan-American Highway that runs from Patagonia in the south along America's west coast to Alaska in the north, a distance of some 30,000 kilometres. In Chile alone, the road runs for 4,000 kilometres.

By the time we turn off the highway just 50 kilometres south, near the town of Ovalle, the skies are clearing and the temperature rapidly rising to around 30C degrees. In our ignorance, we are unaware of the *camanchaca*, or sea mists, which are a feature of early mornings along this coast and which in many places, form almost the only source of precipitation. Although nothing more than early-morning dew created by the fog, it is nevertheless sufficient to sustain many forms of flora along the coastal region of this, Chile's "El Norte Chico" or "Little North", our previous ports of call Iquique and Arica being part of the seriously dry "Big North". We are now in a part of Chile which although very dry nevertheless has a temperate climate that, supported by a sophisticated irrigation system, is suitable for grape growing and wine producing. This is soon evident as we leave the main road and drive through a vineyard before dropping down into the Valle del Encanto, or Enchanted Valley, to view some reputedly 4,000-year-old petroglyphs.

Led by Miguel, we clamber amongst the rocks, dodging the lethal needles protruding from huge cacti to view these early rock paintings depicting strange matchstick figures with antennae on their heads. Sufficiently strange to have provoked speculation of UFOs and alien beings landing in this area hundreds of years ago. Although the path is rough and uneven, it is a relatively undemanding climb through the narrow valley. Nevertheless, by now, some of our party, made up almost entirely of elderly Americans, are complaining. Unperturbed when Miguel asks if we want to press on to see some rocks called the "Inca Bath", we shout, 'Yes,' even though we have no idea if it is worthwhile or not. The "Inca Bath" proves to be a hollow rock situated at the furthest end of the valley, which indeed could have been used for the purposes of a bathtub. As a sight, I have to admit you could take it or leave it. Some struggled to reach our goal, although for the most part this could be attributed not to age or infirmity but to lack of fitness and totally inappropriate dress. The tour company blurb defined this excursion as … *involving moderately difficult walking conditions,* obviously not translating too well into American!

On our first day on board ship we had been walking around the deck when a rasping voice blasted our eardrums: 'Pardon me' in that uniquely American way of saying, 'Move your arse, you're getting in my way.' Despite the loud voice, the female form that pushed past was a waif of a thing with a mass of frizzy hair, dressed in a white jacket studded with sparkly decorations and wearing garish ski pants in strange psychedelic patterns. As this apparition power walked down the deck, I was drawn to the space between her thighs, leaving me with the impression that this was someone whose usual method of going from A to B was riding rather than walking.

As we gather around Miguel to hear more about the petroglyphs, I notice that the same woman is one of our group. Today's ski pants are of a different colour and pattern but definitely from the same wardrobe. By the end of the cruise, I realise she has an inexhaustible supply. Rosie assures me the pants are by Moschino, the jerkin by Versace and the footwear, most definitely not designed for rock climbing, by Jimmy Choo. She is accompanied by what I thought was a much older man with a distinctly careworn expression. It is only now that I appreciate that she is almost certainly much older than I had first thought. Exactly how old, I wouldn't care to guess. She has fallen into conversation with another couple. As her loud nasal tones blank out what Miguel is saying, I have little choice but to listen in. She weighs perhaps seven stone but is relating how to avoid the perils of putting on weight, particularly given the risk of this happening on a cruise ship. The gist of the conversation is that she never travels anywhere without her own personal set of scales. The husband winces as she relates this information. I can't help but think, *Poor guy*.

Miguel, perhaps conscious that he has not been receiving the total attention of this part of his flock, wanders over and asks whether there are any questions. The other couple are much younger, perhaps around thirty, but grossly overweight. The man is sweating profusely from the effort of walking up the valley, damp patches all over his T-shirt.

'Do you always take people to the Inca Bath?' he enquires.

Miguel says, 'Not always.'

'Okay, well, we got value for our money then,' he replies, seeming well pleased with Miguel's response.

From the valley we travel back to the highway, towards what we hope will be the highlight of the day: a visit to a winery. Wines have been produced in Chile since the arrival of the Spanish over 400 years ago, although it is only recently that the quality of those wines has been widely recognised outside of South America. The Francisco de Aguirre Winery is set in beautiful rolling hills in a valley close to Ovalle. It has a distinctly new and clinical feel and as the midday sun is now fierce, we would have preferred to be sampling the product rather than traipsing around the factory finding out how it is made. A cellar has been cut into the side of one of the hills, but it is quite small and is entered down a single set of stairs. When we arrive at the cellar entrance, we are told that it is occupied by another group and we therefore have to wait our turn in the blazing sun whilst the other party of tourists imbibe. Eventually, admittance is granted and in fairness the wine isn't bad but overall, the experience doesn't match winery visits we have previously made in New Zealand and Australia, which even now leave a warm glow.

Next day, we decide to take a short trip from Coquimbo to its nearby sister town, the supposedly more "upmarket" La Serena. Today is a cool but bright morning, and a short taxi ride finds us at after ten in the morning outside La Recovera market. The stallholders are just beginning to lay out their wares for the day's business so we move on and into the main square to visit the cathedral. Worth a look but nothing more. Our guidebook describes this as an attractive resort, but we have seen little evidence to support this assertion. It mentions a Japanese garden, but when we locate it in a backstreet the iron entry gate is firmly locked with a polite notice stating that it is closed for maintenance. We decide that it is time to return to Coquimbo.

There is an irregular but frequent bus service between La Serena and Coquimbo, so when we see a bus clearly displaying *Coquimbo*, its engine already running, we quickly board without any degree of apprehension, paying the driver the requisite *pesos* fare. Twenty minutes later our frustration is growing. We are still stationary. Half a dozen buses to Coquimbo have passed by, but our driver is determined that he needs a few more passengers to make the journey worth his while. Eventually, he decides we are sufficient in numbers. Apart from ourselves, two old ladies sit in the front; across the aisle a native couple, giggly and noisy, maybe high on coca but who will shortly fall asleep on each other's shoulders; at the back, half a dozen students chatting earnestly to one another. At this stage, we are oblivious to the fact that we should have chosen a bus displaying *Coquimbo directo*. This driver is taking us on a circuitous route that will eventually take over an hour driving through the outskirts of La Serena and Coquimbo, constantly playing cat and mouse with other bus drivers so he can reach bus stops where prospective passengers are waiting.

We have journeyed further south to reach Chile's major port, Valparaíso. Here we are leaving our ship before flying to Easter Island but first a couple of days exploring the city. The sprawling dockfront means that we exit the port terminal and take three stops on the modern and efficient metro to reach the main square, the Plaza Sotomayor itself, set on the waterfront and housing the imposing Commandancia Jefe de la Armada, the Navy headquarters building. In the square, a statue reflecting the naval theme, Monumento a los Heroes de Iquique; a reminder of an important battle in the nineteenth-century Pacific War with neighbouring Peru.

We make our way to the back of the square, pay 100 *pesos*, a lot less than it sounds, and take the hundred-year-old funicular Ascensor el Peral. At the top, we browse the numerous art shops and stalls and buy a small watercolour of the funicular. Close at hand is the Palacio Baburizza Museo de Artes, housed in a large and unusual mansion. The former home of a local nitrates magnate, it is unusual in that it combines many architectural styles in one building.

Valparaíso is built on many hills, providing a colourful backdrop to the port, although on the ground, the reality is somewhat less attractive. Graffiti is the bane of Latin America with barely a wall or statue not defaced. As we wander the backstreets beyond the museum, at least most of the graffiti can be described as art, often on an impressive level; not simply roughly drawn slogans but lovingly airbrushed depictions of urban lives and dreams.

We have returned to mainland Chile from Easter Island. I emerge from my post-prandial nap in a pleasantly relaxed stupor, no doubt enhanced by having imbibed a couple of large glasses of a fine Chilean Cabernet Sauvignon courtesy of our travel company. A small gift as an apology for having to share a tour guide with two Americans. A small price to pay.

Through the picture window of our room in the Hosteleria Rio Serrano, I realise that I have been raised from my slumber by the barking of two dogs rounding up a small herd of cattle. Well practised, it seems, their work achieved without any human intervention. The picture window is an architectural feature enabling guests a clear view across to the Torres del Paine National Park. We are blessed here in "Wild Patagonia", where the cold winds are notorious for their intensity and sheer persistence. Today, albeit in late summer, the air is still, the skies blue and the sun high in the sky, generating a pleasing temperature of around 70F.

We are resting after three days of travel from Easter Island. A brief stopover in Santiago, a flight down to the port of Punta Arenas via a very wet Puerto Montt. From here, we had taken a bus rented from one of the many petroleum companies operating in this region together with about a dozen other tourists, heading for an overnight stop at Puerto Natales; a trip through spectacular if barren landscapes, stopping only to visit a colony of Magellanic penguins in Otway Sound. Early the following morning, we were on the road again, leaving behind the pleasant lakeside town with just another 100 miles to Torres del Paine.

You will by now be appreciating the sheer scale of Patagonia. This part of the journey was across a vast flatland of scrub with sheep and cattle ranches each covering hundreds of square miles. North of Puerto Natales, we again left the main road, taking a detour to view the Cueva del Milodon, a cave network set in the slopes of a mountain called Cerro Benitez. The caves are named after a Milodon, a prehistoric creature the skins of which dated as 10,000 years old were discovered in the caves. As you make your way through the cave network, you come across a replica of this frightening-looking beast, carefully placed to startle the unwary. The sheer scale of the caves makes this a worthwhile side trip but returning to the bus we are wondering whether we are in a good place to suffer engine failure. We find our driver with his head under the bonnet. He fails to identify the problem other than to confirm that the engine has expired. Fortunately, we are only a few miles out of Puerto Natales and after an hour or so, a relief vehicle arrives and we are able to continue our journey.

After a few miles, the tarmac road disappears and progress thereafter is at a pedestrian pace. After this arduous journey, it is with some relief that we see the *hosteleria* come into view. The journey is not quite complete. We and our bags are dumped rather unceremoniously by the roadside and we wearily drag them down a rough path and over a rickety wooden bridge to at last arrive.

As an aside, it is worth relating that for Rosie, a retired project manager, old habits die hard, and trips like this are meticulously planned with regard to clothes matching the weather conditions we are likely to encounter, not to mention the medicine bag which would be the envy of any *Médecins sans Frontières* doctor in some remote African country. We can cater for cuts, coughs, colds, bruises, bites, stomach disorders, calluses, skin infections, headaches, blocked sinuses. You name it and Rosie has a cure. Although on many occasions, being slightly accident-prone, I have been glad to take advantage of the travelling first aid kit. It is not needed on this occasion. However, I have been found to be at fault, failing to predict accurately the weather. As we unpack our bags with the outside temperature reaching the mid-70s, I come across a fleece, thick shirt, an attractive array of headgear and woollen gloves and a waterproof jacket.

The latter item at least proves useful. I awake on our third day in Torres del Paine to the sound of rain on our hotel room window. This is a shame because today it is an early start. We are to drive up into the national park and take a boat trip on Lago Grey. After getting washed and dressed, I take a peek out of the window. Dawn is just breaking but even in first light, the clouds above look heavy. By the time we get into our bus, the prospects have worsened. The bone-jarring 50-minute drive up to the lake is in a persistent downpour. From the bus, we walk down to the shoreline to be ferried on rubber dinghies through a myriad of small icebergs to our boat. We are at the southern end of the lake and the plan is to travel the 10 miles or so to the northern extremity and view the Grey Glacier. This is our first visit to view a glacier and to be honest I am feeling depressed with the cold and wet, so from a distance and through the gloom, I am seriously considering whether this has not been $60 wasted. There seem to be dark patches above the glacier and a large amount of degradation on the face of the glacier, judging by the increasing number of icebergs we are encountering as we approach.

My concerns are ill-founded. The captain of our small vessel has done this journey so many times that he knows when it is risky, and today he is content to provide us with a close-up view. Soon we are craning our necks looking up at the white and powdery blue hues of the 50-foot high glacier face. The glacier is divided into two by a solid granite promontory jutting out into the cold waters of the lake. Turning the vessel around, we approach the western side with even more stupendous views. The rain passes and shafts of light break through the low cloud base. Glaciers are magical aspects of nature and during our subsequent travels they will feature more significantly than we can know on this memorable morning.

Our exploration of the park continues. The views are stunning. The park is dominated by three massive and distinctive granite mountains with pointed peaks: d'Agostini, Central and Monzino. Wildlife however proves to be at a premium; our only sighting, albeit very close, is a grey fox.

By mid-afternoon, we are back at the hosteleria and the wind has increased; the now thinning clouds scud past at an alarming rate. A little concern, as in two days' time, we take to the seas again. Our last evening in Torres del Paine, and taking a pre-dinner drink in the bar, we meet up with a group of eight very well-spoken elderly English ladies, ex-Roedean or Cheltenham Ladies' College judging from the accents, now masquerading as a group of merry widows from Ludlow. We like to think we are quite adventurous travellers but discover that they are journeying through Patagonia and all the way to Santiago, driving themselves in a rented mini-bus.

Unbelievably, today we are still in Chilean waters and Arica seems so far away. I can barely contain my acute sense of disappointment as I peer through the rain-splattered, salt-encrusted window, through a near impenetrable grey mist that hangs low over the Southern Ocean. There, less than a mile away, I can make out the outline of land. Screwing up my eyes as best as I can to discern a desolate, unforgiving landscape, high cliffs leading to rolling barren hills above. A few other passengers disconsolately stand around the lounge area drinking coffee and exchanging views on the likelihood of having any chance of going ashore. The consensus seems to be that the answer will be a resounding, 'No.' A quick glance at the clock above the door indicates that we are already fifteen minutes past our intended disembarkation time and still no word from the bridge.

During the night, our tiny ship, the *Mare Australis*, took a fearful battering as we emerged from the relative shelter of the Murray Channel into the open seas. Every few seconds, the dull thud of wave on bow and then the motion of pitching forward into the trough before being hit by the next wave. Rosie has succumbed to, unusually for her, a bout of seasickness, and for the first time, as dawn broke and I looked at her across the cabin, I appreciated the term, "having turned green". It was easy to admire the courage and fortitude of sailors past who have traversed these waters in much worse conditions and in ships a good deal less well equipped for the task than our own. Not to mention the more recent endeavours of yachtsmen and women travelling alone in these treacherous waters. Yet it has been our fervent hope, whilst not trailblazers in any sense, to do something few of them had done: to actually land on Cape Horn.

Then something of a surprise. Our intrepid Captain Strauch announces over the PA system that a zodiac, a motorised dinghy, is being launched off the back of the ship with three crew members who will reconnoitre the landing area onshore. As the tiny boat shoots through our eyeline, nobody on board is surprised to see at the tiller the mad Argentinian Diego. On earlier trips to the shore, on our three-day voyage through the Chilean fjords and along part of the famed Beagle Passage, he has repeatedly frightened me stupid with his antics, his favourite trick being to open the throttle to its maximum as we approach land. Despite his clowning, I think if anyone can make safe passage in these waters, it is Diego. Sure enough, half an hour later, the dinghy hoves back into view and shortly afterwards the captain returns to the PA to announce that although the seas are still rough in the bay, the landing place is sheltered sufficiently for those who feel physically able to go ashore. Rosie is uncertain but I reason that it is better to spend a couple of hours on terra firma than to remain on board bobbing around here in the ocean, waiting for the others to return.

We make our way to the back of the ship, collecting a lifejacket en route. Two dinghies have by now been launched and are circling, making uncertain attempts to tie up at the launch platform. As we queue for our turn, an uncertain feeling. Instead of being helped on board the dinghy, as had become our normal practice over the previous days, we are instructed how to sit and slide to a position where we perch sitting on the outer rim of the craft. The first dinghy fills with some of our fellow passengers and races away into the distance. We are next, and who is at the tiller? None other than the mad Argentinian. I pray that he will on this occasion cut out his larking about.

Well, somehow, we make it. Once on shore, we face a lengthy and treacherous climb up a set of crumbling wooden steps to the top of the island. Here, at nearly 1,500 feet above the ocean, a Chilean Government weather station and lighthouse. Beyond on a small promontory, offering views over the Southern Ocean far below, a monument to all the brave sailors that have passed this way or perished off these dangerous shores.

In the hour or so ashore, we enjoy pleasant sunshine for the taking of photographs but, as the wind suddenly turns and begins to whistle through our warm anoraks and a damp squall passes quickly through, thoughts turn to getting back on board the *Mare Australis* and heading north towards the relative tranquillity of the Beagle Channel.

If nothing proves my point about Chile as a country of extremes, sitting here just off Cape Horn, we are still in Chile and 4,176 km from Arica where we first entered the country.

There must be something compelling about Chile. We are back again. This time, travelling around the Lake District that we encountered on that first journey to South America many years before, when as innocents abroad we had crossed the Andes. Now much more knowledgeable and confident about our surroundings, we pick up a hire car in Puerto Montt and head up towards the nearby Lake Llanquique, arriving at the small family-run hotel where we are to stay for the next few days. This, only after a hairy episode when we inadvertently drive the wrong way down a one-way street in Puerto Montt. We are blissfully unaware of our error until confronted by a large heavy goods vehicle, horn blasting, heading in our direction. I yank the steering wheel sideways and we stall in a narrow roadside pull-off, suitably shaken.

A tip to fellow travellers. Check out reverse on the gearbox before proceeding in a forward direction with your rental car. At this juncture, having failed to heed our own advice and panic-stricken from our near disaster, I pull the gear lever hither and thither in a vain effort to engage the right cogs to enable us to reverse and turn the car so it is pointing in the right direction. By the time we eventually succeed, the atmosphere in the car is heavy with mutual recriminations.

Our hotel is in a beautiful setting beside the lake and with clear views across to the perfectly conical-shaped and snow-topped Volcan Osorno. In need of a drink after our close encounter with the HGV, we settle down in the gardens to enjoy the view, and at the behest of mine host, we are encouraged to imbibe the locals' favourite brew, a *pisco* sour. For the uninitiated, *pisco* is a South American brandy derived from grape, and the sour element is a combination of egg white, sugar syrup and limes. We have been told that after three you feel happy, but don't try to stand up. On this occasion, two seemed sufficient to do the trick.

The following day starts grey and drizzly as we drive north along the side of the lake, intending to reach Puerto Octay, bypassing the lakeside town of Frutillar. However, after skirting the town, the road deteriorates dramatically, slowing progress, and given the unhealthy condition of our hire car, after a few kilometres we decide on a change of plan; we turn around and instead head for Frutillar. It proves a charming little town, much influenced by generations of German immigrants. Alpine-style architecture combined with restaurants serving German cuisine, and a fine museum, largely outdoors, that traces the town's history through the farming heritage of its pioneers. There is a pier, impressive theatre and a tidy promenade with artisan shops and cafés. We stop at one to enjoy a strong coffee and generous portion of Bavarian-style *kuchen*.

Next day, we travel north again, this time to the Puyohue National Park, but we have little time to enjoy the extensive hiking trails and after a brief walk we continue on to visit the provincial capital, Osorno. In the main square, the cathedral, with a truly impressive façade in the neo-gothic style, although not of any great historical note, as it was built as recently as 1960. Close by, we come across a row of striking and beautifully maintained wooden mansions. On closer inspection of the nearby signage, we determine that, dating from the nineteenth-century arrival of German immigrants to this region, they have all been designated as National Monuments.

After taking a late lunch, an incredibly fattening local donut purchased from a *panaderia* and eaten sitting in the square watching local life, we decide to end the day's touring by visiting Puerto Varas at the distant southern end of the lake. We had visited here briefly on that first trip to Chile when we had crossed the Andes from Bariloche in Argentina but frankly had little recall of the town. It proves to be a busy and very popular resort with the usual assortment of cafés, restaurants, small hotels and gift shops. Once again, as we have discovered in this region of Chile, it is a town notable for its German influences. A little research tells us that for a period of about thirty years in the middle of the nineteenth century, the indigenous people were forced to give up land, as the Chilean Government encouraged immigrants from Europe to settle here, coming almost exclusively from Germany.

After four days beside Lake Llanquique, we return our rental car and in Puerto Montt board *Skorpios 2* for the next part of our journey. *Skorpios 2* is a family-owned ship accommodating around one hundred passengers and built to ply the waters south of Puerto Montt. We are no longer on a lake but in a complex archipelago of islands and waterways that ultimately flow into the Pacific Ocean. Over the following five days, we will be exploring this region from the water; the highlight, we are assured, will be to view at close quarters the San Rafael Glacier.

Skorpios 2 has a rustic charm; luxury it is not. Our cabin, situated on the top deck, is fitted out in dark wood furniture with brass fittings. Frugal but comfortable. Our fellow passengers, we discover, are mainly Chilenos with a few Argentinians. We are not just the only Brits on board but from what we can ascertain, the only English speakers. By mid-morning, it is all aboard and we gently ease away from the pier.

Despite a dank gloom, all passengers suitably garbed are on deck to see our departure. Tonight, the ship will sail into open waters to cross the Gulf of Corcovado, and the captain warns that conditions may become choppy, as there will be nothing between us and the Pacific Ocean. In the event, it is a relatively stable crossing, but first glance through our cabin window next morning shows that little has changed weatherwise; grey and foreboding skies and a persistent light rain. We tie up at a small settlement, a large sign on the dockside conveniently telling us that this is Puerto Aguirre on the Islas Huiches. On another day, a two-hour stop here might have been an attractive proposition but on this wet Sunday morning, the locals have made no concessions for our arrival and remain in bed. There seems little incentive to go ashore, but sometimes one has to shake off the natural lethargy and explore. Running away from the dockside and on a steep incline, the main road through the centre of this small settlement.

We are told that a walk will be rewarded with excellent views from a *mirador* at the top of the street so off we trudge. Some local kids emerge to act as guides, but their parents remain determinedly out of view and the village store closed for business. We are dressed for the cold but despite the inclement weather the temperature is a mild 15 degrees and surprisingly humid, so by the time we reach the viewpoint we are in quite a sweat. Even in the murk, we can see that the views are indeed spectacular down across the water to other small densely wooded islands forming this tiny archipelago. As we descend the hill to return to the ship, the skies brighten and locals emerge. We are surprised that most are pure Mapuche Indians, some of the few indigenous peoples still surviving in the whole of Chile.

Sailing through the fjords, there is little to do on board other than spend time on deck admiring the scenery, and here we get into conversation with Gustav, an Argentinian doctor vacationing with his family. Gustav introduces his teenage daughter Florencia, who is delighted to practise her English on real English people, as she is soon to depart on a student exchange visit to the UK.

Overnight, we are at anchor ready for our visit to the now nearby glacier, but the morning brings more despondency, heavy rain and fog. Undeterred, the captain orders the lowering of the two specially designed boats. Hunched together under the rough canopy, we inch forward through the mist amongst the icy detritus that has fallen off the front of the glacier, crunching through, avoiding as we go the larger bergs but, as we do so, the weather mercifully relents, enabling us to view not only the glacier face delineated in every hue of blue but the moraine above.

Skorpios 2 is anchored 1 kilometre away from the glacier for reasons of safety, and we return to the ship in a much better mood for a hearty lunch of stew served with chunks of fresh bread, miraculously loaded that morning from a small boat that has made its way through the gloom from a nearby village. With the weather improving, even a little blue sky emerging from behind the clouds, the captain decides to take us closer to the glacier and we are rewarded when a thunderous crash echoes across the fjord, reverberating around the ship as a huge calving takes place in front of our eyes. Tons of ice falling off the glacier face and disappearing into the water, throwing up a foaming torrent high into the air, and then as we gasp in astonishment at what we have seen, the huge piece of ice dramatically reappears from the deep, surrounded by plumes of spray. Rosie is excited. After patiently training her video recorder on the ice face, she has been rewarded, catching the whole sequence of events to be enjoyed again, maybe sometime in the future when our travelling days are over.

The next day is altogether more relaxing. We are in Quitalco Fjord, where the *Skorpios* owners have a private island, a holiday retreat for the family, accommodation for visitors, with a swimming pool and natural hot springs and hiking trails. The Carcamo family are successful local entrepreneurs, having built a business based on the surrounding waters, shipbuilding, a cargo fleet and two tourist ships bearing the name *Skorpios*. We climb high to a *mirador* for views across the fjord below and come across a tiny *chucao*, a spirited little bird with the friendly characteristics of our own robin. Meanwhile, below on the shoreline, members of the ship's crew are busy preparing lunch: a whole lamb spit-roasted.

Our penultimate day on *Skorpios 2* finds us gliding through beautiful fjords to a place that has long intrigued us: the island of Chiloe. Early afternoon finds us going ashore at its capital, Castro. Chiloe has a certain aura of mystique about it, maybe because of its isolation, its people widely regarded as slightly odd.

The main part of the town is on a plateau, requiring a bit of a climb away from the port. We have been caught unawares by the change in the weather, partly cloudy skies, but the chill wind has been replaced by an ambient temperature in the mid-twenties. Reaching the large plaza, our first priority is to shed several layers of clothing.

Most impressive in the square is the brightly yellow-painted cathedral. We find the post office, send some postcards, and to our surprise nearby an airline office where we are able to check in for our scheduled flight the following day. The square is crowded with people. It looks like a throwback to 1960s hippy culture; long-haired young men and girls in long, flowery dresses and flowers in their hair here for a popular rock festival.

We decide to return to the ship, change our warm clothes for something more appropriate for the soaring temperature and then to head out to look for the famed *palmitos* situated at sea level along the coast road. *Palmitos* are colourfully painted stilt houses, a noted feature of Castro. Once again, the reality doesn't match the tourist guidebook hyperbole. The main street of *palmitos* facing the waterfront are properties in disrepair, although a process of gentrification has begun with some of the buildings having been renovated, and these properties are now holiday lets or small boutique hotels. Further along, we come across a small, almost dried-up lake around which the faded glory of more *palmitos*. Still occupied, not just needing a lick of paint, they sadly have the appearance of a shanty town.

Disappointed, we walk back to the port area and a local market. Our ship is ready to sail and our trip to the Chilean fjords is nearing its end, so too our latest visit to the long, thin country.

Three

Peru: On the trail of the Incas

Peru: The country is dominated by the Amazon Rainforest and the Andes Mountains. However, more than half the population live in the lowland strip along the Pacific coastline. Population 32 million, largely comprising 60% mestizo (mixed race) and 25% Amerindian (pure indigenous). Languages – Spanish, Quechua, Aymara.

It is a place that I have long wanted to visit, "The Lost City of the Incas". Now perched high above the site, looking down with my own eyes, seeing the view that so many photographers have replicated to produce the iconic pictures that adorn posters and travel brochures the world over, I am not in the least disappointed.

Our approach to Machu Picchu has been a little unusual. Two days ago, we left a cruise ship at the northern Chilean port of Arica. From here, two planes had been chartered to take our party of about 200 to the city of Cusco, high in the Peruvian Andes.

We had been bused from the ship to the airport. On the way, we were given clear instructions: 'On arriving at the airport, collect your bags from the bus and take them to one corner of the terminal building.' On arriving, we piled out of the buses to be met by chaotic scenes, a melee of people and suitcases. Most of us did as instructed, albeit with some reluctance, in the absence of any tagging system, adding our luggage to the jumble of bags and cases piled high in one corner of the building. The tour guides assured us that this would be fine, easy to say but more difficult to persuade a sceptical group of seasoned travellers, who could see only a disorganised rabble trying to get us and our luggage onto our planes.

There was no check-in desk; we had been told that we had been pre-allocated seats on the planes. So instead of us queueing, the designated tour company representative, a tiny little Chilean girl with a small voice and limited English spoken with a heavy Spanish accent, started to hand out boarding cards. As the passengers slowly began to realise what was happening, a throng gathered around her as she began to call out names.

'Smeeth, anybody called Smeeth?' Only those next to her could hear. People pressed closer to find out what was happening.

'What did she say, was that Swift?' She seemed determined to find Mr Smith.

We were scheduled to depart in half an hour. This could take days. I decided it was time for action. I grabbed the boarding passes from the hands of the startled girl and leapt onto a chair.

In a very loud voice, I shouted, 'Smith.'

No reply. I placed the boarding pass for Mr Smith at the bottom of the pile.

Next one. 'Jones, David.'

'Here.'

'Quickly take your boarding pass.'

'What about my wife?'

'Sorry, they are in no particular order, just listen out. Next. Wanamaker…'

I had in minutes quickly dispensed about half of the boarding cards to the baying pack around my chair when I came upon the names Le Bargy, Rosemary and Le Bargy, Bernard. I was hoarse with shouting and it seemed the natural thing to pocket our boarding passes and quit my self-appointed role of tour leader. I leapt from the chair, thrust the remaining boarding cards back into the Rep's hands and disappeared into what remained of the throng to join the line waiting to board the aircraft.

Arriving at Cusco presented a timely reminder that South America has a history of political instability, revolution and dictatorship. At the airport, we were shepherded onto a fleet of buses all bearing a large red cross on the side panel. Just before the driver closed the automatic doors, a small woman dressed in army fatigues and a shoulder holster with an alarmingly large pistol almost as big as her leapt on board. The buses were then driven in convoy to our hotel, at the front, a jeep containing armed soldiers with a number of police cars at the rear, all with lights flashing. Along the route, we passed more heavily armed soldiers stationed at every major junction and on footbridges across the main thoroughfare. Our guide rather oddly tried to assure us that this was nothing out of the ordinary. Apparently, we had arrived on a day of a general strike opposing privatisation of the energy industry. It wasn't that easy to convince us; then again, it probably was normal for Peru.

Cusco sits high in the Andes at an altitude of more than 13,000 feet. All the travel literature that we had read recommended several hours, if not days, of rest to acclimatise to being 2 miles above sea level, so it was a surprise to find that we had a schedule providing just one hour of rest, then lunch, to be followed immediately by a tour of the city and its environs. To help the adjustment to the altitude, with our lunch, we were served copious amounts of coca tea. By now, I had a thumping headache, so it was impossible to tell whether the effects of the coca tea were positive or deleterious. Rosie was taken by the taste rather than the therapeutic qualities (or so she claimed) and sank several cups before we ventured forth.

In the hotel lobby, we were introduced to Rosa, a small dark lady. It was no surprise when she told us that despite her Christian name, she was a pure-blooded Quechua Indian. Rosa quickly made us aware that she had little empathy with the Spanish, who had invaded her country and whose influence was already evident from our brief acquaintance with this mountain city. It seemed absurd to be harbouring a grudge; after all, this had happened some four centuries earlier, although I guess Rosa thought that the European influence had negatively impacted on the culture of her own people.

Rosa explained that our first stop was just a short walk across the street from the hotel to the Santo Domingo Monastery, an impressive example of early Spanish efforts to impose their culture on the Peruvian people. Interestingly, though, however hard the Spaniards tried, they had been unable to totally destroy the Inca Temple of the Sun, which lay on this site and provided stout foundations for the monastery. Fortunately for them, given this is one of the few buildings in the city to have survived intact over the centuries, during which there has been a succession of earthquakes.

The temple walls, parts of which are visible and still lie intact within the precincts of the monastery, are an impressive testimony to the architecture and building prowess of the Incas, as well as providing the foundation upon which the Spanish built a temple to their own god. These walls, comprising huge granite blocks hewn accurately into shape, still in place as they have been for over 500 years, stand firm without the use of any form of cement. One couldn't help but agree with Rosa in marvelling at the Incas' building proficiency compared with the more prosaic European constructions on the site.

From the monastery, we take a short journey to the compelling town square, the Plaza de Armas, containing amongst other buildings the Cathedral Jesus Maria. By the time we have toured the grand but stultifying cathedral, we are ready for the next stage of our Cusco excursion. Now it is raining steadily, offering some merciful relief from the attentions of the beggars and hawkers that plague tourists throughout the centre of the city.

Next we board a coach for the steep climb out of the city to the Inca ruins at Sacsaywaman. Here, further impressive evidence of the Inca dynasty and its prowess as builders, where the temple and city built on this site were constructed from huge boulders, many weighing hundreds of tons. Rather like Stonehenge in England, even today it is difficult to understand how huge rocks were manoeuvred and sculpted to create these magnificently impressive structures. Finally, with head now really thumping, to the site at Q'enqo, another impressive Inca temple complex. By the time we return to the hotel, our brains are spinning from a combination of the magnificence of the city and its environs and the effects of the altitude on our near exhausted bodies. We are in desperate need of the hour's rest provided before dinner.

We eat little, instead cutting short our meal to briefly venture out from the hotel for some late-evening shopping, just time to purchase a warm knitted alpaca wool jumper, before retiring for the night. Despite the tiredness from a hectic day of travelling and sightseeing, the high humidity and thumping headache meant it was a restless night.

A very early start and another adventure. Ahead, the main reason for this visit to South America: the opportunity to visit Machu Picchu. After breakfast, we headed by coach out of the city of Cusco to catch the train at the railway halt at nearby Poroy, situated at a mere 11,000 feet. The train itself is a pleasant surprise, very comfortable and with an excellent buffet service. When we pulled over occasionally to allow a local train to pass, travelling in the opposite direction, we realised that our dollars had secured rather superior accommodation to the normal "enjoyed" by local villagers and backpackers jammed cheek by jowl into carriages with bare wooden seats.

The train journey takes close on four hours, descending slowly at first alongside gently meandering mountain streams, passing mixed smallholdings with fields of maize and livestock, usually cattle and pigs, before entering a narrow gorge, the Romatales Valley. Here, the train descends rapidly through a series of switchbacks before entering the vast open Urubamba Valley, where the route continues alongside the fast-flowing Urubamba River. The journey really is downhill all the way, from over 11,000 feet at Poroy to a little over 8,500 feet at Aguas Calientes, where we leave the train. By the time we alighted, my headache had miraculously disappeared and I felt fully refreshed and ready for Machu Picchu.

A stream of tourists queue through the narrow streets of the town waiting to board the fleet of buses which constantly run up and down from here to the entrance of Machu Picchu itself, a precarious climb on a zigzagging road hanging off the side of the mountain and taking around forty minutes, climbing more than 1,000 feet higher atop the mountain overlooking Aguas Calientes.

Now we have arrived, it is late morning and already hot, but clouds are beginning to accumulate in menacing fashion around the nearby mountain range. We have heard that on most days these clouds eventually lead to an afternoon thunderstorm, and we are anxious to climb to the Caretaker's Hut, the highest vantage point in Machu Picchu, and like so many before us to take photographs looking down on the whole complex. That iconic photograph that appears in just about every travel brochure featuring Peru. So, we have left Rosa and the rest of our party at the entrance to the ruins and struck out on our own.

Once through the main entrance and into the city, we are presented with a sight that does not disappoint. Much has been written about this fabulous location, and suffice to say it is a truly awesome sight and more amazing when one considers that it was constructed by some lost civilisation around 500 years ago, and it remained hidden for so long from the view of the conquering Spanish and more recent visits by outsiders until revealed to the world by Hiram Bingham as recently as 1911.

From the gatehouse that today forms the main entrance to the site, we began the ascent to our chosen vantage point. It looked relatively easy and I set off at a gallop, clambering up the uneven paths. It didn't take long before I needed to stop. I pretended I was offering Rosie a helping hand, but she wasn't fooled, describing my pallor as an unpleasant grey. I realised that at this altitude, a slow and steady climb with frequent stops is required, ostensibly to take in the views but in reality, to take in gulps of air.

In the event, the weather is kind but the sunny intervals between the clouds scudding across the sun are hot. The Caretaker's Hut target is achieved and here we sit for some minutes on a rock, taking in the views. It is a magical place. Like the whole of the site, the naming of various locations is rather speculative because in the absence of any written language, the whole purpose of Machu Picchu and the buildings on the site are pure supposition.

Our primary objective having been achieved, we wander in more leisurely fashion around the complex. Many of the early-morning arrivals have left and the site takes on a more serene feel with alpaca roaming freely on the open green spaces between the ruins. An ambition fulfilled and truly one of the most incredible places on the planet.

Time is as ever our enemy in these situations and we have to leave. We take one of the many local buses for the precarious multi s-bend journey back down the mountain to Aguas Calientes far below in the valley. Our attention is deflected away from the hair-raising descent by a little boy dressed in the local traditional garb. I swear he is no more than five years of age. As we board the bus for the trip down the mountain, he comes aboard and waves to everyone before disappearing from view. We then proceed to zigzag our way down the mountain road when suddenly in front of the bus there is the little urchin cheerfully waving. This process is repeated several times all the way down into the valley until he is allowed by the driver, who it transpires is his father, to board the bus and collect dollar bills as a reward. It is an amazing feat doubtless repeated a dozen times in a day as he appears totally fresh and unfazed whilst we, strangers to high altitude, are breathing heavily just at the sight of his efforts. I can't help but muse that this little lad is probably making a darn sight more money in a working day than his father, so free are we foreign tourists with our rewards. A fairly typical example of how tourism can distort a local economy and its reward system.

It is now mid-afternoon and we are back in the town awaiting our train when, true to form, the heavens open, by which time we have seen everything we could reasonably expect in such a short one-day visit.

On the way back to Cusco, we alight from the train at Ollantaytambo to visit the huge agricultural terraces excavated in the hills high above this village. At every stop on our journey today, we have been greeted by hawkers selling their wares, various items of knitwear, hats, gloves, ponchos. The faces become increasingly familiar. An act of entrepreneurship. They have tracked us all day by road, unloading their goods so that every time our train has stopped, there they are with their wares set out on the ground for us to view. Then as the train departs, hurriedly reloading their wares in a couple of clapped-out old Volkswagen camper vans. Quickly heading to the next station in a convoy comprising the two vans and a number of noisy Chinese-manufactured motorbikes to repeat the process.

Here we can say goodbye to the hawkers, as instead of returning to the train, we board coaches for the final stage of our journey back to Cusco. At Pisac, crossing the great Urubamba River and beginning to climb once again onto a huge fertile plateau at over 13,000 feet. Despite the gentle rolling hills and serene surroundings of tranquillity and calm, I am revisited by my thumping headache. Later in the evening, it is with relief combined with a sense of supreme satisfaction that my head gently sinks into the pillow.

Next morning and another early start. Our party had been split into three groups booked on scheduled flights to take us now to Lima and ultimately back to our ship. We have drawn the short straw, being booked on the earliest departure from Cusco Airport this morning. We check in and are pleasantly surprised to find the departure lounge, being very modern and spacious, contains a range of boutiques and gift shops. Not that this is important, given our flight is due to leave in forty-five minutes. At 7.15 am, the passenger information screens indicate our flight is due to land at 7.18, virtually on time for the 7.45 am departure. From the lounge, the picture windows offer the prospect of stunning views up the runway towards the high Andes beyond; the only problem is that visibility this morning with low cloud is such that you cannot see the mountains. This low cloud is a perennial problem at this altitude and with the notoriously violent afternoon storms, this is not a place on which entry or exit can be relied upon. Eventually, we establish that the airport is officially closed and that our plane, although at one time over the airport, has now diverted to Arequipa, over 200 miles to the south.

Within minutes of us receiving this news, the mist begins to clear and aircraft land. Our fellow travellers on the flights scheduled for later in the morning drift into the lounge and then off on their allotted planes pretty well on time. Then more drama. President George W Bush is due to arrive in Lima aboard *Air Force One* later this afternoon, and the airport will close to all traffic at twelve noon. At around eleven o'clock, our plane eventually lands and we are quickly shepherded aboard for the fifty-minute journey scheduled to land in Lima spot on midday. We are on the last scheduled flight that will be allowed to land at Lima Airport today.

We arrive at Lima to find the airport bristling with the military and police all heavily armed. No time to even look around or collect our luggage, we are hustled onto a coach surrounded by Jeeps full of soldiers, and with a rather attractive armed female police officer riding shotgun in the bus, we set off for the short drive down to Callao, Lima's port. Here, another security measure thanks to the President's visit, we discover that our cruise liner has not been allowed to dock nor the remaining passengers on board allowed off to visit Peru. Instead, she lies at anchor about a mile offshore. We are subjected to a thorough search by the port authorities before being taken by tender back to the ship. Another interesting day.

It is to be some years before we return to Peru, and our journey begins in Salaverry where we are visiting the Temples of the Sun and Moon. This is an enormous archaeological site where excavations did not begin until 1991 but where the discoveries are already on an impressive scale. Whilst the two temples have been partly exposed, they sit in a wide valley where it is believed there once stood an important city, remnants of which lie barely disturbed below the surface and yet to reveal its secrets. The site was occupied not by the Incas but by the Moche people between around 200 BC and AD 800 and is believed to have come to a cataclysmic end when hit by a massive El Nino-inspired storm.

We drive past the Temple of the Sun, actually a huge pyramid structure over 40 metres in height, in local legend, built by a quarter of a million men in just three days. We carry on the visit to the nearby Temple of the Moon. Here, evidence of the Moche practice of building one temple upon another. Peeling away the layers rather like an onion, each inner layer is largely intact, not least the extensive wall murals, still retaining the colours as if freshly painted today.

Later, we travel on to the nearby town of Trujillo, which vies with Arequipa in its claim to be Peru's second city. Driving through downtown towards the city centre, the most striking things are the elaborate and often colourful balconies of the colonial-style houses. Although intriguing, they do not prepare the traveller for the sights at the very centre of the city. The Plaza de Armas is hugely impressive, surely one of the finest plazas in all of South America. Here, its buildings contain a microcosm of Peru's history, yet today it is alive with activity, not in any sense a museum to the past. It is difficult to know where to start in describing the buildings that line the four sides of the square so, although lacking the longevity of many of those edifices, there is perhaps no better place to start than in the centre of the square where we find the Freedom Monument, the work of German sculptor Edmund Moeller. A complex piece conveying many messages but none more important than the idea of liberation. The significance of this for the city and for Peru becomes more evident when we visit the Casa de Emancipacion. Here in 1820, the local Governor declared independence from Spain and thus started a chain of events leading to Peru and its South American neighbours casting off 300 years under the Spanish crown. The Freedom Monument was commissioned to celebrate the centenary of independence, although it was not finally inaugurated until 1929.

In one corner of the square, the fine cathedral, but with our limited time to explore we decide to walk across to the opposite side of the square to take the opportunity to visit the Casa Urquiaga, where Simon Bolivar lived for a time in the period after Peru's independence from Spain; indeed, the great man's desk is amongst the artefacts on display. The building, although now owned by the Central Bank, has nevertheless been preserved in its original state. It impresses from its bright blue exterior to its series of three inner courtyards and rooms decorated with the heavy furniture of the seventeenth and eighteenth centuries.

Our visit to Trujillo is all too short, with just enough time left to glimpse the cathedral and the nearby Casa de Orbegoso.

Next stop Lima. Peru's capital has a tired look. Our bus takes us through two large plazas, the 2 de Mayo and St Martin, but despite some interesting-looking buildings, this cursory inspection reinforces our first impression of an underlying sense of decay and neglect. Finally, we alight in the Plaza Mayor outside the Municipalidad, the town hall. It is Sunday afternoon and the square is busy, full of people doing nothing other than taking a stroll. We are fortunate with our timing, as there is a changing of the guard in front of the Palace de Gobierno, the troops in their toy soldier uniforms of white and red.

Arrangements have been made for us to make a private visit to the nearby Casa de Aliaga. An unprepossessing frontage hides a thirty-seven room mansion built by conquistador Jeronimo de Aliaga, trusted ally of Pisarro, the founder of Lima, who granted permission for the property to be constructed in 1535. Eighteen generations later, the house remains in the private ownership of the same Aliaga family. We are told that the Grande Dame of the family, aged 101, is in residence, but she doesn't put in an appearance, the family now residing in a more modern annex at the rear of the property. As old as the city itself, this is a living history of 500 years with an amazing collection of furniture, art and artefacts. If they could speak, each piece would tell a story, but the indelible impression that remains with me is that of solidity and permanence exemplified in the wooden panelling, stout doors, beautifully carved and in a dark veneer, and the *pièce de résistance* centrepiece of a remarkable property: the marble staircase.

By the time we leave, it is late afternoon as we head around the corner to the San Francisco Church and Convent. One of the highlights of the city in the Moorish-baroque style of many Spanish churches and containing the usual excessive use of gold ornamentation typical of so many Catholic churches.

Early evening finds us in Miraflores. In stark contrast to the old city, this area along the coast boasts modern apartments, shopping malls, cafés and restaurants and clifftop vistas over the Pacific. Being a Sunday, the whole seafront area is heaving with people, children playing, families promenading, young couples canoodling; many, it appears, replicating the *El Beso* statue in the centre of one clifftop park. There is a 6-kilometre boardwalk and an impressive lighthouse, but after a heavy touring day, it is time to chill out and people-watch.

The following day and we are in a different part of the city at the Larco Museum in the *barrio* called Puebla Libre. The museum contains an impressive private collection of primarily pre-Colombian artefacts, appropriately contained within what was the house of the eighteenth-century Spanish Viceroyalty but, significantly, on the site of a seventh-century pyramid. The collection itself has an interesting history and Peru has a lot to thank the Larco family for in collecting items which until the museum was created would have been discarded or destroyed. The museum dates back to the 1920s. A wealthy family, the patriarch Rafael Larco Herrera inherited a 600-piece collection from his brother-in-law in 1925. It was his son Rafael

Larco Hoyle who became fascinated with the pieces and their history, and his father encouraged his son to start a museum. This he did with gusto, purchasing several other larger collections and opening a museum in his father's name in 1926. There are exhibits drawn from tribal groups across Peru, many in gold, including fantastical headdresses and nose ornaments. The museum is also noted for its exhibition of erotic pottery in highly explicit forms, with something of a predilection for phallic symbolism that countless visitors, judging from our visit, clearly find highly titillating.

José de San Martin is a hero of South American independence, liberator of Argentina, Chile and Peru from Spanish rule. His contemporary and fellow liberator Simon Bolivar had a whole country named in his honour. In contrast, the port of General San Martin on the Pacific coast of Peru proves to be a tiny, dusty and inconsequential place. The only reason we are here is a desire on my part to see the extraordinary Nazca Lines. Some 2,000 years ago, these geoglyphs were drawn across the arid terrain in this desolate region. Best seen from the air, they comprise both geometric lines as well as outlines of animals and birds.

This is not to prove one of my better travel experiences. We journey the short distance to a local airstrip at Pisco. We together with a small group of fellow passengers are all weighed to ensure the aircraft loading is balanced. As a result, Rosie and I are allocated seats in different parts of the aircraft. Anticipating a tiny six- or eight-seater prop, I am surprised when we are led onto the tarmac and directed to board a small executive jet-style plane. The omens are not good. I have drawn the short straw. I don't even have a window seat and I am sat next to a complete stranger. It is a one and two seat configuration. Luckily, Rosie has been allocated a window seat. Soon after take-off, my travelling companion is clearly not enjoying the confined space. Within minutes, we are flying low over the Nazca Lines, but being a jet, the sights below are little more than a blur. Completely disoriented, the man next to me hides his head in a sick bag, puking violently. Whilst he has his head between his knees, I take the chance for a few quick photographs through the window. Minutes later, we are back on the ground. Not one of my most satisfying travel experiences. Sadly, this is to be my final glimpse of Peru.

Four

Ecuador: Highs and lows

Ecuador: Straddling the Equator. It is home to Cotopaxi, the world's highest active volcano, just one of twenty-seven in the country. Perhaps the best-known part of the country is offshore, the Galapagos Islands. Population 17 million. Official language – Spanish.

On landing at Quito Airport, we make our usual rapid exit through Immigration and Customs to be met by? Nobody. We are scheduled to rendezvous with a guide and as we emerge from the Customs Hall, we pass the customary huddle of men holding cards bearing the names of their intended charges. I take careful note, but there is not one for Le Bargy. Something similar had happened on an earlier trip to Chile and only a few months before, I had a furious argument at Sydney Airport; when telephoning the travel company, the Rep had told me, 'Be patient, mate' when I had already waited for half an hour for a driver and car that he said was still somewhere in the middle of the city rather than at the airport to meet us. This time, after the long journey from London via Amsterdam and Bonaire, I am less than happy that this should have occurred yet again.

We once before briefly visited Ecuador, paradoxically the home of the Panama hat. Landing by ship at the port city of Manta, we had travelled a few miles up the coast to Montecristi where the famous hats are made by the ladies of the village and sold in the local market. In Latin America, the hat is popularly known as a "Montecristi"; the label "Panama hat" dates back to the Gold Rush days. Miners making their way to the west coast of America through Panama found the hats on sale, and seeing them as an ideal addition when working in the hot sun, they made purchases, and having acquired them in Panama, it was that name that stuck.

We had been told that the secret of a good Panama is that it can be rolled and fitted into a small balsa wood box, and when unfurled the next time you want protection from the hot sun, with but a little manipulation, it should readily return to its original shape. In the market, it was difficult to differentiate the good hat from the shoddy, but we asked around and prices seemed very similar. Eventually, we made a purchase from a couple of brothers who spoke some English and who had a smooth sales patter. We negotiated a price and as several years later we still have our hats in their original balsa wood boxes, I guess on this occasion the locals did not take us too much for mugs.

Some ports suffer from not really having much to show your average tourist and Manta was a good example, as having exhausted the sights of Montecristi and its Panama hat emporium, our next visit was to a button factory.

I am going to come clean here. I wasn't big on button manufacturing before arriving at the Bototagua factory in Manta. I hadn't really given the subject much thought, but if pressed, I would have guessed that your average button is made of plastic. But then hold up a minute; don't buttons predate plastic by some considerable period of time? Yes indeed. So to those readers as ignorant as myself on the button question, I can reveal that the secret lies in the *ciclantacea* plant that grows in the tropical rainforest of Ecuador. The plant, similar to the palm tree, produces a nut called the *tagua*. The nut is sliced and dried and the slices become very hard and shiny, what the locals call vegetable ivory. With the application of some simple engineering, the slices are formed into buttons. Amazing what you can learn in an afternoon when you have nothing better to do.

Given the evident shortcomings of Manta as a tourist destination, we arrange to visit Isla de la Plata, situated way out in the Pacific Ocean, some 17 miles from the mainland.

A heart-stopping bumpy ride in a high-speed launch brings us to the small harbour and within minutes of climbing up a rough path, we are amidst a colony of what is to become our favourite bird, the blue-footed booby.

That very short visit had whetted our appetite to see more of Ecuador, and in any event, the country is custodian of another of those places that were on my "must see" list: the Galapagos Islands. So this, our return to Ecuador, was to be for a longer duration.

Back at the airport, the auguries are not good. We stand around trying for once to look as conspicuous as we can as our fellow passengers make their way out of the Customs area, but nobody approaches us. After a few minutes, I decide to check out the guys with the name boards once again and sure enough there is one with *Le Bargy* being held aloft by a very small dark man with glasses. I introduce myself and he apologises profusely for having 'slipped away to the little boys' room' just as we must have appeared through Customs. As he quickly ushers us towards our transport, he tells me his name is Ramiro and within minutes, we, together with Ramiro and our driver, Francis, are on the Pan-American Highway heading south.

As we pass the old city of Quito on our left, Ramiro explains that we are headed down through the famed Avenue of the Volcanoes to Cotopaxi for an overnight stay. He says that he appreciates that we must be very tired after the long journey from London and we can make our way to the hosteria for a rest as many of his clients prefer to do or, alternatively, he can take us on some interesting diversions along the way. We naturally choose the latter option and give Ramiro carte blanche to vary the itinerary whenever he feels there are worthwhile local sights that can be readily included in our tour, within the constraints of time. With the rules firmly established to the clear satisfaction of both parties, we have within minutes a strong bond with Ramiro as someone likely to prove an exceptional guide. In the next hour, we learn that Ramiro is single and has honed his excellent command of English whilst attending the Chicago Business School.

An hour or so later, we leave the main highway and head off along a rutted side road to the market town of Saquisili. Market town in this case is an accurate description. On the edge of the town a large open area where the buying and selling of animals is taking place. Later in the centre of the town we will find both craft and food markets, but here at the livestock market, it is apparent that most of the business of the day has been completed, with local farmers herding their purchases onto the backs of small pick-up trucks or driving them on foot towards their new homes. The animals are an eclectic mix of pigs, sheep and llamas. In the town centre, activity is more frenetic, and parking the vehicle at the first opportunity and ignoring a persistent drizzle, we stride out along the street with Ramiro to catch some of the atmosphere. Viewed from this the main thoroughfare, Saquisili appears a poor and rather dispiriting place, with rows of undistinguished breezeblock buildings along a muddy road that eventually opens up into a large square set on two levels, the upper containing endless rows of stalls selling an amazing variety of locally made craft goods.

Within a few minutes, we make our first purchase from the stallholder at one of those stalls. He is a young man, I guess mid-twenties, and speaks excellent English. I establish that he is an artist and that his name is Edison Posso. He tells us that although trained as a painter in classical Western techniques, he has become increasingly fascinated by indigenous art forms from pre-Columbian and Inca periods in his country's history. His works reproduce traditional symbols painted onto a canvas that the artist describes as being made from "natural material", although he is not prepared to be drawn on the exact nature of those materials. The sun and the calendar are prevalent in his work, as they were in those civilisations, so too animals and birds, such as the condor, although he is anxious to explain that he has not confined himself to merely replicating traditional symbols but inputs his own creativity into the works. We agree to buy two pieces. He is a confident young man and refuses to enter into any bartering on price, and after feigning to walk away, we agree to pay the asking price before moving on.

Further along, we come across a row of men sat with ancient hand- or foot-powered sewing machines. We have one at home in the attic. It is something of a family heirloom and hasn't seen any action in the thirty-five years I have known Rosie. I'd date it around the 1920s, and none of the machines on view are any newer. The men are undertaking many different tasks repairing various items of clothing. We stand watching for several minutes, the men demonstrating incredible dexterity, before Ramiro ushers us on.

Down some steps onto the lower level and here in the vegetable market we are amazed at the potatoes: of different shapes, sizes and colours. Ramiro explains that there are something like 170 varieties for sale in this market alone. Despite the choice, the potatoes appear to sell for a uniform $3 for a 50-kilo sack.

I have remarked that Ramiro is "a small man", certainly by European norms, standing little over 5 feet tall, yet here in the hustle and bustle of the market I am conscious that by local standards he is by no means short. Some of the older women, I swear, stand Hobbit-like at no more than 4 feet in height. Most have dark brown leathery skin weathered by both the sun and the cold temperatures found here, and despite the deep wrinkles, I would not hazard a guess with any degree of certainty as to their ages. The older women in particular are wearing traditional dress with embroidered blouses and colourful ponchos.

In the market, the produce is well presented. Apart from the infinite variety of potatoes, there are many fruits and vegetables with which we are familiar. We notice that the local practice is to sell peas and broad beans freshly shucked. We stop at one stall where the main product is large round brown objects the size of a cannonball and Ramiro tells us that this is sugar. At another stall, he purchases a snack in an inverted cone of brown paper. He tells us that it contains a protein-rich mixture of broad beans, corn maize and lupin seeds and invites us to join him in an impromptu snack. At another stall, we see something unusual to our eyes and encouraged by Ramiro purchase a couple of red bananas to sustain us until we stop for lunch.

This is taken a further one-hour drive from Saquisili at the impressive Hosteria la Cienega, housed in a large more-than-400-year-old mansion at the end of a long tree-lined avenue of pine trees. The first of several fine meals to be taken in equally beautiful period properties during our stay in Ecuador. Although we have been in the country for only a few hours, I am already beginning to think that this country is another hidden gem that over the next three weeks will have much to offer.

From the hacienda, we have had our first sighting of Cotopaxi, perhaps the most famous, although not the highest, mountain in Ecuador. An active volcano with more than fifty recorded eruptions over the past 200 or so years. Our day is not yet complete. We stop to visit a farm producing industrial amounts of roses for export to the UK and other countries, most notably the United States and Russia. Another interesting diversion as we meander down the Avenue of the Volcanoes.

The living room of the Hacienda San Augustin de Callo has a distinct lived-in appearance to the extent that we feel just a little uncomfortable invading someone else's privacy. The present owner, Mignon Plaza, is away in Quito and despite a promise from her urbane Estate Manager that she is due to return for an important local festival, she does not appear whilst we are in residence. Instead, we have the run of the hacienda as the only guests. Ramiro and our driver, Francis, are to stay in a nearby village, this obviously being deemed a little too grand for them, but before leaving us for the evening, Ramiro provides some background, telling us that Mignon is part of the Ecuadorian aristocracy. Apparently, her grandfather, a former president, first purchased the property in 1921. Ramiro tells us that he has met Mignon several times but on the first occasion, flustered at meeting one of the most famous figures in Ecuadorian society, he worried about getting her name wrong so tried word association – Mignon became Filet Mignon in his mind. Unfortunately, on that first encounter, he forgot to translate that to Mignon Plaza and introduced her to one of his clients as Senora Filet Mignon.

The absence of our hostess means we will not suffer the same embarrassment and so we make ourselves comfortable. We take care in our travels to check out the weather conditions well in advance but despite the planning, I am finding the temperature cooler than expected. As usual, Rosie is prepared for every eventuality but here at close on 10,000 feet above sea level, my one thin sweater is most definitely inadequate. The living room contains a huge wood-burning stove but it now holds just the dull embers of what a few hours ago must have been a blazing fire. We wander around looking for someone to help. A young man is summoned and soon the fire is roaring, but given the size of the room and the ambient temperature, I am still feeling the cold. I mooch around the room in an effort to get warm. The walls are adorned with oil paintings of family members and photographs, many featuring a bullfighter, who on enquiry we discover is Mignon's father José Maria Plaza, an amateur matador of some note as well as part of the Plaza political dynasty.

We make our way back to our room to prepare for dinner. Outside, it is grey and gloomy with heavy rain. I decide to stoke up the log-burning stove in the bedroom to give some much-needed warmth, little realising that the pungent smell of wood smoke will hang on my clothing for the rest of the trip. Dinner is served in splendid isolation. Tonight, we are the only guests. The dining room is dark, with walls at least a metre thick, and instead of it being atmospheric, as is surely the intention, it is rather cold and dank, but praise be, the service is attentive and the food is good.

When morning arrives, the weather has cleared a little. Now a fine drizzle hangs in the air and soon Ramiro arrives to take us up into the Cotopaxi National Park. I say "up" advisedly because we begin a slow climb on a rutted and by now wet and muddy track, ascending for a further three to four thousand feet to a high plateau. After about an hour's drive, Ramiro suggests a walk. I am happy to stretch my legs, enjoy some exercise and learn from Ramiro a little of the local flora and fauna. It takes only a few steps to realise that this will be more difficult than I had anticipated. Ramiro leads us along a path on a gentle upward gradient. Immediately my heart starts thumping at an uncharacteristically fast rate; my head is pounding and each step can only be undertaken after a deep intake of breath. I am a little disoriented. When we had travelled to Cusco in Peru sometime before and at similar altitude, I had adjusted with almost no reaction. Now the reverse is true.

Ramiro, for whom the altitude is no problem, is sympathetic and takes things at a slow pace to enable me to take deep breaths as we make our way along a defined yet clearly little-used path. Almost immediately we come across carpets of the beautiful orange flower called *chuquiragua*. Ramiro explains that it grows only here on the *altiplano* at above 3,500 metres and is important in the culture of the local peoples. The *chuquiragua* is also called "flower of the Andes", having a significance here in the same way as the edelweiss in the Alps and is noted not only for its colour but its medicinal properties.

We return to the car and climb higher. Soon the scale of the huge plateau becomes apparent and despite the low cloud and drizzle, we can see that it is covered with small alpine flowers and lichen of purple and yellow, in the distance the outline of Cotopaxi itself, the upper reaches and summit still shrouded. The landscape is of lunar proportions, strewn with rocks and huge boulders, yet the flatness of the plateau belies the fact we are over two miles above sea level. As we make our way across this vast wilderness, it is strange to see a building set high upon a natural promontory overlooking the national park. I point the building out to Ramiro, who says that we are heading there for lunch.

The Hosteria Tambopaxi is the only restaurant to be found within the national park but the lack of choice of eateries is not a problem, as we soon discover that it serves an excellent local speciality: a potato soup that has already found favour with our palate. In a country with so many varieties of potato, it is perhaps no surprise that the potato soups vary from restaurant to restaurant, but always they please. The cuisine is proving a positive experience in a country in which the guinea pig is commonly eaten, much to Rosie's distaste, she being a vegetarian.

The only other diners are a group of Italians clad in lycra of varying colourful hues. I ask Ramiro what they are doing here and Ramiro calls over mine host and after a lengthy exchange Ramiro explains. They are mountaineers loading up on carbs for an ascent on the mountain. The proprietor, himself apparently a noted local climber, is about to drive them to base camp about a third of the way up Cotopaxi. Here they will spend the rest of the day acclimatising, tomorrow progressing to a higher camp and then tomorrow night, around midnight, making their attempt on the summit. Climbing at night seems odd but our host explains that with Cotopaxi so close to the Equator, the snow is fundamentally unstable in the warm daytime temperatures, meaning that the serious climbing has to be attempted at night. The time frame to climb a mountain peaking at close to 6,000 metres seems ambitious until you realise that because of the plateau, base camp is at something over 4,000 metres.

On our return drive across the plateau, Cotopaxi periodically, for short periods, emerges from the gloom and we are able to clearly see base camp. Ramiro, conscious of my struggle with the altitude, wants to take us to a canyon at a slightly lower altitude to look for a rare species of owl. The terrain is to say the least craggy, and although we embark upon a hike, we fail to spot any owls, although we do come across many colourful hummingbirds, a species I in my ignorance have associated more with tropical climes.

Putting behind me the tribulations of yesterday, caused by the altitude, today we continue our journey south towards Riobamba, where we will say our farewells to Ramiro and Francis. Before that we have a long drive, during which we will pass the erupting volcano Tungaroha, which has been causing such disturbed weather patterns in the area.

As we have spent time on the road visiting towns and villages along the way, one thing we have discovered about Ecuador is how each town or village adopts or develops a specialism in a craft such as woodcarving, weaving, leatherware, ceramics, etc. In the small town of San Miguel de Sercedo, we come across the oddest form of this tradition – ice cream making.

When Ramiro mentions that Sercedo is famous for its ice cream, we imagine that perhaps it is home to a large ice cream making factory but no, we are wrong. Ice cream making here in Sercedo is a true cottage industry in which almost every local family participates. Along the main thoroughfare, on every street corner, up alleys and side streets, literally dozens of *heladerias* or ice cream parlours, each with their own version of the local product. The ice cream parlours all look remarkably similar, so we ask Ramiro if we can stop at the best he knows to sample the product. He instructs Francis to pull up beside his chosen shop and we all pile out. The ice cream, I have to say, is not what I had expected. A menu listing the different flavours appears on boards outside every shop, but what you get is a lolly on a stick. I choose a variety, largely on colour, and only when eating do I discover my combination consists of *taxo* (passion fruit), blackberry, avocado, strawberry and good old vanilla.

Beyond Sercedo, we pass through the substantial town of Ambato. A modern and architecturally insignificant municipality that was flattened by an earthquake in 1949. It is salutary to understand about life on a tectonic plate when we learn that 30,000 people died here. At the roadside, in quick succession, two examples of local life. A restaurant outside of which spit-roasting guinea pigs, a popular local delicacy in a country virtually devoid of any natural livestock before the arrival of Europeans. Then outside a small shop, a young man wrestling with what at first appears to be a thick rope. Rosie comments on his physique and for sure the rippling biceps and upper body muscles are testament to a tough occupation requiring considerable upper body strength. Ramiro tells us the man is kneading *alfenique*, molasses, being formed into a local version of toffee. He gets Francis to stop the van and steps out, returning with a sample for us to try.

Two days later. Ramiro and Francis have returned to Quito and we are at Riobamba Railway Station early in the morning. Over a hundred years ago, a railway line ran from the port city of Guayaquil to Riobamba, here in the centre of Ecuador, and from this point north to Quito. It was a truly incredible piece of civil engineering for its time, yet perhaps also one of the greatest white elephants built by man. Now, just two short sections of the line remain operable, including this one from Riobamba to just below the town of Alausi, a journey that will take us about four hours this morning. Today, the line is nothing more than a tourist attraction, and despite the early hour, there are dozens of other travellers like ourselves milling around the renovated station concourse.

Today, our "train" is a brightly painted bus mounted on locomotive bogies. We are due to board the commercially run Chiva Express and have been told to arrive early to get a head start on the two near identical vehicles run by the Government that already stand on the adjacent platform. There are only about a dozen of us on board and ready to go, whilst on the other two trains people are already packed in cheek by jowl and we are feeling quite smug. As always in these situations with lots of shouting in an intelligible foreign language, our departure is delayed. Eventually, we ascertain it is because a group booked to travel with us has failed to arrive. The Government trains depart, and after about half an hour, two young backpackers arrive, the rest of their party apparently still sleeping after a heavy night on the town; and a decision is made that we shall leave without them.

Our driver, Gonzalo, speaks not a word of English, yet we somehow establish that until his retirement (and I will hazard a guess here that it was many years ago) he was a train driver for the National Railway Company. In those days, he may have cut a handsome figure; he may also have sported a set of teeth.

Despite the small number of passengers, Gonzalo is ably supported by a crew of two. A young girl serving drinks and a gawky boy sitting next to Gonzalo who as we edge our way out of the station has a role that is not immediately apparent. He then leans out of the cab and makes what appear to be rather rude signs suggestive of self-abasement. I am momentarily baffled until I realise that his sole purpose is to indicate to the driver when to sound the horn as we approach the first of what I soon appreciate are many unattended and unregulated crossings, roads and paths that criss-cross the line.

Soon we leave behind the jumble of breezeblock houses that are Riobamba and begin to make our way through a beautiful lush and fertile valley with a fast-flowing river never far below the rail track. A landscape scarred only by the occasional quarry or cement works.

It is a cool morning and over his smart black uniform with red trimmings Gonzalo wears a heavy royal blue poncho embellished with Inca symbols celebrating the sun god, his hands warmed by a pair of equally decorative thick woollen gloves.

As we look back up the valley we are fortunate. Momentarily, through the broken cloud, we get one clear sighting of Chimborozo, at 6,268 metres, Ecuador's highest mountain, before the clouds finally close in and extinguish our view.

After about an hour, a short photo stop becomes elongated due to a rather large American woman who insists on clambering rather indecorously down the carriage steps and starts rooting around beside the track to find rock samples for her geology class.

The Chiva Express has passenger access to its roof where although your bottom sits in extreme discomfort on a seat set a few inches above the top of the carriage, knees up to your chin, one's viewing of the spectacular scenery is infinitely improved. I try this but the early-morning temperature is cool and the wind chilling, and in the absence of a suitably thick sweater, I return to the comfort of the saloon. It seems a shame not to take advantage of this facility, as climbing on the roof has been banned on the state-run trains after a catalogue of accidents.

We stop at the small town of Geamote. The sign indicates an altitude in excess of 3,000 metres. We have time for a leisurely coffee and *empanada* in a small café. We are served by a young Belgian volunteer worker who explains that he is working for a charity running educational projects for kids from the local ethnic Kichwa community.

We clamber back on board and continue through the valley where, despite the near vertical sides, fields are clearly delineated in a patchwork quilt from the valley floor up to the very tops of the mountains. The American woman demands we stop again and calls for her husband Bill to start taking photographs of a long since extinct volcano. She wants to collect more rock samples, but after the last episode, Gonzalo stoically stares at the line ahead and keeps the train moving forward.

As we approach Alausi, the Ecuadorian guide Miguel who is escorting us, implores everyone to take a seat on the top of the bus. We soon realise why; as we come to a halt in the centre of the town, a throng of tourists press forward and soon fill every remaining seat on the bus, upstairs and down. Only later, as the train fully laden with passengers slowly edges forward to leave the town and we are able to look down into a valley deep below, do we realise that the Chiva Express is about to embark on the most spectacular part of its journey, albeit on a journey to nowhere.

Years ago, El Nino rains destroyed the track in the valley a few miles beyond Alausi. Repairs have never been effected so we are about to make a spectacular descent through an intricate series of switchbacks before a rather more laborious return journey back up the slopes to Alausi.

However, before that, back on board the Chiva Express, an international incident. I am going to plead guilty right away to a bit of stereotyping, but the tourists who piled onto the bus at Alausi prove to be a group of Germans. Poor old Bill, on the instructions of his wife, the loud American lady (more stereotyping), has momentarily vacated his seat to go and take a photograph. On his return, he finds it occupied by a middle-aged German complete with pince-nez glasses and armed with an impressive Zeiss camera complete with a huge telescopic lens. You can see where I am coming from here. Anyway, the German point-blank refuses to cede his seat to Bill, despite Miguel intervening on his behalf. I am impressed by the German's implacable belief in the justification for taking someone else's seat and we have a serious stand-off as nobody seems prepared to compromise. Then the guide with the German group is asked to intervene and eventually, and with the utmost reluctance, the implacable German agrees to move to allow Bill to return to his seat. Miguel is totally mystified by this whole incident, and we quietly explain why European history is one with lots of wars.

It is a shame that the Chiva Express can only take us down into the valley, where we can see the mountain outcrop that gives the train its alternative name of the Devil's Blue-nosed Express, before returning us to Alausi.

From here we leave the train and take a bus. This part of the journey is in no sense anti-climactic as we initially zigzag our way up to the small town of Chunchi, where the people live in an almost perpetual grey mist as the cloud hangs across the mountain peaks. Then we make our way down towards Canar, capital of this province, home to the distinctive indigenous Canari people. Initially across a high mountain pass where for a time we emerge above the low clouds hanging over the mountains before descending back through the clouds to view the impressive Inca ruins at Incapirca.

The Canari people have their own distinctive culture which survived through the period when the Inca ruled much of what is now Peru and Ecuador. Fiercely independent, it seems that the two groups achieved some sort of mutual accommodation which might account for Incapirca as an important staging post for the Inca on the Royal Road between the major cities of Quito and Cusco also having elements of Canari as well as Inca relics on the site.

Incapirca is quite extensive and dates back to around the 14th century AD. As a staging post, the site most likely contained storehouses and an inn. A complex system of underground waterways also suggests there would have been baths. However, the most significant building on the site is the

Temple of the Sun, the size and intricacies of the build sufficient to confirm the importance of Incapirca.

Late in the day, we reach the UNESCO heritage city of Cuenca.

At the end of an exhausting yet exhilarating day, we check into the impressive Mansion Alcazar in the middle of the old city. We receive news that our trip to the Galapagos Islands is in doubt. The ship that we are due to join has technical problems and our cruise has been deferred for five days. We have the option to cancel but we tell our travel company, 'No problem.' Instead of making our way to the coastal city of Guayaquil from where we are due to fly to the islands, we accept the option of returning to Quito for a few days, later flying from there to the Galapagos Islands to take the now delayed cruise.

At dinner, we are the only guests in the restaurant. We are presented with an impressive menu and, perhaps with the benefit of hindsight, I can say that rather foolishly I choose a pork dish. I awake in the middle of the night violently sick and next morning, decidedly under the weather, face the prospect of a walking tour of the city.

In the splendid guest reception area of the Mansion, we are met by our local guide, Diego. A handsome young man with a laddish air. I explain my predicament and Diego assures me that we can walk the city always within a short distance of toilet facilities, so we set off just one block north to the Plaza San Sebastian and just around the corner the Old Prison now housing the Museum of Modern Art. Here I discover that although weak and hungry, the worst of my discomfort has passed and encouraged I am, already appreciating that this is a fine city with much to offer visitors like ourselves.

After the museum, as interesting as it has been, we pass a rather more intriguing building housing the Alcoholics Centre for Roman Catholic Priests! From here, a short walk finds us in stark contrast at the Carmelite Seminary. With a spiritual emphasis upon contemplation, this is one of the oldest monastic orders. Despite this emphasis upon meditation, the Order is also strong on providing public service and here through a small grill in the wall that looks like a prison cell, we discover nuns selling *leche*, honey and cures for ailments such as arthritis.

Cuenca's historic centre being a UNESCO World Heritage site, we find history at every turn. Our walk takes us next to the Parque Calderon, the main city plaza. Unusual in that the square contains two cathedrals, one at each end, the old and new. Behind the new cathedral we find the colourful flower market, a proliferation of colour. Cuenca is the orchid capital of Ecuador.

We take a drive alongside the Rio Tomebamba which runs through the centre of the city. Shortly before our arrival in Ecuador, the country suffered from heavy rains and flooding and the river is still perilously high, with a huge volume of tree trunks and other debris passing downriver at great speed. Having stopped briefly on the riverbank to view the carnage, we are then driven up to a *mirador* with stunning views over Cuenca to conclude our city tour.

After only a few days here, we are enchanted by Ecuador, a hidden gem. We speculate that whilst many foreigners come here to visit the Galapagos, relatively few stay to enjoy a country with an interesting history, both pre- and post-arrival of the Spanish, creating a complex mix of cultures together with its truly stunning scenery.

Fortunately, by the next day I am fully recovered from my bout of food poisoning and we make our way out of the city to Las Cajas, a national park set in the hills above the city. Diego is most pleasant company; well educated, he comes from a wealthy family and frankly he does not have to work but clearly enjoys telling visitors about his city and more importantly taking the opportunity to indulge in his first love: nature and the great outdoors. So once up in the national park, we take a ramble with Diego explaining the flora and his particular interest, the birdlife. A light drizzle and low cloud have clearly deterred the birds, noticeable only by their absence. Diego has a gadget with various birdcalls, although he himself is quite adept at imitating many of the birdsongs. All of his efforts however go unrewarded.

Back in the vehicle, we climb higher into the national park and with the weather improving, so do the bird sightings. We have challenged Diego to find us a toucan; they prove elusive but thanks to frequent stops, we see *blue dacnis, metaltail* and the evil *caracara*.

We come to the Tres Cruces Research Station where they are experimenting with trying to grow alpine plants. At 14,000 feet, this would be above the snowline in other parts of the world. We thought we were now acclimatised to the altitude, having had no breathing difficulties since my problems at Cotopaxi but, although only some 2,000 feet higher than where we had taken our morning walk, the air here is noticeably thinner.

We take another hike. Diego again produces his birdsong iPod, much to our derision. He is finding our sense of humour a little unsettling and seems a little hurt by our response. However, with the improved weather, the birdlife is becoming more active and much to his delight this time he has more success, and after getting a response to his call, we get an appearance from a particular type of *tanager* that he says is quite rare to sight in these parts. Blue and brown, it comes and sits on a rock in front of us as if to have its photograph taken. The amount of birdlife here is amazing, given the altitude and the cold: the trees and bushes look like a petrified forest hanging heavy with frost. However, today, no condor or toucan to be seen, but with a contented Diego, we make our way back to the city.

After Cuenca, because of our delayed trip to the Galapagos, we return to Quito. Ramiro told us when he took his leave of us at Riobamba that he is already booked to guide a tourist group on the days when we will be back in the north, but we have a sneaking feeling that he will find a way to resume his role as our guide and, sure enough, at the airport he is there to greet us like old friends. The only change is that he has a new driver. We are introduced to Rex. A typically swarthy man but unusually stocky, it is difficult not to be drawn to a vicious slash mark or scar across his left cheek. Rex, we soon come to realise, understands English well but lacks the confidence to speak it but follows our banter with Ramiro, laughing in the appropriate places and occasionally getting Ramiro to pass on his comments.

As the days pass, we learn that Rex has a colourful past. A one-time member of the criminal fraternity, his scar was the handiwork of a rival gang member. Having fallen foul of the gangland world, he slipped into alcoholism then seeking redemption from his criminality and the downward spiral brought about by his drinking, Rex sought his personal salvation. He joined a particularly pious Catholic Order in which verbal communication was frowned upon, and he spent three years as a monk before deciding that penance paid, he would return to a normal life. Putting his past firmly behind him, Rex still remains a devout Christian and teetotal. We had become very fond of Francis, our first driver, but Rex proves more interesting and, in his way, an equally warm character.

With these additional days added to our itinerary, we are delighted that we have the opportunity to see more of Ecuador and begin to explore Quito and its environs. On our first day some 25 miles north out of the city, I ask Ramiro if we can pull over to view a strange edifice, part of which is still under construction. A sign indicates that at this point we are exactly on the Equator; the site is called Quisato, or Middle of the World, and the construction is a giant sundial. Given the Equator stretches for more than 40,000km around the globe, it is something to claim that this particular spot is indeed the middle of the world.

We are in luck. On the site, we meet up with the architect behind this project, Cristobal Cobo Arizaga. He explains that he is using the knowledge of the modern world in terms of science and the universe and combining it with the ideas of past civilisations that lived around here to understand the subject of astronomy. His language is arcane and I am still, many years later, not sure if this is deep science or dottiness in the extreme. All I can confirm is that in the intervening period since that encounter, the site has developed into a major tourist attraction, all proceeds apparently used in the furtherance of Senor Arizaga's research.

After that interlude, we reach perhaps the most famous street market in the whole of South America in the town of Otavalo. Here, stall after stall of the very things Rosie has been looking to purchase throughout this trip but has resisted until now: ponchos, shawls, wall hangings. For the first time in Ecuador we are conscious of being amongst significant numbers of tourists, and the stallholders have developed their patter to would-be customers similar to that we have encountered elsewhere in the world, such as in the bazaars of Tangier, Istanbul and Cairo.

I am no fashion guru, but it is easy to note the change in the dress worn by the ladies here in the north compared with Cuenca, which we left only a few days ago. Here, the ladies wear predominantly white blouses and black *anukus*, a wraparound skirt. In Cuenca, dress was more colourful with a shorter skirt or *polleras* hanging just below the knee, with a distinctive embroidered hem said to identify the actual town or village from where they originate. The straw hat or Panama seems fairly universal wherever you go, worn by both men and women, although more so by the women.

As I have mentioned earlier when we were travelling down the Avenue of the Volcanoes, each village tends to focus on production of one particular product, and the same applies today as we travel from village to village. A very unusual example we came across shortly after leaving Quito in the village of Calderon, where the locals specialise in making and carefully painting tiny figurines made out of bread dough. We were sufficiently intrigued to purchase a set of napkin rings depicting ladies in different local costumes.

From Otavalo, we travel a short distance out of town to take lunch at Hacienda Cusin, another beautiful period house. Set in gardens, the house, painted white, is approached across a cobblestone forecourt and up an imposing set of stairs. An excellent lunch matches the surroundings. From here, replete, we travel the short distance to Peguche. In the centre of the village, the customary plaza dominated by the church. A ceremony is taking place to celebrate the solstice. The procession moves in a strange shuffling motion to the rhythm of guitars, and I cannot help but think this makes it appear more pagan than Christian.

Across the square and outside a smart-looking house, Ramiro announces, 'This is a village of weavers. Let us look in here.' Inside, an Aladdin's Cave of weaving and I have to acknowledge articles made to a far higher quality than anything we have seen in the markets. After viewing some of the goods, we are led down a narrow staircase into the basement area, where in a very confined space members of the Perugachi family are hard at work. The husband is busy producing thread whilst his young wife is weaving on a loom. Ramiro says the technique she is using is now very uncommon; this is a traditional backstrap loom, and to find a woman working such a loom is equally unusual. She was taught by her father, a technique passed down through generations, in the past only father to son. Ramiro says that she is highly accomplished in using the method, and the articles she has made confirms this on our close inspection. Also, the family only use natural dyes in their products; sweaters, ponchos and elaborately designed wall hangings. Despite having made some purchases in the market the previous day, Rosie is encouraged to purchase some items.

We move on, travelling further north to San Antonio de Ibarra, a village close to the town of Ibarra and noted for its woodcarvers. Most of the products have a religious theme; figures of Jesus, the Virgin Mary and angels proliferate, although there are statues with a secular theme such as animals. The craftsmanship is bordering on the incredible, the detail and the delicate painting of the artefacts. You can walk from workshop to workshop watching the craftsmen at work with no pressure to buy. A quarter of the population of the town are woodcarvers, so there is no shortage of choice. Although the refined skills on display are amazing, we are not tempted to buy, given the subject matter.

As we drive out of the town, we pass a gathering outside the village church. The crowd, almost exclusively women, carrying effigies. Ramiro gets Rex to slow the car for us to take in the view and take a photograph, but this attracts the attention of a demented old lady who is much agitated by our presence and she screams at us and bangs her fists on the side of the car. More of the women come and join her screaming at us through the car windows, clearly unhappy with our presence. Time to move on. As Rex accelerates away, we ask Ramiro to explain, but he appears as nonplussed as we are about why we have upset the local women in such a way.

Overnight, we stay over at the impressive 300-year-old Hacienda Pinsaqui and next day head towards the Cotacachi Cayapas National Park.

The route takes us through the town of Cotacachi, noted for its leatherwork, particularly coats and jackets. I am thinking Rosie might be seeing this as another opportunity for some retail therapy but today I am in luck. As we approach the town, we find the main thoroughfare blocked off. It is an important Saints day: the Day of Saints Peter and Paul, and the main street is filled with crowds of bystanders. With all the shops closed and with no prospect of driving through the town, we leave Rex to park up our vehicle whilst we walk down with Ramiro to join the crowds, watching what proves to be an apparently never-ending procession. There are pure marchers, many smartly dressed school children in school uniform and other groups; people representing a multitude of community groups. Interspersed are bands; all are dressed in traditional costume and playing musical instruments, some familiar but others very specific to this region, notably *bandolin*, a stringed instrument similar to a mandolin, and what appears to be a cut-off version of pan pipes, which of course are common throughout this part of South America.

Although there are often subtle differences in local costumes between regions and even towns and villages, the men here favouring the fedora as a headcovering, a blue poncho and white knickerbockers, and the ladies a white blouse and blue skirts and shawls, Ramiro points to something that the casual traveller would not naturally note. In this region, marital status and age is denoted by the number of strands in their gold bead necklaces.

Once the procession has passed, we are able to continue towards the Cotacachi Cayapas National Park. The park is dominated by the Cuyabeno Lake and as we take the lakeside road, Ramiro relates the story of Martin the circus bear. Poor Martin has his teeth extracted in the circus to make him less dangerous to his trainer then one day Martin manages to escape. He roams far and wide, but without teeth and unused to foraging for himself, he nears starvation until he is adopted by friendly villagers. They nurse him back to health and eventually he is released into the wild in the national park where eventually he finds a partner. Maybe apocryphal but nevertheless a good story. I have to report that we failed to sight Martin or indeed any of the spectacled bears that do reside in the park. Nor the elusive jaguar.

After two delightful days touring north of Quito, time to return to the city.

This is the first time during the trip that we have the chance to explore Quito itself, and it proves to be another fine South American city. We are staying in a hotel in Casco Colonial, the old city, and within easy walking distance we have the impressive Plaza de la Independencia, also, for good reason, known as La Plaza Grande. The square is dominated by the Catedral Metropolitana by virtue of it sitting on an elevated position at the top of the square. The square contains other noteworthy buildings. The presidential palace is also significant not only for its architecture but for the uniformed guards in their blue, white, red and gold uniforms dating from an earlier age. There is easy access to view the inner courtyard with its fountain. Opposite is the City Hall, and the plaza is completed by the Archbishop's Palace. In the centre of the square, the Monument to Liberty constructed in marble and bronze. This is one of the great city centrepieces in the world, not only to come and admire the fine architecture and absorb the history on all sides but with space to sit under the oases of trees, relax, watch the world pass by, or meander, avoiding the host of kids wanting to polish shoes or simply wanting a dollar. No wonder it is a magnet for not only tourists but the locals residing in the surrounding old city.

More amazing, though away from the *centro*, is the Basilica del Voto Nacional. This enormous edifice based on the Notre Dame in Paris is a project started in 1890. Built in the neo-Gothic style, it was blessed by Pope John Paul II in 1985 and officially opened in 1988, yet it remains unfinished. The scale is impressive, so too the stained glass windows, but once in the nave you can look around and realise that even after 120 years much more building work remains to be done. The project has taken so long that locals actually believe the story that if it is ever completed, it will signify the end of the world.

After two days in Quito, the time has come to make our way to the Galapagos Islands. As a final act of sightseeing, Ramiro wants to take us to somewhere he says is special. We drive up to the Cima de la Libertad to enjoy views over the city below and to take photos of us together with Ramiro and Rex.

Our week in the Galapagos is fruitful but largely uneventful. Rosie overcomes her fear of lizards; handy, as they tend to be typically about 4 metres long and prevalent on the islands; continue our love affair with the blue-footed booby and see the mating rituals of the albatross. We also see the giant tortoise Lonesome George in his latter days before he died at over a hundred years of age. Sadly, the last of his species.

When you travel, you have to accept that you win some, you lose some, and as a footnote to our Ecuador trip, when we return home: good news. The Galapagos cruise ship company, impressed by our willingness to stay with our booking despite the delay, have decided to refund half the cruise cost, and even better, our own travel company, grateful for our flexibility and understanding, have matched that offer. Effectively, we have enjoyed our week's cruise around the Galapagos Islands free of charge.

Five

Bolivia: Tales from the Altiplano

Bolivia: A landlocked country with a population of 11 million and the highest percentage of indigenous people in all the Americas. Its capital, La Paz, is the highest in the world at 12,000 feet above sea level. In 2005, Evo Morales became the first elected indigenous president in a South American country. Languages: Spanish, Quechua, Aymara, Guarani.

You can see the Great Wall of China from space. I have often pondered the truth of this claim, given many other larger and physically more prominent man-made structures, and even more conspicuous geographical spectacles on our planet. The Grand Canyon and Mount Everest, for example. It does appear to be another urban myth. I have since read that oceans and continental land masses apart, the only discernible physical feature is in fact the Salar de Uyuni.

If perchance on that October afternoon, Russian cosmonaut Ivan had glanced through the small circular porthole of the International Space Station and looked down towards Planet Earth, he might have seen two bedraggled figures making their way across the outer edges of the aforesaid salt flats high on the *altiplano* of south-west Bolivia.

Now days later as I sit beside the tranquil waters of the mysterious Lake Titicaca, in local legend the belly button of Mother Earth, I cannot but reflect: Liz, how did you get us into such a fine mess? But here at 12,500 feet above sea level, I am slightly light-headed and I apologise for getting ahead of myself, for we have already been in Bolivia for two weeks and there is much to tell.

That first afternoon, we had flown into Santa Cruz from Northern Argentina, our flight arriving three hours late. We were collected at the airport by Andreas, a young twenty-something guide from a local travel company who hurried us to the car park to be introduced to our transport: an ancient Fiat 600 with an engine designed for a motorcycle. I remember being a less-than-proud owner of a new model of the very same car back in the 1970s, myself young, recently married and short of cash. This was of the same vintage, with many more miles on the clock. I was aware of the limitations of a pristine version of this motorcar and with driver, guide, two passengers and our not inconsiderable luggage, I expressed to Rosie my doubts as to the statistical likelihood of our reaching our hotel, an equation involving snowflakes and a hot place beneath the ground. Andreas had no such reservations, and ably assisted by the driver, our four substantial bags were tied somewhat precariously, held only by a stout rope, onto the car roof. Chugging through the city outskirts, as we sweated profusely in the humidity of the tropical lowlands, Andreas imparted news that after depositing our bags at the hotel, we would embark rather belatedly on a planned city tour.

Santa Cruz is a cross between Las Vegas and Naples. A lowland retreat for well-off Bolivians from a life at high altitude; a place where they can let their hair down but equally a border town attracting a high percentage of lowlifes and chancers.

Proof positive of this assertion came quickly at the hotel, where we were greeted not by the usual flunky dressed in a uniform fit for a general in the Ruritanian Army but by a security guard with a sub-machine gun in hand. After a frantic check-in, we were ushered to inspect our room, passing the swimming pool and sunbathers in what in all respects appeared to be a holiday resort hotel, albeit hundreds of miles from the sea. Having ensured our luggage was secure here, in the gathering gloom of early evening with the temperature still hovering around 30C degrees, we set out on our scheduled city tour.

Santa Cruz has little to offer the tourist as opposed to the holidaymaker, whose only interest is sun, a swimming pool and cheap booze. It is a sprawling metropolis of breezeblock buildings and American-style strips with endless rows of small businesses and fast-food outlets, so I will mention only the highlights of the tour. We passed a full-sized airliner parked incongruously on a major intersection in the city centre, to later discover that it was forced down by the air force many years before, suspected of containing illicit drugs. Incapable of safely taking off, it has remained in the same spot ever since, now totally surrounded by a burgeoning city landscape.

We stop to change money and to take a brief stroll. Andreas suggests a soda as relief from the heat and pollution and produces some liquid refreshment from a cooler in the car boot, nonchalantly flipping the lid off with a flick knife that he assures us he carries for our protection. Andreas leads us to a small museum where exhibits depict local traditional dress and elaborate headwear, but clearly uneasy at his inability to answer our questions about the indigenous people and their culture, he hurries us back to the car where after an animated conversation with the driver, we make our way somewhat more purposefully through the city streets.

In gathering gloom somewhere in the city suburbs, we cross a bridge. A crowd has gathered. We ask the driver to stop. It is a protest by disabled people, and a number of wheelchair-bound citizens protesting against the Government are being suspended in mid-air over the side of the bridge – still in their wheelchairs. We would have liked to stay longer and engage with the protesters, particularly given that the final destination on this evening city tour finds us peering over a high blank wall at an estate of largely incomplete executive houses built for employees of some large multi-nationals setting up business in Bolivia.

Back at the hotel, my head is in a spin as I lean back on the pillow in the relative normality of our hotel room. By now, Rosie already fears the worst and is in a mild panic. Welcome to Bolivia; we have been in the country all of five hours and the portents are not good.

Next morning. We are due to take the short flight from here in Santa Cruz to Sucre. Our guide, Andreas, has told us to be in the hotel reception at 8.30 am. It is nearly nine. No sign of Andreas. We talk to the concierge. The airport is half an hour away by car and we have no contact number for our guide, so we decide to take a taxi. By the time we reach the airport, the flight is only thirty minutes from take-off. Entering the terminal, we hear our flight being called. We join the back of a long and slow-moving queue.

Time for extreme measures. I push to the front. The man at the front of the queue looks startled.

'Sucre?' he asks.

'Si,' I reply in an anxious tone. He kindly ushers me forward towards the desk.

Seconds later, boarding passes in hand, we race up the staircase to Departures. More delay. We have no stamp to show we have paid the departure tax. We try to explain we are in transit and paid tax on leaving Argentina. Another passenger intercedes on our behalf but to no avail. We travelled yesterday so this is now regarded as a separate internal flight and we are no longer technically in transit. We have to pay the tax. I rush headlong back down the stairs, find the desk and pay over my 26 *bolivianos*. My boarding passes are stamped and I clamber back up the stairs. Through security, down to the gate, we dash down the gangway and on to the plane, the doors close behind us, we are on our way.

At Sucre Airport, we are met by Liz. Long dark hair, late thirties. She speaks good English and is clearly well educated. On first impressions, she seems altogether likely to prove a more reliable guide than Andreas. Within minutes, we are in the city. The skies are blue, the temperature cooler but pleasant. Thank God the airport incident happened at sea level at Santa Cruz and not here at 12,000 feet as we get our first sensation of altitude. A headache, breathing a little heavily. We stop in Bolivar Park. Sucre is known as the "White City". Despite the thin air, it is fresh and cool, everything looks good and it feels good. Fine buildings at every turn, a slower pace of life. Our mood changes.

The rest of the day we are free to roam the city. Our hotel is around the corner from the impressive Plaza de 25 Mayo, symbolic heart of the nation where independence from Spain was declared in 1825 and home to both the cathedral and the House of Liberty, where the historic events leading to the declaration took place. The one-time Jesuit University now contains a museum and our sightseeing takes us to the beautifully maintained hall where the original legislature was held. There is also the inevitable bust of Simon Bolivar, who of course gave his name to the country. As a point of interest, most assume that La Paz is the capital of Bolivia. It is indeed the administrative capital, whilst Sucre remains, as it has been since independence, the constitutional capital.

The following day, Saturday and Liz is to take us on a more formal city tour, including the Museum of Textiles and Ethnography. A subject close to Liz's heart. Here she demonstrates her enthusiasm for the work of the indigenous people as she shows us around the exhibits. Even after this museum visit, I am not going to profess great knowledge on this topic other than to say that the main purpose of the exhibition seems to be to reflect upon the historical significance of weaving within two distinct local ethnic groups: the Jal'qa and the Tarabuco.

From here, Liz leads us to her old school, a former convent still run by a strict Catholic order of nuns. Liz, from her demeanour, clearly feels comfortable here, although her bravura is abruptly halted when a matronly figure, not one of the nuns, slips into the small chapel whose history Liz is explaining to us, ushers her to one side and quietly but firmly tells her that she is no longer free to visit some parts of the building. Liz is plainly upset. She soon regains her poise and not to be thwarted, the "rebellious child" element of her personality emerges and she ushers us through a heavy and clearly rarely used door that leads us up a narrow stone staircase on an apparently never-ending climb. At the top of the steps, we are faced with another obstacle: a tiny wooden door firmly locked and bolted. Liz, now oozing confidence, reaches up and from a tiny, totally hidden alcove high in the wall, she produces a large metal key, unlocks the door and leads us onto the rooftop, high above the convent quadrangle. From here, we have magnificent views across the old city, and Liz is able to point out many of its historic buildings.

From this discreet viewpoint, as we admire the vistas, Liz relates stories from her time here as a student, including narrowly avoiding being expelled. On consecutive end-of-year celebrations, Liz, with a small group of her friends, had embarked upon ever more daring and outrageous pranks. One year putting laxatives in the party food. When it came to Liz's own last year at school, and from this very rooftop, the girls launched their most daring prank. She and her friends filled balloons with helium and applying their physics lessons, added papier-mâché weights then dropped them from a balcony upon their fellow students, nuns and parents gathered below, with obvious hilarious consequences. It was all laughter until many of the assembled guests began to be violently sick. If not already evident, we can see that Liz still clearly retains some elements of free will from her schooldays.

We are getting to know Liz and she has already told us that she has a teenage son and an estranged husband. She is volatile, sensitive and more than a little highly strung. Tomorrow, more revelations as we are travelling to visit her family home.

It is an early-morning start but another beautiful day, with blue skies and crisp mountain air as we take the road in a south-easterly direction out of the city and into the moonscape mountains. Firstly, we are heading to the famous local market at Tarabuco, a journey of some 60km. The market is vibrant and colourful, the women in their bowler hats and striking and unique traditional dress. The long, fringed *manta* or shawl around their shoulders and the voluminous *pollera,* or skirt. They are selling local produce, mainly fruit and vegetables, chillies, potatoes, beans, onions and a number of root vegetables and fruits that we do not recognise. There is a central market contained within a cavernous building, but the stalls spill out from here into the surrounding streets and the main plaza. In the central hall, we watch as transactions take place. One lady sits with tidy piles of carrots set out in front of her. Another comes along, a bunch of herbs in hand. Words are exchanged, a deal consummated. The goods are exchanged. The deal done, the carrot lady turns to a sack behind her and picks another handful of carrots and offers them to the herb lady in a goodwill gesture.

We are largely anonymous in the crowd, but Rosie, videoing a large sticky mass of molasses, is accused by the stallholder of "stealing her soul", clearly believing she is being surreptitiously filmed, and it requires Liz's intervention to pacify her.

People have come from villages dotted around the mountain valleys near the town, many travelling on foot, others on big open-backed trucks onto which they now begin to pile their purchases, ready for the journey home.

We have anticipated more local handicrafts but this is definitely not a market for tourists, simply a place for local people conducting their daily lives. The non-food stalls are selling practical products, colourful ponchos widely worn by the men, wide woven belts and the heavy tightly pleated skirts worn by the women, the elaborately decorated hats signifying a single woman and the ever-present coca bags worn at the waist, used to hold the daily ration of coca leaves. The leaves which are formed into a tight ball and placed into one cheek.

We take lunch at a rustic open-air restaurant sitting on benches rather crudely fashioned and welded from old bedheads, before picking up a dirt road taking us high above the town towards the south-west.

We press on, heading for Candelaria, Liz's family home. This seems an odd side trip until you appreciate that Liz and her mother own the tour company. It is called Candelaria, as is the village where we are headed, and their hacienda is situated within the village.

I need to introduce you to our driver, Eric. He will feature much more in this story, but we are getting to know that although his English speech is limited, he understands much of our conversation. He drives in a way that gives confidence, a definite positive on these bumpy dirt roads, often climbing along precarious narrow mountain roads without any guard rails, only air between you and the valley floor hundreds of feet below.

Candelaria is set in one of these valleys, and when we arrive, Eric drops us off at the edge of the village so we can walk through whilst he heads on up to the hacienda. The village has about 800 inhabitants and once in the distant past, everything here was owned by Liz's family.

From the main road, most of the houses are set away to our left on a small hill, and Liz leads us up a path towards these dwellings. A small boy, maybe ten or twelve years old, comes towards us, and after he and Liz exchange words, she tells us that our arrival has been noticed and that we have been invited to visit his mother's house. It is one of perhaps a dozen similar concrete buildings that Liz explains are relatively new, the construction of which has been funded by a US charity seeking to reduce disease and eliminate poverty amongst the local population. The boy's home is in fact a number of small buildings set out around a tiny courtyard, and we are greeted by the boy's mother, who ushers us into the largest of the buildings that we realise is both the living room and her place of work, as she is a weaver. She has a small hand loom and shows us how it operates and her current work-in-progress. The boy and his younger sister then appear with two large bin bags, the contents of which they spread across the stone floor. These are the product of their mother's labours. We choose a piece and after a contrived piece of bargaining settle on a price close to the asking price.

As we walk back down the hill, an old man emerges from the next house and urges us to follow him. He is persistent so we oblige, although we know what to expect. In the courtyard, his elderly wife is hastily setting up her loom for us to view her handywork. Even with our untutored eye, we can see that the quality of her work far exceeds that of the piece we have just purchased. We have paid 180 *bolivianos* and she is asking 900 for a piece of similar dimensions. The woman has a heavily lined face and although I know life expectancy here is low, I still guess that she is in her seventies. She has a helper, a teenage girl, I assume her granddaughter, although having seen the women in the market at Tarabuco I am not sure, and we are not surprised when Liz, overhearing our conversation, whispers, 'She is in her early fifties and this is her daughter.' We leave without having made a purchase, feeling a little uncomfortable, and it is with some relief that, as we leave, I notice Liz passing the woman a small denomination banknote for her trouble.

This whole process is repeated a little further down the hill. This time, it is an old lady, a real old lady. She too hastily sets up her loom and shows us her work. It is poor and shoddy and I can see that although she wears glasses, her eyesight is clearly failing, no doubt explaining her poor workmanship. Thunder begins to rattle around the valley, and with rain in the air, we are able to make our excuses, hurriedly retreating down the hill before we are spotted by any more of the householders. Turning sharp left at the bottom and crossing a small bridge, some yards beyond we find ourselves at Hacienda Candelaria.

We walk through the arched entrance into an inner courtyard where Liz's mother, Elizabeth, greets us. Although the hacienda has been in the family for generations, times have been hard since land reforms in 1953 led to the confiscation of much of the surrounding estate and dispersal of the lands amongst local peasant farmers. The hacienda has lost most of its former grandeur. Set around a courtyard of low buildings, opposite the arched entrance a small chapel but first, we are led to the kitchen. We pass an aged retainer at the entrance stooped over huge pots on open fires, boiling the day's washing. Inside, it is dark with the harsh smell and smoke from another wood fire immediately filling the eyes and nostrils with a burning sensation. We are invited by Elizabeth to sit at a large simple kitchen table. The servant, relieved of her washing duties, serves us generous portions of broth ladled from a large ironware pot suspended over the fire. This is accompanied by enormous chunks of freshly baked unleavened bread just removed from the oven by the cook, another aged retainer from a former time.

Here in Hacienda Candelaria, one thing is evident: Liz is subservient to her mother, the undisputed head of the family. Elizabeth, it has to be said, is an impressively worldly, opinionated, highly intelligent and articulate lady, part of a dying breed. She from the old order now marginalised in this country where the people have spoken and have elected an indigenous native and leftist president. We are also introduced to Liz's disabled brother and her grandmother. We all sit around the table and chat amiably about the history of the hacienda and more recent world events, before Liz is instructed to take us on a tour of what is left of the estate.

First to the Cornstore where corn is spread on boards to dry. Liz explains that whilst they still cultivate their remaining land after the agrarian reforms, the estate was left with just 5 hectares of land from the original 1,000 hectares. On to the chapel. Here, we find stored sacks of dried corn. It is obviously some time since this was a place for religious ceremonies.

The main hacienda is a frankly dark and dreary series of rooms. The family has been here since 1873, and much of the furniture and paintings adorning the walls may well date from the time the hacienda was built.

Life here is clearly not what it was in the heyday of the estate, but by establishing and running her travel company, Elizabeth has generated an income so that the family can at least retain what is left of the ancestral home.

According to our itinerary, Uyuni is to be a two-day side trip from Sucre, spending a night in Potosi en route and another in Uyuni before returning to Sucre. On this basis, close to our hotel we find a laundry and leave a bag of washing to be collected on our return to the city. We take just overnight bags, leaving most of our luggage in the hotel to await our return. On our return, we will spend a further two days in Sucre, before continuing our journey by travelling north to La Paz.

Potosi is the old capital from Spanish colonial times and the region the source of much of Bolivia's wealth, mainly silver extracted from one mountain overlooking the city, the Cerro Rico. This is the reason the Spanish built a city here when they arrived in the sixteenth century.

Following a long drive through the mountains from Sucre, we arrive in Potosi. After we've taken lunch at a smart converted factory, now an upmarket restaurant, Liz takes us for a drive around the city. We take a stroll by a parade of small shops where she shows us how easy it is to buy explosives and detonators. We stop at a shop selling a range of groceries and soft drinks. Here Liz picks up a stick of dynamite and a crude piece of thin rope which will act as a detonator, both openly on display alongside those other goods. Liz says that this stick is packed with nitroglycerine. Any explosion in the confined space in which the men work in the mine will be too powerful and given the cost, the miners will cut a stick like this to create three separate explosives adding fertiliser and attaching detonators, and pray. Liz hands us several sticks and takes photos of us, dynamite in hand.

Still, after hundreds of years of extraction, this remains a mining city. Now most mines are run by large corporations, but freelancers still work in and around the main mines on a piecework basis, taking enormous risks to dig out sufficient silver to make a living. Liz takes us up to the entrance of one of the largest mines run by the Corporacion Minera de Bolivia. The sign at the entrance says it stands at 4,180 metres above sea level, which I calculate is close to 13,000 feet. Liz offers the chance to visit inside, and kids probably no older than eight are scrabbling around the van, touting for business, prepared to act as guides. We are in two minds, because it would give a couple of them a few dollars in their pockets rather more easily than a ten-hour shift deep in the darkness. My mild claustrophobia finally leads to us declining the opportunity.

Instead, we take in some more of the sights in the city before checking into our hotel. It is an odd experience. We are offered a ground-floor room but being adjacent to the hotel reception, it is noisy and smoky; a former guest had a definite penchant for cigars. We decline and ask for a quiet room on an upper floor. I notice the receptionist give Liz a querulous look. We have obviously declined the best room in the establishment. Strange to say, just climbing up a little higher from the ground to the first floor has us gasping for breath. Once alone in the room, we decide to check out our finances as we tend to do on a daily basis during our travels. The arithmetic is simple, but neither of us can manage to add up accurately, both of our brains being scrambled. Perhaps a combination of the altitude, tiredness from an early start to the day and the long journey.

We spend the next day around the city taking in more of the sights, including the National Mint, surely one of the most impressive and historically significant buildings in the whole of Bolivia, if not South America. We are honoured. Arrangements have been made for us to be guided around the building by the curator. Built in the middle years of the eighteenth century and to a solid specification as befits a factory making valuable coins, the first thing that strikes you as you enter the courtyard is the rather incongruous mask of Bacchus positioned over the top of a large hallway. This was apparently added some hundred years after the original construction for reasons nobody seems to really understand. Known locally as the "Mascaron", it has become something of a local icon. Although the museum includes an extensive art collection, most impressive are the huge wooden machines used to produce the coins, and the safes, huge boxes for keeping the coins safe, with elaborate lock mechanisms.

We leave Potosi early the following morning for what Liz anticipates will be a six-hour journey to Uyuni. Although the mountain scenery is spectacular, the road is fraught with danger, the biggest obstacle to steady progress being the rather haphazard programme of road building that leads to stops and starts and off-road diversions every few miles. After the long and tiring journey on these narrow, dusty and often hazardous roads through the mountains from Potosi, we descend towards the town of Uyuni. It is yet another town with a frontier feel, a town of some 10,000 souls sat on the edge of the enormous wasteland, the Salar de Uyuni. It is here that we get the first inkling that there may be trouble ahead. We draw up outside a café, an obvious hangout for backpackers with a chalk board notice outside, advertising rooms at incredibly cheap prices. Liz spots another guide that she knows and goes off for a chat and is followed by Eric, who has also spotted an old friend, leaving us sitting somewhat frustratingly in the vehicle.

Liz and Eric eventually complete their lengthy conversations and once back in the van suggest that we head out to the edge of the town to view the famed "locomotive graveyard".

As we drive, Liz and Eric are in earnest conversation and I enquire as to what has caused them to appear so concerned. Liz says that both of their friends they have been talking to in the town have told them about a strike planned for Uyuni, which is due to start tomorrow. Truck drivers at a mine some distance away towards the Chilean border are in dispute with the mine owners, who are planning to build a railway to transport ore across the border into Chile. Liz says this is not a problem, as the strike is due to commence at midday, by which time we will have concluded our visit to the salt flats and will be on our way back to Sucre.

The loco graveyard has become an unlikely tourist attraction, much to the surprise and incredulity of the locals. It is literally a place to dispose of unwanted railway engines. Many were clearly dumped here on the edge of the salt flats many years ago to slowly rot, but as the collection has grown, so has the interest of railway buffs around the world, and now ordinary visitors to the area like ourselves. Rosie can't really see beyond piles of rusting metal but, as a one-time train spotter, albeit half a century ago in my early teens, some of the locomotives on display have a curiosity interest and certainly justify some snaps on the digital camera.

Soon we are on our way again, travelling through the outskirts of Uyuni. It is a grey place, wide rutted avenues with unmade roads and low corrugated-roofed buildings. We join the road north without realising that when we come this way tomorrow it will be with dire consequences. We are skirting the salt flats clearly visible away to our left and soon we leave the main highway and head towards what is to be our overnight accommodation, the Hotel De Sal Luna Salada or Salt Hotel.

Something akin I guess to the idea encompassed in an ice hotel in northern Norway, it is genuinely unique. A not insignificant building in terms of size, it is literally constructed from blocks of salt. Once inside, we discover that the corridor floors consist of loose salt that can be readily swept away and replaced when dirty; in the restaurant, there are salt tables and salt chairs and, in the bedrooms, salt beds. Of curiosity value, probably unique but with an inherent problem.

We rise very early. The definite downside of a hotel made of salt, as you may have guessed, particularly given this location, is that it is very cold. I have slept fitfully, fretting over the gas stove in the room exuding unhealthy vapours. I still have a headache from the altitude and the cold is bearing on my weak chest, causing further discomfort.

Make no mistake; I am happy to have the opportunity of visiting this amazing place. I nevertheless look forward to returning to the comfort of our hotel in Sucre later in the day. The plan is to drive onto the salt flats to the Isla de Pescadores from where on the higher point of the island it is possible to get panoramic views of the sheer scale of the Salar.

In the event, it has been a great morning. The Salar has not disappointed: a sea of salt the size of Wales. The views from the island are great, the island itself a weird place, covered as it is in huge boulders and dotted with enormous cacti. The morning tour is coming to a conclusion; time to head back to Sucre.

We need to drive through the centre of Uyuni and pick up the Sucre road on the far side of town before midday, when the strikers plan to impose their blockade. We make quick progress across the flat open space that is the Salar and arrive on the main road some 5 miles outside of the town. It is still only around 10.30 in the morning. Shortly, we make out a local bus ahead at the side of the road, and as we approach, we can see people standing around.

We assume the bus has broken down but then we see a lorry parked across the road. The blockade has started early. As we pull up behind the stationary bus, some men come across to our vehicle. Eric winds the window down and joins an earnest discussion with the men then after several minutes, he starts the engine and we turn and begin to drive back down the highway away from Uyuni. Uyuni is closed to us and so too our escape route to Sucre.

Liz assures us that at worst there is a backroad across the mountains to Sucre, avoiding the need to drive through the middle of Uyuni, but Eric says driving that road will be very slow and hazardous. Instead, he favours going off-road and picking up the main road again on the far side of Uyuni by making a wide sweep so that the blockers do not see us. To this end, we leave the road and pick up a track heading back towards the Salar. The terrain is rough but the track, although rutted and dusty, appears well used. After maybe twenty minutes, we are passed by another vehicle heading in the opposite direction but we guess on the same mission: avoiding the blockers. Then a second vehicle approaches; a pick-up truck with four or five men on board. They signal for us to stop and Eric goes to talk to them. The men look rather intimidating; one carries a rifle. At first, we think the worst, but the conversation appears convivial. Eventually, after some minutes, the men climb back into their vehicle and drive off in the direction from where we have just come. We assume Eric has been trying to find out from them the best route, but bad news, despite the appearance of a friendly encounter, the men are blockers. They have already persuaded the other vehicle we saw to turn around and have told Eric the same, not to proceed. If we continue, we will be trapped in Uyuni for the next two days, as that is the length of their protest, and all roads in and out of the town will remain blocked.

We gather through Liz that Eric knows another way around the town and from our map we can see the route he has in mind, running south of Uyuni then through the mountains before rejoining the Sucre road to the north, almost certainly beyond any blockade. We are in favour, as we don't fancy the prospect of another cold night on the edge of the Salar.

We set off again and soon Eric leaves this well-worn path for another track, deeper into the Salar. The track forks and forks again and it becomes obvious as the quality of each track reduces that the journey is becoming increasingly fraught. We see wading birds and what appears to be water, although it might be a mirage. Any doubts disappear as the track dips and we splash through a shallow stream. Then a deeper recess in the road, the track churned and deeply rutted where other vehicles have clearly found navigating difficult, perhaps impossible. Eric stops to consider our options but the answer becomes plain. As he engages the gears, our wheels are spinning, and despite four-wheel drive being engaged, any forward motion has ceased. We are firmly stuck in the Salar de Uyuni.

It is still only late morning but in the pit of my stomach I already have an uneasy feeling about unfolding events. Eric and Liz try to extract the vehicle. I know from experience that the wheels need grip, and simply spinning the wheels will dig the vehicle deeper into trouble. I help pack some stones and small boulders under the wheels but Liz doesn't want her guests getting dirty, and Eric, despite his experience as a driver, seems convinced that turning the wheels at high speed is the answer when I know what he needs to do is completely the opposite. Soon, with the vehicle up to the axles in mud, it is apparent that we have no means of escaping without outside help. Liz tries to call the Salt Hotel on her mobile. The signal is weak and it is only after numerous unsuccessful attempts that she eventually succeeds in contacting the management and there is a promise that help is on its way. Although the hotel is perhaps five or so miles away, giving the rescue vehicle our exact location proves somewhat problematical, and it is a further two hours before that help arrives in the form of a small truck with four-wheel drive. We gather up our hand luggage and soon find ourselves back at the Salt Hotel.

Initially, Liz joins us, but after an hour or so, anxious about the fate of Eric and the vehicle, she leaves, together with a member of the hotel staff, to go and help Eric in recovering the vehicle, insisting she will be back in two hours at most.

We sat on the verandah most of the afternoon sipping coffee. It provided a wonderful vantage point for looking out upon the endless expanse of the Salar and spotting the occasional vehicle making its way across the salt flats. The skies were crystal clear, the sun high in the sky, but the temperature stayed stubbornly low, hovering just above freezing, and we remained wrapped in our cold-weather clothes. In late afternoon, we spotted what we thought must be Eric and our 4x4 heading towards the hotel. At first just a speck on the horizon, its course indeterminate, then confirmation that it was indeed heading our way. When it drew up at the hotel we realised that despite our expectations, it was not Liz and Eric. It proved to be the lead vehicle of what was a party of Argentinean professional photographers who had come across the border on a photo shoot. This first vehicle being shortly followed by two more. A middle-aged woman clearly in charge of organising the trip spoke good English, and through her we gathered that her group had been due to arrive the previous evening, but having crossed the border, the party had encountered hostile groups of blockers on the road and like us had headed across the salt flats, where they had eventually bedded down for the night in what she described as incredibly low temperatures. They looked tired and bedraggled after their ordeal and in desperate need of food and hot drinks. It was to be another two hours before Liz returned to the hotel, minus Eric and our vehicle.

I was very angry with her for abandoning us, supposedly for no more than two hours, yet she had been away more than five hours with no word. She took my tirade in sullen fashion, slinking away without response, further raising my ire, but later she returned with news that rescue was at hand. A taxi had been hired from Uyuni and a car was also on its way from her company in Sucre. Whichever was able to navigate around the blockade and reach the Salt Hotel would get the assignment to return us to Sucre. I told her that rather than stay another night and despite the late hour, we were still up for taking the circuitous route north to avoid the blockers and return to Sucre even if it was three or four in the morning before we arrived, so as soon as a car arrived, we were ready to leave.

By around eight in the evening and despite Liz's continuing assurances, we began to seriously doubt whether we were going to get away from the Salar that night. She spent a lot of time trying to make telephone calls and at the end of one animated conversation I was called to the phone to speak with Darius. He proved to be the Chief Executive of the largest travel company in Bolivia and ultimately responsible for organising our trip. Liz was in total awe of him and told me that I was privileged, as he never normally speaks directly to customers. He seemed charming but, despite my arguments, was adamant that he could not be party on safety grounds to arranging for our return by road to Sucre. He said the blockade was widespread and the blockers by now would be drunk, making them belligerent and dangerous and more importantly, armed. Instead, he said we would have to stay overnight at the Salt Hotel. He would arrange for us to travel north to La Paz to avoid the blockers, and our luggage left in Sucre would eventually find us somewhere along the road. I reluctantly agreed and eventually arrangements were made to evacuate us the following morning. The plan involved the hotel owner, who needed to replenish dwindling stocks of food at the hotel, driving us north to the town of Oruro where we would be met by a car and driver sent by Darius from La Paz. The charm of the Salt Hotel was by now wearing thin, and we reluctantly spent another very cold and largely restless night on the edge of the Salar.

The following morning, we set off on what was a long and, in light of the happenings of the previous two days, uneventful drive past the improbably named Lago Poopo to Oruro, where as promised we were met by the car and driver sent by Darius.

By early evening, we are driving through the centre of La Paz when the strangest of things occurs. Looking out of the car window, we simultaneously notice two men walking down the street, pulling what unmistakably are our suitcases. We later discover they and our laundry have been recovered from Sucre, and the following day they appear in our hotel room in downtown La Paz. Soon we are checked into a pleasant modern hotel that is to be our home for the next two nights.

That morning, back at the Salt Hotel, we had said our goodbyes to Liz, but even after sleeping on it, I could not bring myself to proffer her other than a small tip and left a rather more generous amount for her to give to Eric, our beleaguered driver. To this day, I wonder if the rescue vehicles from Uyuni and Sucre ever arrived, or were they a fiction of Liz's imagination?

Minutes after checking into our hotel there was a knock on the door. On opening it, I was confronted by a matronly figure dressed in a smart business suit. She introduced herself with some grand job title, although in essence she was Darius's PA. She apologised profusely, telling us that Darius would arrive shortly but had been temporarily delayed by a summons to the presidential palace for an audience with President Morales. It seemed a tall story but we were content to discuss our ongoing itinerary with the formidable Madame Gockman so were surprised when half an hour later, another knock on the door and there was Darius himself. Darius was charm personified, and apart from apologies for our problems in Uyuni, he offered all sorts of variations in our planned itinerary, at his company's expense. We declined, given that our intended next stop was the magical and mysterious Lake Titicaca, a much looked-forward-to part of our planned itinerary.

Before leaving for Lake Titicaca, however, two days to explore La Paz. Apart from the altitude, it presented few surprises for travellers like ourselves who have previously visited other Latin American cities such as Quito and Lima.

After Andreas and Liz, our latest guide, José, seems quite normal; a bright young man in his mid-twenties. Our tour of La Paz, however, gets off to an odd start as we head to the Witches' Market.

It is probably the simplistic outsider's view, but the various potions and animal parts on display on the many stalls and in the small shops appear to be aimed at three broad areas: medicine, fertility and "black magic". In the latter case: the casting of spells on your enemy or to bring you good fortune.

Key to Bolivian culture is the figure of Pachamama, or Mother Earth, so one of the most common sights is dried llama foetuses. Typically, this is buried in the foundations of a new house as a present to Pachamama to bring good luck to those who come to reside there.

Judging from the many stalls, other favourite victims from the animal world appear to be the poor armadillo and birds, whilst no witches' coven would surely be complete without snakes and frogs, which seemed to be in abundant supply in various forms: dried, powdered or liquid. The good luck charms invariably feature images if not of the sun then the puma or the condor.

José tells us to look out for the local witch doctors and fortune tellers that operate in numbers around the market. They are women and wear a distinctive hat like a trilby. Known as Yatiri, they derive their insight not from tea leaves or crystal balls but from the coca leaf that they carry in a pouch around their waist. They are deemed to have inherited powers, and their role reminds us of our encounter with a shaman in Guatemala.

Our interest aroused, we wander into one establishment and find ourselves trapped at the back of the tiny shop, our exit barred by the effusive shopkeeper, and finish up in possession of a small Pachamama doll that is still in residence in our apartment, warding off evil spirits whilst we continue our travels.

Moving on through the narrow cobbled streets, we emerge in the central square Plaza Murillo where a large crowd has gathered. It is a demonstration. I am keen to see what is going on and use my limited Spanish to read the placards to try and understand what the protesters are demanding. Armed policemen stand around in large numbers, and José, I am sure encouraged by Rosie, ushers me away to the nearby Museo de Etnografia y Folklore. The most impressive of a number of museums around the city that would grace any major European city.

José, maybe thinking I am too dangerous to be left wandering the city, for our final sightseeing of the day takes us out of town to visit the Valle de la Luna. As the name implies, this is a lunar landscape of jagged rock formations and has become a popular tourist destination, thanks to the creation of a circular walk on a paved path. Rocks in their odd natural shapes have been attributed names: Mother Moon, The Lady's Hat and Turtle Hill. It is a welcome escape from the city, even if the presentation of this entirely natural occurrence is a little over-contrived.

After two days, it is time to leave La Paz and we make our way via a stop at Tiwanaku, ruins of an ancient city, to a hotel on the banks of Lake Titicaca. Tiwanaku was the hub of a civilisation about which little is known, except that it was at its height between one and two thousand years ago but had by AD 1200 become another "Lost Civilisation". The lack of knowledge about the people who lived here close to the shores of Lake Titicaca has been compounded by the site having been constantly looted over generations. With many structures still in place, it nevertheless has enough of interest to the passing tourist heading for Lake Titicaca.

We have reached the lake and here we are looking across the dark, mysterious and mythical waters. Already some amazing discoveries. In our hotel, we discover a small museum containing a replica of Thor Heyerdahl's *Ra II*, which successfully crossed the Atlantic from Morocco to Barbados in 1970. What could be the reason? Heyerdahl had become famous as far back as 1947 when he sailed his raft *Kon-Tiki* from the coast of South America to the Tuamotu Islands to try and prove his theory that the original settlers of Polynesia came not from the west, as most presume, but from the east. By the 1960s, he wanted to test the technology of the Ancient Egyptians, constructing the first *Ra*, which ultimately sank mid-Atlantic. Undeterred, he elicited the help of the Limachi brothers, resident boatbuilders of reed boats living here on the banks of Lake Titicaca. And in this backyard of a tourist hotel by the lake, we find two of the very same Limachi brothers, only too ready to tell their side of the story.

If that is not enough of a surprise, on our second night after dinner, the hotel manager leads us out into the back garden past the museum to another building. Here, he reveals the presence of a powerful telescope that offers us an amazing look at the Milky Way and beyond, the clear Andean skies being perfect for stargazing, sufficient for NASA scientists to make an annual pilgrimage to this very spot.

Today is to be spent on Lake Titicaca. First, we travel to the nearby town of Copacabana. It is a busy lakeside town with a seventeenth-century Basilica of the Lady of Copacabana set in the main plaza. This church attracts thousands of pilgrims and is the scene of an important religious festival in the Bolivian calendar. Today, we will witness a somewhat more mundane but, nevertheless in my experience, unique ceremony. In the square, many stalls with local ladies selling flowers, doing good business. We arrive in time to witness this unusual ceremony. Recent purchasers of new cars have gathered. Their cars are decorated with garlands of flowers. The proud owners have assembled to have their new autos blessed in a service conducted by the local priest.

After this diversion from the purpose of our visit to Copacabana, we head for the quay to join our hydrofoil for the trip on Lake Titicaca. First, we head for Moon Island. This is but a small islet where we tie up at the jetty and disembark for a climb up a steep incline to view some ruins of an Inca temple. The island has an interesting history, reputedly being inhabited by virgin women, and the ruins are those of Inakuyu, the "Palace of the Virgins of the Sun". Women actually held a position in Inca society, the Emperor apart, above that of the men, so the reason for an apparently elite group of women living here in isolation is not entirely clear. Was this the Inca equivalent of a seminary? Some have actually dubbed the temple complex a nunnery. Or, as others have speculated, were the women here prior to being the subject of human sacrifice? Plausible, there being no higher calling in Inca society.

Once we have climbed to the temple site, it becomes clear that it is built on a plateau commanding views back across the lake. The temple has been subject to extensive restoration, providing some idea of how things looked before the Spanish arrived and decimated the site. Beyond the temple, further up the hill and still clearly delineated, a series of terraces where crops would have been grown, suggesting the women resident on the island were largely self-sufficient.

This is but an interlude as we now return to the boat and progress to the larger nearby Sun Island. Although the main purpose of stopping here is to enjoy lunch at a pleasant lakeside restaurant in Inca folklore, Sun Island, like its near neighbour, has a significant role. It is believed to be the birthplace of the sun god and latterly that of the first two Inca, Manco Kapac and Mama Ocillo. They were the children of the sun god Viracocha, the Inca equivalent of Adam and Eve in Christian belief. That said, many of the ruins on this island predate even the Inca civilisation.

We transfer to a smaller boat to visit Chisawa, one of the floating islands of the Uros tribe. These people genuinely live on islands made of *tortora* reeds floating on the surface of the lake. They have a unique culture, having cut themselves off from the outside world several hundreds of years ago to avoid becoming vassals of the Incas. Today when we visit, tourism is at an early stage on these floating islands. I wonder how these islanders have coped in the intervening years since our visit. Already at this time there were concerns about the number of visitors to the floating islands on the Peruvian side of Lake Titicaca, where there is a much more developed tourist industry.

All I can report is that the people we meet are genuinely friendly and welcoming. Through a local guide, we discover that the Uros people live largely off fishing and the birds which frequent the lake, like the ibis, which over the centuries they have domesticated and which are kept for both their meat and eggs. This diet is supplemented by eating the soft part of the reeds so key to their very unique existence. Life is hard, however, so it is only natural if they view tourism as an attractive new source of income. Part of that is selling their wares. Their clothing is very colourful, and one item they push hard for us to buy is the multi-coloured knitted hat. As we head back to port, it is time to reflect on another interesting day in Bolivia.

José has returned to La Paz so we have a free day. Being the only guests at the hotel, we have become friendly with the manager and he tells us that there is a festival in the nearby village of Huatajata, so following his directions we set off walking along the main road adjacent to the hotel. On a hot day, it seems a long way but perhaps on reflection only little over a mile before we come across a large open greensward where events appear about to begin. We chat to a couple of young girls, thinking they may speak some English but they don't. Nevertheless, using our limited Spanish, we do establish that this is a celebration of local fishermen at the end of the fishing season, the Fiesta de Pescadores.

A stage has been erected and after an interminable version of the Bolivian National Anthem, played by a less than tuneful brass band, local dignitaries, all wearing garlands of flowers, begin a series of opening speeches with a large picture of President Evo Morales as a backdrop. Some locals gather around the stage but most are in small groups chatting. This is an annual gathering and we guess people have travelled from many different villages to take a rare opportunity to meet and greet old friends. Speeches over, a loud cheer and events get underway.

There are booths selling the usual items of clothing – dresses, hats and ponchos – and fast-food stalls emitting pungent smells. *Saltenas*, savoury pastries; whole hogs on spits; skewers of meat of uncertain origin and much more. The highlight of the fiesta appears to be the bands. There are many, each finding themselves an area in the large open field. First tuning their instruments and then starting impromptu concerts, gathering around them a crowd. The music and the instruments vary. Most popular are guitars, that we would immediately recognise, but there are other stringed instruments, like the *charango,* but also flute-like instruments, the inevitable panpipes and large drums. However, this remains first and foremost a social gathering of people coming together to talk.

Later, when we head back to the hotel, we come to a rise in the road where there is a small cluster of buildings and a petrol station. Parked on the forecourt and spilling onto the road, the National 2, are about thirty taxis. A poster indicates that they are owned by members of the Taxi Drivers' Union having some form of social get-together. Wives are preparing food, kids are playing and the men are sitting around chatting and supping beer. Rosie tries to engage one of the men in conversation, but he and the other men sitting next to him cannot tune into her Spanish. Instead, as a gesture of friendliness, he serenades her on his guitar, singing *Frère Jacques*. Much laughter all round.

Our journey around Bolivia is coming to an end. It has proved to be one of the more memorable countries we have visited. We return briefly to La Paz before continuing this particular trip in Argentina, but that is another story.

After two weeks in Bolivia, apart from the minor incident in Potosi, Rosie has not been affected by the altitude, but now as we drive to the airport she appears quite distressed, disoriented and gasping for breath. It is not until we are aboard our aircraft and airborne that she recovers. Altitude sickness is a strange and unpredictable affliction.

A final footnote to this chapter. A few days after leaving Bolivia, we receive an email from Liz confirming that she, Eric and the vehicle have all returned safely to Sucre, but not before poor Eric had spent a further freezing cold night on the salt flats with his beloved vehicle.

Six

Brazil: Sugarloaf, Amado and more

Brazil: The world's fifth largest country with a population of over 200 million. A significant number of the inhabitants live around the two metropolises of Sao Paulo and Rio de Janeiro. The country is also home to the bio-diverse Amazon region, encompassing the Amazon River, second longest in the World. Portuguese speaking.

Like Argentina some years before, we rather liked what we found when we made our first visit to Brazil. Yet it hadn't started too promisingly.

I was really annoyed with myself falling for the scam. Our first morning in Rio de Janeiro. We decide to venture out from our hotel and take a walk along Rio's famous Copacabana Beach, supposed home of the "beautiful people". We were promenading along, minding our own business and taking in the sights, the scantily dressed beach people, when this shoeshine kid suddenly appears at my side and asks if I want my shoes polished. My first reaction was to look down at my shoes before realising I was wearing trainers and that the suggestion was absurd. In that brief instant, our attention distracted and without either of us noticing, he manages to squirt some odious-looking substance on Rosie's new red sandals. He quickly draws her attention to the offending brown blob and we stop in our tracks. He now kneels down to inspect at close quarters. 'Dog shit,' he quickly confirms.

There was a little bit of a tussle as Rosie tried to clean off the mess whilst the kid pronounced, 'I will do it, it is my job.' He cleans off the muck and tries to polish the sandals. Rosie senses the scam, and the fact that these were a brand-new and shiny pair of sandals means she is very firm in telling the boy to clear off. Sensing danger, I look around for an accomplice. It's a one-man (or -boy) job, however, a scam pure and simple and finally evidenced when he demands, 'You give me 10 *reais*.' That is over £2 and to a Rio street urchin worth a hell of a lot more. Much to Rosie's disgust, I give him a 1-*real* note and without hesitation he takes it and moves along to find his next victim. A warning of things to come, although fortunately on this particular trip, it proved to be a one-off. As in most South American countries, the disparity in Brazil between rich and poor is huge and as tourists you are foolhardy if you do not remain on your guard, particularly if you choose to pursue your sightseeing away from the mainstream tourist attractions.

Although we liked Brazil and its people, to be honest, this first taste of Rio was a little disappointing in terms of its status as one of the great cities of the world. Yes, it had the statue of Christ the Redeemer located in a magnificent viewing point high above the city and an awesome feat of twentieth-century construction, but the crowds were suffocating. Sure, there was Sugarloaf Mountain and of course there are the famed beaches of Copacabana and Ipanema. Not, after all, full of beautiful people; a beach full of all body shapes and sizes. It could be Brighton beach except the tans are better and with scant concern about melanoma. As a city, though, Rio had left us feeling that we had not really got under its skin and our visit was too short to do it justice.

We were staying at the prestigious Copacabana Palace Hotel on Avenida Atlantica with views over Copacabana Beach. An old-fashioned hotel dating from the twenties and recently refurbished, it is an oasis of charm amidst a brash and noisy waterfront and regrettably the planners have allowed high-rise buildings to be constructed so that it has now dwarfed into insignificance amidst the concrete jungle, one downside of which is that the pool area is in shadow from about two in the afternoon as the sun disappears behind the palace's neighbouring buildings. A shame, as the Copacabana Palace is one of the few character buildings still standing in this part of the city.

The charm of the Palace Hotel is enhanced by its very special breakfast buffet, the centrepiece of which is the array of fresh fruits. On one morning, we counted no less than forty different fruits on display, ranging from familiar tropical fruits like pineapple, guava and papaya to *mangosteen* (rather like a lychee in texture and encased in a leathery and crimson-coloured skin), *jabuticaba* (a small purple fruit the size of a grape but with a tougher skin) and the *abiu* (bigger and yellowy with a white chewy flesh), all beyond our previous experience, and others so obscure that even the waiters could not put a name to them.

In this sanitised world of the tourist, you are only from time to time reminded of that extreme difference between rich and poor. And it is true not only here in Brazil. There is a common thread; almost every country in Latin America has been ruled for generations by a privileged elite, reluctant to share their accumulated wealth, often, it has to be acknowledged, under a two-party political system. A duopoly of power in which both ruling parties are dominated by a few wealthy families yet, masquerading as a democracy, only recently have they been challenged by leftist-leaning populist politicians like Chavez and Morales.

Our first taste of this ambiguity came many years ago on another visit, albeit brief, to South America. We had arrived on a cruise ship at the Venezuelan port of La Guaira where we had arranged to meet a distant relative of Rosie's. We hung around the dockside for half an hour or so, assailed by taxi drivers, before deciding that her relatives were not going to show and we agreed with one of the cabbies on a fee for a day of sightseeing in the capital, Caracas. A motorway cuts its way through the mountains and as the road emerges on the outskirts of the city, there hanging precariously off the side of a steep hillside was our first sight of a shanty town that only a few months later, in a torrential rainstorm, slid down into the valley below with many hundreds dying. With this in mind, it was something of a surprise a week or so before leaving home for Brazil that we read a travel article saying that an enterprising travel company was arranging tours to visit the comparable *favelas* on the edge of Rio.

As we drove towards the city from the airport, our driver, Marcelo, pointed out the vast swathe of these very slums to our right. At best breezeblock-built, corrugated-roofed constructions, more usually a timber frame covered with tarpaulin; the *favelas* of Rio. When we mentioned the possibility of a visit, he could not have been more vehement in his advice to stay well clear. Rio is clearly delineated into two parts by a range of mountains, and his distinct instruction was, 'Always stay on the coast side.'

He said the *favelas* were like a war zone and the military had recently moved to confront head on the drug barons that ruled the streets.

Once we reached downtown Rio, the idea of a war raging on the other side of the hill seemed improbable, but we later discovered that one of these ghettos is actually known as Gaza City, a place where the death toll in fact far exceeds that of the city it is named after. In the past twenty years preceding our visit, Brazil has recorded 300,000 murders, most gang- and drug-related; more casualties in fact than in the Angolan Civil War raging in West Africa during the same period. Despite these incongruities, as privileged visitors protected from the seedier aspects of the countries visited, we continue to have strong positive feelings towards Latin America.

Before leaving Rio on that first visit, we of course did all the touristy things. Our guide, Lima, was overtly homosexual, mincing his way from location to location. At first, we thought that his over-the-top theatrical performance was largely for the amusement of his guests until passing a historical building of note, he announced to us and the bus full of our fellow tourists, 'If there is any more noise, I am not going to tell you anything more. After all, I know all there is to know about Rio, which is more than I can say for you.' At that point, we realised his was not an act. He succeeded in quietening the recalcitrant, but at that moment, I couldn't help but think that this prima donna had destroyed his chances of picking up any tips today.

The tour took us to visit the statue of Christ the Redeemer, crowded but impressive. Next to Sugarloaf Mountain. By the time we reached Sugarloaf, it was late afternoon. You take two cable cars to reach the summit and by the time we'd alighted from the first cable car at Morro da Urca, heavy cloud had blotted out both the mountain summit above and views over the city below. The second cable car was closed for safety reasons, so we were left with no choice but to return to ground level on the next available car. A hectic but not totally rewarding day.

On our final evening in the city, Lima escorted us to watch a samba show, all long legs, feathers and sparkly costumes. This was preceded by a visit to another Brazilian favourite: a *churrascaria*. These essentially beef restaurants are certainly popular. I read that they date back to *gauchos* in the 1800s barbequing their meat, although I also read this type of "meat only" restaurant had been popularised more recently by roadside truckers' cafés.

We were seated on long tables whilst a seemingly endless line of waiters with an amazing range of meat spit roasted and carried on long skewers came to the table. Mostly it was various cuts of beef, but also served were lamb, pork and chicken and a spicy local sausage. As a concession to those who are not carnivores, there were plates of puffed pastry filled with cheese. The restaurant was popular with locals, mainly large family groups, and we few English speakers were placed together at the end of one of the long tables. Apart from ourselves, the small group of foreigners comprised a rather over-dressed middle-aged lady from Oregon, a GP from North London and a Filipino businessman and his daughter.

By chance, we had met the Filipino gentleman the previous day on a sightseeing tour. He had announced himself rather strangely: 'I am Mr Wee from Manila. I am fifty-seven years old and this is my daughter. She is fifteen.' At first, I thought that perhaps reaching the age of fifty-seven was something significant in the Philippines. On reflection, I decided that perhaps he had learnt his English through one of those courses where the language used is frankly too formal and unnatural, having had a similar experience with our own attempts at self-taught Spanish.

Mr Wee, we had noted at lunch the previous day, had a liking for his food and had subsequently spent most of our tour asleep in the bus. Today, true to form, he consumed every cut of meat brought to the table. At the samba show, although seated in the front row close to the bright lights and noise from the stage, he slept through the whole performance.

Time to move on. The Falls at Iguassu are spectacular. I have seen Niagara and Victoria but for sheer scale these are the most impressive. Yet my first reaction had been, okay, but not stupendous, little realising at the time the sheer magnitude that we were subsequently privileged to view from a helicopter by way of a birthday present from Rosie to me. The important thing about Iguassu Falls is to view them from both the Brazilian and Argentine sides and of course if you are lucky enough, from the air as well. The Brazilian side of the Falls is within a nature reserve that contains only one hotel, the Cataratas del Iguazú, splendid it is too, however, a little old-fashioned.

Checking in, we find in our room a copy of the *Rules internal for hotel guests*.

These include a request that guests:

- *Turn out the taps when not being used*
- *Turn off the lights and air conditioning before leaving the apartment*
- *Close the door before leaving the apartment*

In addition, guests are not allowed, amongst other things:

- *to throw waste paper through the window*
- *to bring in pets of any kind*
- *race or size (sic)*
- *to drive nails in the walls*

Abiding by the rules did not in any way detract from the charm of the place; a feeling of well-being towards the whole establishment enhanced after a busy day sightseeing when we imbibed a welcome sundowner by the hotel pool. We ordered what we had been told is the national drink, a cocktail called *caipirinha*. Made from a sugar-based liquor called *cachaca*, a Brazilian rum with a quite distinctive taste, it is served long with lime, sugar and ice. As I rarely drink alcohol but for the occasional glass or two of wine over dinner, the *caipirinha* had the effect of making me legless in a manner that I could only recall once before in my life when as a hapless teenager I had overindulged at my first work's Christmas party.

It is nearly ten years later and we have returned to Brazil. This time, Rio de Janeiro, we discover, has many facets that passed us by on that first visit, and now we can see it as a truly great city. Perhaps that first visit had suffered from its brevity and the inclement weather that meant our visit up Sugarloaf Mountain had terminated so abruptly. This time, we visit Sugarloaf again; the weather is kinder with cloudless skies and amazing views back towards the city and beyond to the Christ the Redeemer statue.

After a day sightseeing, we take an early-evening stroll downtown, but sensing a change in the weather, we narrowly avoid getting caught in a horrific thunderstorm that floods large parts of the city in minutes to the extent that pictures of a flooded Maracana Stadium make the BBC World News bulletin later that evening.

Our evening exploration seemed to suggest that the city is fairly safe to walk in, certainly in daylight, so it is the following morning and we set off for one of our marathon walks starting in the main thoroughfare of Avenida Rio Branco. We will typically do some research, have some ideas about where to visit – museums, galleries, monuments – but be prepared to go "off-piste" if we spot something else of interest. This is such a day. Off along a side street to the left we see a bell tower and decide to explore. Shortly, we find ourselves in the Praca XV de Novembro, the former main square of the city when Rio was the Brazilian capital. Here, old and new are juxtaposed, skyscrapers and fine old buildings side by side. Our marathon walk takes us past the National Museum to Cinelandia, the artist colony known as Lapa and the modernistic Metropolitan Cathedral.

In need of sustenance, we have read that a good coffee can be had at the café in the Teatro Municipal. Instead of a coffee, we find ourselves in a line queueing for a tour of the recently renovated theatre. Built in 1908 in the style of the Paris Opera House, this proves a useful diversion, but we emerge an hour later still in need of liquid refreshment. Relief is at hand when we come across the famous coffee house Confeitaria Colombo in Rua Concaves Dias. The ambience and decor are superb examples of another age; we could be in Paris or Vienna at the turn of the last century. The coffee is even better and the cake beyond sublime.

Next I want to introduce you to Salvador. At the end of our first visit to Rio, we flew north to take some time to relax by the beach and to visit the colonial city of Salvador. For various reasons, our first two choices of location were unavailable and we ended up at Costa do Sauipe, some 80km north of Salvador. It was a resort complex that our guidebook (fortunately inaccurately) described as "Disneyland in Brazil". The beaches were great, the resort eco-friendly and being off season the whole place nearly deserted. From here, we took a trip down to Salvador and it proved well worth a visit; in fact, the old part of the city is one of our favourite places to simply walk and absorb the atmosphere.

Salvador was once the capital of colonial Brazil. On my birthdate in 1500, Pedro Alvarez Cabral with a fleet of a dozen ships searching for the Indies espied land, naming this area Terra de Santa Cruz. From here, Cabral turned east and using the trade winds sailed across the Atlantic past the Cape of Good Hope, eventually reaching India. His was therefore but a brief visit, and many years passed before the Portuguese were to return as colonists and begin building the city of Salvador.

There seems to be an inverse relationship between the poverty in a locality and the grandeur of the Roman Catholic churches set in its midst. Salvador is certainly a good example, with the Church and Convent of San Francisco a structure awash with gold. It adorns walls, ceiling and altar, and it is not even the Cathedral. This is located close by and is another impressive building, sitting in a prominent position at one end of the Praca de Se.

Since then, our two subsequent visits to Salvador have seen us arrive by ship. This in itself provides a grand introduction to the city, which sits high on a plateau overlooking the port. The most popular way to access the old city from the port is to walk the short distance to the Elevador Lacerda, passing along the way the former Customs Building which is now the Mercado Modelo, a market with some 300 stalls selling local crafts and tourist tat.

On our second visit to the city on the way from the port, we take a cursory look inside the market, but it is pretty ordinary by contrast to markets in other Brazilian cities that we have visited, like Manaus and Belem, so we quickly move along. Crossing the road, you come to the imposing entrance to the near 150-year-old Elevador Lacerda, the lift to Cidade Alta, the upper city. We pay our 15 centavos and take the Elevador. Pick your time; over 50,000 people use the lift every day and the crowds can be large and the wait in the steamy tropical temperatures tedious. On this occasion, there is no queue and we are soon alighting onto the Praca Municipal.

Amidst the throng of tourists, it is easy to pick out dubious-looking characters, likely scammers or pickpockets, so we are on our guard. We begin by taking a look in at the recently opened Afro-Brazilian Museum, dedicated to a history of the slave trade, and visit the nearby Palacio do Rio Branco. Later, emerging into the bright sunlight, we make our way up to the Praca de Se, the main square, to make another visit to the famed Iglesia San Francisco, one of the most highly gold-encrusted churches that we have ever encountered in all of our travels. Emerging, we hear the sound of music from a side street and go to investigate. A lively street band has attracted a significant audience and after enjoying the entertainment we decide to give our planned visit to the cathedral a miss and continue down the narrow street into the area called Pelourinho, itself a labyrinth of narrow lanes and passages. This is what was the upper-class part of the city, built as the residential and administrative centre by the Portuguese colonists but later, after independence, left neglected for more than a century. Now it has been beautifully restored to its former glory and enjoys UNESCO World Heritage status.

On this our second visit we discover Amado. We are looking for the city museum but as the narrow cobbled street we walk down opens onto a square, we come across an intriguing house. The impressive building painted in pale blue is the former residence of Jorge Amado and now a museum and archive of the works of the most famous of Brazilian literary figures. In the ground-floor café we come across Martin, a fellow shipmate of ours, who explains that he is an avid reader of all the books of this prolific writer.

Jorge Amado was born in 1912 in the state of Bahia, of which Salvador is the capital, and which is the setting of his stories of lives of "ordinary people".

Born the son of a plantation owner and subject to a strict religious education, Jorge soon rebelled. By the age of twenty he had become involved with a group of political activists, written his first book and joined the Communist Party. His writing reflected his fascination with the different strata in Brazilian society and particularly the role of those with Afro traditions. These interests were reflected in his early works, such as *Jubiada* and *The Beach Waifs*. He was twice exiled because of his political views, although in between was elected to Congress. Five years in Paris in the 1940s saw him mingle with intellectual thinkers and artists, including Sartre and Picasso.

A new Amado emerged on his return to Brazil in 1952. His political enthusiasm for Communism was on the wane and in reflective mood, viewing his own early work as too serious, he decided that a more comedic, even satirical, look at Brazilian society would have more impact.

Amado the storyteller emerged in a series of novels. *Gabriela, Clove and Cinnamon,* published in 1958, increased his reputation at home and abroad, and a series of socially based novels followed. The most acclaimed was probably *Dona Flor and Her Two Husbands,* published in 1966. Some regarded his novels as formulaic, with sexual undertones, racial stereotyping and common characterisations. This criticism may have been justified but was also a strength, as many of the books have been turned into films and TV series, the television version of *Gabriela, Clove and Cinnamon,* made in the 1970s, proving a huge hit and further enhancing Amado's reputation as a national institution.

Amado died in 2001 but by then the house in Pelourinho was well established. During his travels in the United States, a number of universities had approached him about donating his archive for preservation and subsequent research, and he was minded to accept one of these offers. However, his wife and fellow author, Zelia Gattai, interceded and insisted the material must be retained not only in Brazil but specifically in Bahia, the setting for his novels. Thus, the Foundation House in Pelourinho was established in 1987. Although much of the house contains material of interest to the academic researcher, the ground floor has exhibits of his colourful book covers published in multiple languages, many personal artefacts and a clever mural illustrating the some sixty languages into which his works have been translated.

These naturally include English, and a copy of *Dona Flor and Her Two Husbands* now sits on my bookshelf, a reminder of our inspirational visit to the blue house in Largo do Pelourinho.

Our third visit to Salvador and all now seems familiar; the market, the lift, although this time a long queue, and once up in the old city, the crowds in the square in front of San Francisco, but today something different; it is carnival. The crowds are even more dense than normal, lining the streets in anticipation. Music plays and soon the procession arrives. Lacking the structure and formality of carnival in Rio, this is more akin to carnival as we know it, albeit on a grand scale. In fact, the event continues over a six-day period and has been described as the world's largest street party, so we are very much viewing just a microcosm. Noise, music, scantily dressed girls and most impressive, the enormous papier-mâché characters.

It has to be said that as much as we like the country, we have also visited many uninspiring and frankly uncomfortably frightening towns in Brazil. So, on this particular journey, it is with some relief having travelled some 200 miles south from Salvador that we find ourselves in Ilheus, a town with buildings of note and an interesting back story: the rise and fall of the cocoa industry and of the "Colonels" who dominated that industry and made their fortune here. However, more importantly for us this is the town where Jorge Amado spent his formative years, so our first mission is to find Amado's house. We seek out Tourist Information. The young man in the booth is singularly unhelpful. No town maps to be had and he feigns no knowledge of Amado's house. Annoying, as we subsequently find it barely 100 metres away.

Firstly, though, we come across the cathedral. It is not a building to pass by. On a grand scale for a town the size of Ilheus. This as we later learn emanating directly as a consequence of the boom years in cocoa production. The cathedral is relatively new, having been built from 1931, although it was not dedicated until 1967. It is built in the neo-classical style, with an impressive dome and spires. I think I counted five. The interior is comparatively modest by Roman Catholic standards and certainly when contrasted with the cathedral in Salvador.

Close by, we come to the Teatro Municipal, built in 1932 and about to undergo renovation and opposite the Amado house. The Casa de Jorge Amado is where the great writer lived and grew up and where, staying with his parents, he wrote his first novel, *Gabriela, Clove and Cinnamon*. The book is set here in Ilheus. The impressively frontaged building in yellow and white has now been restored and turned into a museum honouring his life. A bronze statue of the author stands outside. We naturally take the opportunity for a modest 2.50 *reais* to look inside. The museum contains a collection of photos and manuscripts of his life and gives a further insight into the man we discovered earlier on our travels in Salvador.

Moving on to the central plaza, we find it is home to some historical buildings of note: the Piadade Palace and the Bataclan, one-time house of ill repute now a coffee house.

We make our way back to the cathedral where on the steps a local guide introduces himself as Hector. He is obviously looking to escort us around the town, but we tell him we have done that already. He asks if we have discovered Bataclan. When we answer in the affirmative, he relates some of the history of the town that we had not appreciated. He tells us that this part of Brazil was once called the "Cocoa Coast". The city has a long history and in the earliest days, the local economy depended on sugarcane production. A combination of factors – the end of slavery, overproduction in the Caribbean islands and the use of sugar beet as a source in Europe – led to a steep decline in the price of sugar, and this region went into decline. Then in the late nineteenth century, a new crop, cacao, or white gold, led to another era of prosperity. The industry was dominated by the "colonels", a handful of powerful cocoa barons with huge plantations that not only dominated the burgeoning industry but also the town of Ilheus and local society. Hector says you can see the impact around the town; the cathedral, the theatre and some of the grand mansions still evident were down to the colonels and their largesse and excesses.

Returning to the subject of the Bataclan. Hector says he will tell us a story, although he has been barred from the cathedral for relating this story to tourists. The colonels would attend Mass, greet the priest, take their seat but during the service would slip down an alley at the side of the cathedral to Bataclan. The priest was privy to their clandestine activities, being paid to give extraordinarily long sermons. As the service reached its conclusion, he would signal for the church bells to be rung as a sign for the colonels to hurriedly return to rejoin the congregation. We ask what happened to the colonels, and Hector tells us that they continued to be a major influence here until the 1980s, when a blight, *vassoura de bruxa,* or witches' broom, decimated the trees and left the cocoa industry in ruins. The colonels' dominance was at an end.

We thank Hector, who incidentally is not looking for any payment for his unsolicited services, but he does say, 'If you have time, I recommend a visit to one of the few remaining cacao farms.' We decide that this might be interesting and he kindly waves across to one of the waiting taxi drivers and we are on our way. A soft sell but we do not feel victims.

Arriving at the cocoa farm, we are in luck. A guided tour for a group of tourists is about to begin, so we tag along as if we are part of the group. This presents the opportunity to follow the full lifecycle of cocoa, beans growing and being harvested, followed by a demonstration of the drying process, a chance to taste the juice and finally to sample some chocolate. We ask the guide about witches' broom and he responds that it was all a Communist plot to get Lula into power. I couldn't help but think that there was something of a disconnect. There was a gap of over twenty years between the incidence of witches' broom destroying the cacao crop and the presidency of Lula, the popular name of Luiz Inácio Lula da Silva, Brazil's thirty-fifth president. I don't pursue my questioning.

Back in town. Rosie wants to do some shopping so we return to an artisan shop we saw in the morning and buy some pictures. The shopkeeper is very persuasive and somehow convinces us to top up our purchases with a jar of local honey, not the most practical item to buy when on a long journey.

We pass the Vesuvio bar, former haunt of Jorge Amado, and from where he observed much of the street life reflected in his novels. It seems impolite not to pay homage so we decide to stop for a drink. Sitting here in his youth, close to his family home and watching the world go by, Amado began to develop the characters and scenarios played out in his first novel, *Gabriela, Clove and Cinnamon.* It is easy to visualise; little will have changed. I am expecting to order coffee but to my surprise, after the experience in Iguassu, Rosie orders a *caipirinha.* Happy days.

Moving on. We are in Santos, a city made famous around the world by Edson Arantes do Nascimento. An avid football fan since attending my first football league match at the age of ten, by the time of the 1958 World Cup finals in Sweden, now a teenager, I was totally absorbed by the "beautiful game". I can therefore well remember when a new star emerged on the scene. He was a little older than me, just seventeen. I am of course talking of the man we know better as Pelé.

Pelé and Santos FC have a shared history, as he played for the team from the age of fifteen until his retirement twenty years and 650 goals later. Voted the player of the 20th century, he was a three-time winner of the FIFA World Cup. It is no surprise therefore when we take a tramcar ride around the city to orient ourselves that we pass, under construction, the Pelé Museum. If the museum not being completed is a disappointment, imagine Rosie's delight when I suggest that we are left with no choice but to head for the Estadio Urbano Caldeira, the home of Santos FC, especially when she discovers the stadium is located some distance away, in a suburb of the city called Vila Belmiro.

Well, a bus ride later, we have made it to the stadium and I have to report I am quite relieved to find that it is located in a fairly affluent part of the city. Fortunately, the trip proves worthwhile, even for the non-football fan, as Santos FC boasts a very decent museum, the Memorial das Conquistas, dedicated to the history of the football club. Naturally, Pelé features highly amongst the well-presented exhibition of trophies, medals, shirts, posters and photographs.

Whilst Rosie is reasonably engaged by the football paraphernalia, she is less impressed when returning to the city we get disoriented, exiting the stadium at a different place from where we entered, finding ourselves on a road devoid of buses or taxis and leaving us with an uncomfortably long walk back into the city.

Santos of course had an existence before Pelé and was once hailed the "coffee capital of Brazil". The old coffee exchange, The Bolsa, ceased operations in the 1960s. The fine but unpretentious art nouveau late-Victorian building in which it was housed was left to rot and at one point was due for demolition. Fortunately, a restoration project was put in hand and today the Bolsa e Museu do Café is a highlight of the city not to be missed. The trading floor, or Bidding Hall, has been beautifully restored, the sheer opulence of a room used simply to sell and buy coffee, a tribute to the wealth of the former coffee barons that dominated the industry. Marbled floors, seventy huge walnut chairs around the outer part of the cavernous room where sat the brokers and on an elevated platform the chair of the president, surrounded by those of his assistants and clerks recording the transactions.

The room is completed by the hugely impressive stained glass window with the title *The Epic Feats of the Pioneers*, a truly magnificent work of art.

A fervent hope that you are keeping up with this whistle-stop tour of Brazil. We are back to Rio for the third time, ostensibly to attend Carnaval. If you are visiting Rio at this time in February, it had better be to see Carnaval. For five days before the start of Lent, everything else stops; shops, public buildings, museums, galleries and even most of the churches close and, in most cases, actually board up their doors.

Our first foray onto the streets is on the Saturday morning. Bands play, crowds gather, gaggles of the Policia Militar stand on street corners. It is difficult to tell if people are heading home from Friday night out or setting out for Saturday's festivities. We stroll the downtown area and the only building of interest that we can find open is the Cathedral Metropolitana; an element of good fortune, as we have visited most of the museums and of course the theatre on previous visits but have never been inside the cathedral.

The cathedral is big and modern. Built between 1964 and 1979, it can hold 20,000 people. On size alone, it is impressive. The style, oddly, here in Brazil, is a shape redolent of a Mayan pyramid. The main feature is the stained glass windows, some 200 plus feet from floor to ceiling. Given the condition of the external fabric of the building, one thing I will predict is that unlike churches built in the Middle Ages across Europe, this one will not be still standing in 500 years from now.

Sunday morning. Seeking out the Confeitaria Colombo that we had enjoyed so much on our last visit, we find ourselves just a block from where we want to be. I have no sooner remarked to Rosie that we have inadvertently strayed into a slightly insalubrious neighbourhood than I spot a couple of characters sitting on the kerb on the opposite side of the road. One stands up and I say to Rosie, 'Watch out, trouble coming.' She is on my wavelength. Although we avoid eye contact with the two men and begin to walk a little more briskly, out of the corner of my eye, I can see the man who has stood up is now heading straight across the road in our direction.

Seconds later, he is in my face, but strangely the first thing I notice is his body odour, deeply unpleasant. He grabs at my trouser pocket and demands, 'You give me money.' He is a weaselly man, not of an intimidating stature, wearing a dirty old T-shirt and shorts. Although you cannot predict how you will react in such a situation, I push him away, perhaps more influenced by the wish to get the pungent smell from my nostrils rather than any act of bravery.

At the same time, Rosie shouts out loudly, 'Back off,' and swings her day bag, giving him a good whack across the chest. He makes a desultory grab at her wristwatch before running off empty-handed. I glance across the road to check out his companion, a rather physically larger specimen, but he is quietly slinking away, obviously not wanting any trouble.

As we gather ourselves, a passerby who must have witnessed the incident, a smartly dressed man with a briefcase in hand, asks us in English if we are okay. But no damage done, we say thank you but we are fine. We quickly make our way to the main street, Avenida Presidente Vargas, only a block away and relative safety. Here we stop and reflect on events. Rosie is euphoric; her self-defence classes taken thirty years ago have paid off. Shout loudly being lesson one, although I am not sure her tutor would have recommended her counterattack on the would-be assailant. Perhaps we were lucky; he had failed with the element of surprise, and perhaps most importantly, no knife had been drawn. Despite being quite streetwise and consciously avoiding ostentation, there are no guarantees of immunity from this type of circumstance and in the coming days, we hear plenty of stories similar to our own.

However, this incident aside, let us not detract from the purpose of this visit to Rio: to attend Carnaval. Whilst week-long street celebrations are taking place throughout the city – singing, dancing, drinking and generally having a good time – the main event is the parade, which takes place in the Sambodromo on the Sunday and Monday nights. This is the serious business, Premier League Carnaval. Twelve samba clubs, six performing on each of the nights, all trying to win the prize of one million *reais*.

The Sambodromo is a purpose-built stadium, inevitably designed by the great Brazilian architect Oscar Niemayer and opened in 1984. The whole edifice is rather like the grandstands around the start/finish line at a Formula One racetrack and measures about half a mile in length, with towering concrete terraces either side, and the inevitable VIP hospitality boxes. The whole place filled to capacity, a crowd of some 250,000 fee-paying spectators, on both nights.

Each team in turn parades through the stadium. They have between sixty-five and eighty minutes from entering to leaving the stadium. During this time, they are adjudicated under various headings such as dance, costume, float design, bands, fantasy and theme by a panel of judges. The accumulated scores are calculated and the winners are announced on the

Tuesday. The winning team subsequently parades through the city on the following Saturday. The teams are samba schools, usually linked with a particular community within the city, hence the parallel I made earlier with Premier League football. The oldest of these schools is nearly one hundred years old, whilst one that we watched, Grande Rio, was formed as recently as 1988. The whole procession is highly stylised, with a minimum number of 2,500 participants, or *passistas,* in each team, a band of at least 200 musicians and various clearly defined roles. These include the Mestre Sala, or Dance Master, and the Porta Bandeira, the standard bearer lavishly dressed in the style of an eighteenth-century costume redolent of a European royal court.

It is Sunday evening and we are making our way slowly through the heavy city traffic to the Sambodromo, thanks to a temporary one-way system by the most circuitous of routes, a journey from downtown which normally takes a few minutes taking us two hours. Eventually, we are in our seats, or more accurately sitting on our allocated square metre of concrete. It is 9.30 pm and proceedings are just about to begin. The band strikes up, the volume maximised through the stadium loudspeaker system, fireworks explode and the first procession begins to make its way slowly through the Sambodromo. This is a serious assault on the senses.

Six hours later, and having watched four teams parade through the stadium, we decide to head back to the comfort of our accommodation on a cruise ship moored in the harbour. It is now 3.30 am, and action in the Sambodromo will continue until well after dawn, ending at about 7.30 in the morning.

As we make our way from our seats, we are quickly engulfed in a melee of humanity. There are droves of tourists like us heading back to the port or to downtown or to their beachside hotels in Ipanema and Copacabana. We have been assured that buses will be running back to the port every fifteen minutes during the night, but despite the promises, there are none heading in our intended direction. One cruise company has hired a bus just for its clients. We try and hitch a lift but the girl in charge insists it is only for her flock. To prove we have paid for entry to Carnaval, everyone has a ticket which is worn around the neck via a piece of string. We notice that the girls' clients all have a red sticker attached to their ticket, obviously a way of identifying them in the crowd. Armed with this knowledge, we join the back of the bus queue and tuck our badges inside our shirts. As we approach the steps up into the sanctuary of the bus, we hold our breath but she doesn't recognise us as she busily counts people onto the bus. Half an hour later, we are back at the port.

Next day, we discover that our fellow passengers have been less fortunate. Buses eventually arrived to collect them but the drivers had been drafted in from out of town. Not knowing the city and confused by the complex one-way system set up for Carnaval, they took two hours to reach a point about a mile away from the port. Here the drivers, unable to fathom how to get closer to their destination, had unceremoniously abandoned their passengers on the pavement and left them to find their way back to the ship. Sometimes, even if a little unedifying, a little bit of blagging is justified.

Just to conclude, Carnaval is a truly amazing spectacle. Colourful costumes, dancers by the hundreds, marching bands, floats and tableaux depicting phantasmagorical scenes, and all on a huge larger-than-life scale. One of those experiences that will live with you forever.

Seven

Paraguay: Brief encounter

Paraguay: Landlocked country of just 7 million people surrounded by Brazil, Bolivia and Argentina. Spanish and Guarani are the official languages. Noted for the longtime dictator Alfredo Stroessner, whose 35-year rule ended in 1989.

I pick up my pace to keep up with Mario as he threads his way through the throng of people making their way across the bridge. I glance around and realise that Rosie has become detached. Through a mass of dark, swarthy faces, I can see her some twenty metres back trying unsuccessfully to push her way past a man with a huge bundle on his back. She looks a little distressed and I call to Mario to stop. To my surprise, Rosie has agreed to my madcap idea that we should cross briefly, from our trip to the Iguassu Falls in Brazil, to visit the neighbouring country of Paraguay. And here we are, halfway across the bridge linking the two countries between the towns of Foz do Iguassu and Ciudad del Este.

A poor and landlocked country, Paraguay did not figure high on my list of places to visit, but this one-off chance to make a visit, albeit brief, seems like an opportunity too good to miss. When we first arrived in Iguassu, it had seemed an unlikely proposition when our guide, Ricardo, made it clear that he was not in favour. He had handed me an outline programme of things to do during our visit, insisting these were just some ideas but of course it was entirely down to us. When I replied, 'How about visiting Paraguay?' he asked, 'Why?' The following day, he asked again about our plans and was equally dismissive when I mentioned the P word.

However, having sensed his reluctance, I had by then my contingency plan in place. At our hotel, I had discovered a small room the size of a broom cupboard. Its occupant was Carlos, who I quickly established was the local Mr Fixit for tourists. When I sounded him out on the possibility of travelling across the border, he immediately told me with a conspiratorial air, 'It can be arranged.' We agreed a price and a time for a car to come and collect us. I asked Carlos about the sights we might expect to see across the border. He didn't raise my expectations with his response: 'There are no churches, missions, monuments or buildings of note, only the shopping. It is a new city.' How right he was to manage my expectations.

So it was that this afternoon I located Carlos in his tiny office and he introduced me to Mario, who was to be our driver.

Introductions completed, Carlos confides, 'There is a problem at the border. We sent a car three hours ago and they are still stuck on the bridge trying to enter Paraguay.'

For a moment, my heart sank.

My immediate thought was *So close and we aren't going to make it. Oh, Carlos, you raised my hopes, now this.*

'If it is okay with you, Mario will take you down to the bridge and park the car and you can walk across.'

I of course readily agreed but Rosie, standing behind me, was, I have to admit, a little less enthusiastic than me about this whole venture.

However, she was encouraged when Carlos confirmed that, 'Of course, Mario will accompany you.'

So here we are quite literally between the two countries. When we arrived at the Brazilian side of the bridge, the traffic was indeed gridlocked without any sign of movement. The bridge is 300 metres in length and spans the Paranha River below, which forms the border between the two countries at this point. There is a two-lane road across the bridge, separated from walkways either side by a high wire fence. People are abandoning vehicles to clamber over the fences onto the walkways, whilst others like us have obviously forsaken buses and cars on the Brazilian side and are making their way across the bridge on foot. We join the melee. Mario, whose English is far from perfect but good enough for us to understand most of what he says, exclaims, 'There must have been a manifestation.' A comment which leaves us just a little perplexed.

Having reconnected with Rosie, we soon find ourselves across the bridge and faced with an imposing archway spanning the road, extending a *Welcome to Paraguay*. Despite an office block with various officials sitting around, people are coming and going quite freely in and out of Paraguay without any document checks. We could pass into Paraguay unannounced without any formality; however, I produce our passports. It is Mario's turn to be perplexed, pushing them away and motioning with hand gestures that they are not required. I persist and eventually he gets the message.

Mario takes our passports and after some discussion with an official in a roadside booth, he secures the rubber stamp that we desire from the official, obviously unaccustomed to such requests and, hey presto, here we are in Paraguay. A wide road stretches uphill away from the border, and looking around absorbing what we see, I think we both quickly form the same impression from the condition of the roads, buildings and look of the people that this is a poor country, even by contrast to Brazil, so close a neighbour just across the bridge.

Mario says he will take us to some shops and leads the way up the hill. The pavement is formed into a series of steep steps and on each level to the left are stalls and to the right small shops. This area is covered by a canvas canopy, doubtless protection from the hot sun, enclosing us in something reminiscent of an Arab souk. The pavements are crowded with the stallholders calling, 'Amigo, come and buy,' immediately demonstrating that we stand out from the crowd as tourists. There is an apparently endless marketplace here, and as we later realise, this is but a fraction of the stalls in this downtown part of the city. The strange thing is that one stall is much like another. The products are limited to what I assume are pirated CDs and videos, sunglasses, shoes and cheap T-shirts and rather alarmingly knives of many shapes and sizes. For variety, Mario leads us off to the right into a small precinct of shops, maybe ten in number, all offering cheap electrical goods: TVs, DVDs and cameras. It all seems rather anachronistic, given the evident poverty of the locals.

Mario, noting our indifference to the electrical goods, leads us back onto the main street and eventually the canopy gives way to sunlight and we emerge onto a major intersection of four roads. Darting between the stationary traffic, Mario leads us into the Mona Lisa Shopping Mall. The first impression is of entering the first-floor perfumery department of a large West End store. Missing is only one ingredient: customers. Apart from the well-dressed staff moving between the bottles of Estée Lauder, Givenchy and Cacherel perfumes, there is nobody else in the store. We check out the prices and they are no cheaper than in the UK. We beat a retreat.

By now, Mario is utterly confused about our motive for visiting Ciudad del Este but unfazed, he leads us onwards, past many more small shops and throngs of people until we find ourselves outside a small store selling local craft products such as handbags and tableware. We decide that perhaps we should show some interest, and go inside. We feel rather trapped, as Mario is clearly running out of ideas about where to go and what to show us. The goods seem authentic and locally crafted, and as we potter around, we manage to select a number of small gifts to take home with us. We don't have any local currency but we are told that there are 5,800 *guaranis* to the dollar. A sure sign of rampant inflation. We pay for our purchases in US dollars and head out.

A knowing glance to each other is enough. We decide that this is probably sufficient of Paraguay and after telling Mario, 'Time to go,' we meander back through the streets and alleyways in the general direction of the bridge. Outside of every shop a uniformed and heavily armed security guard. Even outside the shop where Mario stops to purchase some toys for his children.

Then here we are back on the bridge heading for Brazil. About halfway across, we hear a loud whistle from behind and stand aside as four guys come running past, each of them rolling a giant tractor tyre. Shortly afterwards, we hear a soft, shuffling noise and once again stopping and looking around, we see a line of men approaching, each bent almost double, carrying enormous boxes on their backs. I ask Mario what they are carrying and he replies, 'Cigarettes.' We soon come upon a milling crowd of people and realise what is happening. Beneath the bridge at this point is the Brazilian bank of the river, and far below us we can see that there too a crowd has gathered. The tyre men are obviously awaiting a signal from below, whilst the cigarette men, better organised, have handed their contraband to another group that have already tied ropes around the boxes and are lowering them over the railings to awaiting accomplices below. I tell Rosie to take a photograph, but she says that she doesn't want a knife in her back so I don't pursue my suggestion, and we decide that perhaps it is best not to linger too long observing the comings and goings. A few yards further along the bridge, we pass a uniformed official, presumably a customs officer, doing nothing in particular. Nelson and blind eye come to mind.

Our visit to Paraguay is over, it being a brief interlude in a rather longer visit to Brazil.

Eight

Uruguay: Finding the real gauchos

Uruguay: A population of less than 4 million, tending to be overshadowed by its large neighbours Argentina and Brazil. For such a small country, has the enviable record as twice winners of the football World Cup. Spanish speaking.

Uruguay is to South America what Belgium is to Europe. Small and fairly inconsequential in relation to its larger and more prominent neighbours. In this case, not France and Germany but Argentina and Brazil. Not on the face of it the most exciting place to go but, like most countries, with a little bit of probing and investigation, it is not without interest or merit. Despite some drug and social problems, it remains by most standards a gentle place, populated by charming and friendly people. A pleasant little country where little of note ever happens. This a premise based on the experience of several short visits to Uruguay.

These previous visits have been notable only for the brief periods we have spent in the country. Twice we have taken the Buquebus, the high-speed ferry from Buenos Aires to Colonia, the well-preserved colonial town on the opposite bank of the River Plate on day trips, and on two further occasions we have stayed a little longer, spending a few days luxuriating in a posh hotel and playing golf a little further west from Colonia along the banks of the River Plate near the town of Carmelo. Incidentally, to those who know their corned beef, Carmelo is the last town on the river before you reach Fray Bentos.

Now we have decided that it is time to get to know this country, squeezed between those giant neighbours Brazil and Argentina, a little better. We fly in from Chile where at Santiago Airport a noisy group of football supporters in yellow and black replica shirts try and push to the front of the queue as we board the aeroplane. They are firmly put in their place by the airline official manning the desk. Once on board, I try to read the local newspaper and despite my limited Spanish realise from the sports pages that these are not football supporters but a football team, Penarol, champions of Uruguay and fresh from a victory the previous night against Chilean opposition in the Copa Libertadores, the equivalent of Europe's Champions League.

At the end of the short flight at Montevideo Airport, we are met by Isabel, a convivial lady to whom we relate that our fellow travellers were a football team. Isabel proves to be something of a football aficionado and gives us a potted history of the club. Penarol is a *barrio*, or district, of Montevideo, deriving its name from the hometown of a nineteenth-century Italian immigrant. The football club it seems has a strong British connection in that it was founded in 1891 by a group of English railway workers, its original name being the Central Uruguay Railway Cricket Club. Since then, the club has won fifty major titles, including five-time winners of the Copa Libertadores. As we drive from the airport towards the city centre in the upmarket suburb of Carrasco, Isabel reinforces her football credentials by pointing out the family home of Diego Forlan, who spent a short and unproductive period at Manchester United but who she tells us is nevertheless far more of a national hero than the free-scoring but highly controversial former Liverpool player Luis Suarez.

Isabel also has some startling news to impart. The city we are visiting is pronounced as two words, *monte* and *video,* not, as most English people say, with the emphasis upon the last syllable. Her explanation for the name is one widely held by locals, although it appears frightfully convoluted on first hearing, namely, that when the Spaniards first arrived, they annotated maps of the area where the city now stands, numbering hills visible from the sea. Thus, the city location is at Mount 6, navigating from the River Plate east to west. ***Monte*** (mount) **vi** (6 or VI) ***de*** (of) **eo** (east and west, in Spanish *este a oeste*). It sounds plausible, and I congratulate Isabel on being able to tell a good story.

Before long, we are entering downtown, travelling along the Rambla or seafront, before turning two blocks north into the Plaza Independencia where our hotel is located. We have three days to explore the city and there is no better place to start than right here, as the square has many buildings of note together with an imposing centrepiece: a statue of Artigas mounted on his horse.

Throughout Latin America, the names of Simon Bolivar and José de San Martin are ubiquitous, with frequent use of their names on streets and squares in almost every town or city and barely a town or city without a statue of one or the other. Uruguay is an exception; here Artigas is the man. José Artigas was born in 1764 and was to have a distinguished military career. With nationalistic tendencies, he variously found himself in opposition to the British, Spanish and Portuguese. Strangely, though, for a national hero his last battle ended in defeat and he spent the last thirty years of his life in exile in Paraguay. In fairness, the Uruguayan fight for independence was complicated. Whereas in most of South America it was a case of removing the Spanish, the colonial power, for Uruguay their road towards independence was more challenging. Once again, those dominant neighbours Argentina and Brazil loom large. Having achieved their own independence from Spain and Portugal, respectively, both had designs on what is now Uruguay. Eventually, in 1830, with British mediation an independent Uruguay was established.

Back in Independence Square, the Artigas statue apart, the most imposing sight is the Palacio Salvo, built in the 1920s in the style of, and intended to be the South American equivalent of, New York's more famous Empire State Building. By all accounts a perpetual white elephant, it now houses local people in fairly modest apartment accommodation. Along the south side of the square the Palacio Estevez, for the best part of a century the home of Government and now the Presidencia, used for formal receptions. Along this side of the square the Torre Ejecutiva, housing the offices of the president. Isabel lives around the corner from here and relates recently passing the president outside her local supermarket chatting to a friend. Not the typical behaviour of a president but this one a populist octogenarian former communist member of the 1970s' revolutionary group the Tupamaros.

On our first evening, we content ourselves with a stroll around the square, but the next morning we cross the square and pass through the arch of Puerta de la Ciudadela, the only remaining part of the walls of the old city built in 1746, and from here we enter Ciudad Vieja.

Sarandi is the main shopping street, now pedestrianised but almost entirely free from the hustle and bustle of the comparable Florida in Buenos Aires. Our leisurely walk takes us along to the Plaza Matriz where in the gardens there are market stalls selling locally produced wares, most typically *mate* sets. The drinking of *mate* here is almost a religion; it is popular in Argentina but even more so here. *Mate* is made from the dried leaves of the plant *yerba mate*. It would be easy to describe *mate* as the South American version of tea, but that would be too simplistic and understate its role in the culture of this country.

A typical *mate* set selling in the market comprises a calabash gourd in which the drink is mixed, the leaves first infused with cold and then hot water. With this comes the *bombilla,* or straw, through which the drink is imbibed. This drinking straw is usually made of silver and has a sieve device preventing the drinker from ingesting the leaves. Typically, and just looking around this busy city street, we can see evidence of this, most people leaving home will take with them their *mate* equipment and a thermos of hot water.

We spend the next three days exploring the city. Not too difficult to take in almost all of the sights as Montevideo is a relatively small and walkable city with few "off limits" areas. We visit museums and admire the many fine buildings. There is even time for some shopping and on the advice of the hotel concierge we find, tucked away in the corner of one of the squares, a leatherwork workshop where after some haggling Rosie treats herself to a new handbag.

The Carnival Museum housed in an old warehouse close to the port has a modest display of carnival costumes but an excellent explanation of the carnival tradition in Uruguay, so very different from that of its neighbour Brazil. Two major differences are that the Rio Carnaval, for example, takes place over five days leading up to the start of Lent, whilst in Uruguay the carnival season is forty days long. Similarly, the essence of carnival in Brazil is the procession; in Uruguay the main focus is on the tableaux, each created on a permanent site in different communities. Each municipality or *barrio* prepares its display to which visitors from other parts of town come on a particular night to view and party.

Strangely, given that unlike its neighbour Brazil very few Uruguayans have African origins, here the carnival tradition is closely and inextricably linked through *candombe*, dance and music of the African slaves.

The Palacio Legislativo or Parliament building is situated in a part of the city we have not yet visited and is atop a hill someway from downtown, so the walk provides us with some useful exercise. An impressive neo-classical structure and quite imposing. The Parliament is in session so today it is not open to visitors. We take the customary photographs of the exterior and are then quite fortunate. We spot a group of German tourists with a local guide on the steps of the Parliament building. They seem to have some pre-arranged booking, allowing them to visit inside the building, so when they move towards the entrance we tag along at the back of the group. Fortunately, the flunky on the door who ushers us inside has not been given a specific number of visitors in the group or hasn't bothered to count, and our presence as interlopers remains undetected. Our cheek is rewarded. The interior is impressive, with marble and granite on a grand scale and guarded by soldiers in a traditional uniform of green and white.

Montevideo is a likeable kind of city. Not too big, not brash in a "look at me" kind of way. But whereas in Buenos Aires even after six or seven visits there are still new things to discover, you can pretty well cover all the things worth seeing here in a few days.

So, after three days it is time to take our leave of Montevideo and in our hire car we head east back along the Rambla through the suburbs and beyond the city, taking the coast road, carefully avoiding the brash resort town of Punta del Este. We are to stay for a few days at José Ignacio, until recent times a sleepy fishing village but now described in our travel guide as, *a chic resort and favourite hang-out for some of the beautiful people.* From the car registration plates, it certainly seems popular with visitors from across the River Plate. This is borne out when we check into our "boutique" hotel, as it is run by an Argentinian family and, us apart, all the other guests are also Argentinian. If "boutique" means minimalist then this property conforms with the definition, but although still quite new, it already seems a little careworn. Our room is dominated by an enormous Jacuzzi yet lacks some of the basics such as a hanging space and drawers.

José Ignacio is a pleasant enough little village, dominated by the old lighthouse, but most of the buildings are modern holiday homes interspersed with a sprinkling of restaurants and a general store. We are not attuned to the Latin American habit of dining late. Most restaurants in Uruguay open at 9 pm. This is when we would normally be contemplating our supper, so we have adapted our habit to comply with the locals by eating a late lunch around four or five o'clock in the afternoon and making this our main meal of the day.

It is a Sunday and we find ourselves in a cosy alfresco eatery that includes a deli and the local bakery. The food is good but overpriced. Every so often, a large car cruises by and very often after a short interval the occupants appear and take a table. One particular couple take our eye. We have seen them drive past in a large open tourer, could have been a Bentley. They arrive a few minutes later. The man calls the head waiter and they are found a table in the corner of the now busy restaurant. The man is late middle-aged, stereotypical Latin suntanned, thick black wavy hair combed back and a lived-in face with craggy features and deep lines. Dressed simply in a T-shirt, chinos and sandals yet every item of attire screaming, *I cost a fortune.* His wife (or dare I hazard mistress) wears a flimsy cover-up over a swimsuit and sports a pair of over-sized sunglasses. Both spend most of their time staring blankly into sophisticated-looking mobiles. Their first course arrives, a "to share" salad served on an enormous platter. She looks at it disdainfully. The waiter is called, the plate removed. It returns minutes later, some magical ingredient no doubt added to make it palatable. Later, two identical-looking plates arrive. Their main dishes. The food looks remarkably like their starter, with lots of green leaves. He picks at his food whilst engaging in a long conversation on his telephone. She meantime disposes of her dish of rabbit food. His conversation ends and without any consultation with the woman, he clicks his fingers. The bill is brought, quickly settled and doubtless with a large tip added. The couple sweep out of the restaurant. Moments later, the Bentley passes, driving slowly in the direction from whence it came.

We have no such luck at managing a grand exit. When our bill arrives, the excellent but highly priced meal comes to an amount way beyond the number of *pesos* in my wallet, so I produce my credit card. For some unfathomable reason, it is rejected, not once, not twice but three times, which of course means that until I contact my bank it is completely useless. The waiter reacts impeccably and says we can return tomorrow to settle the bill, adding, 'After all, you are British,' and adds with a little twinkle, 'of course, it is not a favour I would have extended if you were French.' Charmer.

In stark contrast, the following day, we venture further along the coast to the east. After several kilometres, the dirt road comes to an abrupt end at a river. The far bank is a mere 200 metres away and on the other side, protruding into the water, a partly constructed bridge. Our only way across is to drive onto a primitive ferry and pay two local men a few *pesos* to turn a huge wheel on a pulley system to propel us and our car across to the far side.

We later learn that with ribbon development all the way along this coastline from Punta del Este, the locals at this point on the coastline had by direct action decided enough was enough and opposed officialdom by preventing the bridge construction being completed, there being no doubt that a bridge here would undoubtedly change the remoteness of this coastal area. This is confirmed once we are across the other side and continuing our drive. A few properties but a largely deserted road and completely empty, pristine beaches. The road is rough and dusty so after an hour we decide to cut our losses, and after taking a beach walk, we head inland to pick up the main road back to José Ignacio.

Back in town, we again take a late lunch, this time avoiding the over-priced restaurant of yesterday, and find ourselves in the local pizza bar. Although our Spanish is normally good enough to manage reading a menu and ordering food, this one is full of words to which we are unaccustomed. The mystery is solved when the waitress explains that it is written in what she describes as "Indio-Spanish", a form of local dialect. We order ourselves a pizza followed by a *dulce de leche*-flavoured ice cream. *Dulce de leche* is boiled condensed milk, a process producing an incredibly sweet, gooey mixture that has been a favourite of Rosie's since our first visit to Argentina many years before.

Replete and on this occasion only a few *pesos* lighter, we take a stroll down towards the beach close to the *faro*, the lighthouse, where we come across an excited crowd. A huge bull elephant seal has hauled himself up on the shoreline and is basking in the early-evening sun. Judging by the animated reaction of the locals, a rare sight around these parts. The seal has a remarkably calm disposition, given the excited and noisy horde of people that have gathered around him, unlike many of his brethren we have encountered in more southerly climes like South Georgia, much further south into the Atlantic. He seems to be in good order, save for the extensive scarring around his face.

The following day we are back on the road, driving west for some distance before turning north at a junction in a small town called Pan de Azucar. (Translated meaning: bread of sugar!) Our guidebook describes the town as a living museum, with extensive wall murals depicting local history scenes. Clearly little of historical note has occurred here because despite a slow drive through the town centre, the only mural we see is a modest painted wall at the end terrace of what could pass for a row of English council houses.

By mid-morning, we are looking for a break and stop in the town of Minas. Once a booming gold-mining centre, it is now a little quieter and more sedate. A typical small market town, it is the capital of Lavellaja Province. A statue of Lavellaja himself, an independence hero, sitting astride his horse, dominates the small park, centrepiece to the town plaza. We find a parking space but no obvious place to feed a meter or secure a parking ticket. Next to us, an old man sits in the driving seat of a clapped-out old motor, window open. We ask him if we need to pay and without hesitation he climbs from the car and shepherds us along the pavement and into the *confiteria*. A short conversation ensues between him and the shop assistant and we are led from here along the street to the *farmacia*. Inside the shop a small booth where we pay for two hours' parking and are issued with two chits, one for each hour.

Time for coffee. Our guidebook says that the Confiteria Insano was opened in 1898. The decor suggests little has changed in the ensuing years. We order our coffee, and given Rosie's predilection for *dulce de leche,* we take it accompanied by *alfajores.* They consist of two round biscuits conjoined by a sticky layer of thick *dulce de leche.* Rosie is sufficiently taken to purchase two more packets for the road. These covered in chocolate; one packet of dark, the other in white.

After this sickly sweet elevenses, we take a stroll around the town. The cathedral is unusually not situated in the town square but a block back and to our surprise the door is locked. Little more success at the museum. A sign on the door indicates afternoon-only opening. Peering through the door, we see an interesting exhibition of traditional *gaucho* clothing and equipment. Time however is not on our side. We decide to move on.

Once outside of Montevideo, the driving in Uruguay is easy. Although one of the smallest countries in South America, it is also thinly populated and you can drive long distances without ever passing another vehicle. Wending our way north along the major Ruta 12, we pass through no further towns of any size before we approach the village of Cerro Colorado. Here, a rough hand-painted wooden sign indicates that our destination, the

Estancia San Pedro de Timote, lies a further 14km east along what is clearly an uneven dirt track.

As we approach, we are met with the sight of cows grazing on the front lawn of the beautifully preserved house. The former Jesuit mission, now a hotel and our base for the next three days. We check in, discovering that none of the staff speak any English. At dinner, we meet the four other guests, amazingly also English.

Next morning, the opportunity to explore the extensive grounds of the estate. Our guide is Bebo and our transport is a trailer drawn behind an aged tractor. The cows on the front lawn are explained; this is a working ranch. As we trundle through the fields, we see a mare and her newly born foal, extensive birdlife, including the flightless rhea, and come across real-life cowboys, or *gauchos*, on horseback rounding up cattle.

Later, Bebo takes us on a tour around the *estancia*. He speaks not a word of English, and the local dialect means comprehending his Spanish is difficult, but he takes us to the chapel, the impressive ceramic-tiled library and to the main house where he shows us the room in which he was born. Bebo is a large man with an ambling gait; in truth, he cuts a sad figure. His whole life, and probably that of his parents and grandparents, has been spent around the *estancia,* working in the kitchens and with the horses and other animals. Today, things are different. Bebo, the old retainer, now lives some 10 miles away in the local village, an outsider in his own world.

Today, the Brits depart and three French Canadians arrive but are only staying overnight.

Day three and we are now the only guests at the *estancia*. Since our arrival, there has been intermittent rain and today by lunchtime it has settled into a consistent heavy downpour. We take afternoon tea and, much to his delight, tell the chef we will miss dinner, effectively giving him the evening off. The rain continues unabated through the evening and during the night. When we awake, the courtyard is awash and drains overflowing. After taking breakfast, we intend to depart, but at breakfast the staff tell us that it is now impossible to leave due to the flooded roads around the area.

By mid-morning, the rain has finally ceased, to be replaced by a wan and hazy sun. Our intended route is to take the unmade road on which we arrived, not returning in the direction from which we came but instead continuing past the *estancia* for some 20 kilometres. There it meets a major road to the south, towards our next destination. By lunchtime, a member of the staff arrives from the direction of Cerro Colorado, and we are advised that it is safe to leave if driving with care, but not along our intended route that passes through several fords which will be flooded. Instead, we must return along the road on which we arrived three days previously. In truth, taken carefully, the journey back to a tarmacadam surface is not too difficult, and soon we are making speedy progress, albeit on a slightly circuitous route, to our next destination, Colonia del Sacramento.

Founded in 1680 and fought over by the Spanish, Portuguese and even the British, Colonia sits on the banks of the River Plate about 100 miles west of Montevideo and an hour by fast ferry across the river from Buenos Aires. The Barrio Historico, the old town, is a designated UNESCO World Heritage site and for good reason. A well-preserved area of narrow cobblestone streets with an amazing history, here at the very boundary between the sphere of influence of two colonial powers, Spain and Portugal. From the founding of the city until Uruguay achieved independence in 1828, control of the city changed no less than nine times.

Having visited Colonia several times, after checking into our hotel, we feel comfortable about taking an evening stroll downtown in the old city and finding ourselves dinner at a local eatery. A film crew have taken over a large part of the old quarter, so we find ourselves a quiet restaurant a short distance away from the centre. Whilst Rosie contents herself with an omelette, I order *dorada*, a large bream, which eventually arrives complete with head, grilled and served upon a huge platter.

When we return to the old town the next day, we find that the filming continues. I see a beautiful actress being interviewed by a television crew under a large *jacaranda* in the square. I wonder if I should recognise her. Dozens of film extras are standing around dressed in a fashion that I guess reflects action taking place perhaps in the very early years of the twentieth century. Then the filming starts. Some revolutionary activity, an angry mob confronted by armed soldiers. Shots ring out and the mob disperses in disarray. I ask some of the crew what is going on and they point to a young woman who they say is the assistant director. Although I quiz her on the film title, she is tight-lipped, saying only, 'It is a secret.' Later, I discover they are filming a rather elaborate advertising feature for Bacardi. The scenario features a true-life son of the founder of the famous distillery, Emilio, and the setting is not here in Uruguay but Cuba 1896, a country perhaps not available for this film for obvious reasons. The Bacardi company was founded in Cuba but was forced to relocate after the Castro-led revolution, and is currently headquartered in Bermuda.

Nine

Brazil: Up the Amazon
without a paddle

French Guiana: Set on the north-east coast of South America and technically a Department of France, it remains the only country in the Americas still a colony. A population of just 300,000. Of significance: it is the home of Kourou, the European Space Station.

Prelude. Before our ship enters the mouth of the mighty Amazon, an interesting side trip to Devil's Island, somewhere Rosie has wanted to visit since she saw the epic 1970s film *Papillon* starring Steve McQueen and Dustin Hoffman. The film based on the book of the same title written by Henri Charrière and published in 1969 in which he wrote of his escape from the island together with another inmate, Sylvain, who died close to the mainland shore after they had drifted at sea for three days, clinging to sacks of coconuts.

No sooner have we landed ashore than disappointment abounds. Here we are greeted by a local guide who reveals that we are on the Iles du Salut, an archipelago comprising three islands, and we are on the one called Ile Royal. From here on the shoreline, we can see a second island, Ile Saint Joseph. Ile du Diable, or Devil's Island, we will see later in our tour, but it is not accessible to visitors. What is more, she breaks the news to Rosie that the real-life Papillon was never incarcerated on Devil's Island. He was only ever held in a penal colony on the mainland some miles distant.

This, Ile Royale, the largest island, is where most prisoners were held. Ile Saint Joseph was where prisoners were held in solitary confinement. Devil's Island was for political prisoners; perhaps the most famous, in its century-long history beginning in 1852, being Captain Alfred Dreyfuss.

Not to be deterred, we embark on an island tour. Our guide today is Ronaldo, a young man with a thick accent combining both French and Caribbean. An odd combination of *'Allo 'Allo* and a Rasta. We ask Ronaldo if he lives on the island but he says no; he comes from the mainland by speedboat on days like this when a cruise ship is visiting.

From the seashore, we climb a steep unmade road before we reach the settlement: an assortment of buildings, a church, police post, school and the old hospital. Beyond the central square a large and imposing prison block known as the Crimson Barracks, the scene of frequent prisoner-on-prisoner murders. The regime was brutal. Barely half the prisoners brought here survived the first year of their sentence, if not dying by the hands of the pitiless regime of the guards, or at the hands of their fellow prisoners, then from malaria. Other buildings we come across evidence that many prisoners could roam the island with a degree of freedom and self-sufficiency, cooking their own food and doing their laundry on the clear supposition that any attempt to escape to the mainland seven miles distant would be futile.

At the far end of the island, we are shown around the cemetery. Most of the graves are those of children of the prison staff. Bodies of the inmates dying here on the islands were simply thrown into the sea.

There is a perimeter path around the island which we take, and leaving the cemetery, we soon get our first view of Devil's Island.

The Dreyfuss Affair still leaves a stain on French history. In 1895, Captain Alfred Dreyfuss, a serving French Army officer, was accused of treason, spying for Germany, found guilty and sent to Devil's Island. Later, despite clear evidence emerging that another officer was the real traitor, he remained incarcerated on the island. He continued to protest his innocence and after a retrial and a lengthy legal battle, he was eventually pardoned in 1899. The conviction was not rescinded, despite it being clear that his fellow officer was indeed the guilty culprit, but Dreyfuss reluctantly accepted the pardon as a way of getting off Devil's Island. Eventually, in 1906, he received official exoneration by the military and was formally restored as an army officer, later being awarded the Légion d'Honneur. He was to be back in the Army for only a year before he was discharged on medical grounds, the whole lengthy process getting justice having taken a toll on his health. He did later enrol in the Army again in World War I in a non-combat role, being promoted to the rank of lieutenant colonel.

The Dreyfuss Affair is still writ large in French history. It is said that the French Establishment was never able to accept that they had put an innocent man through hell. Furthermore, many believe that Dreyfuss being Jewish contributed to how long it took him to gain some degree of justice and in the end the less than entirely satisfactory outcome.

As we get closer, we can see that the distance between the two islands is maybe just 100 metres, but the waters are fast-flowing and subject to extremely dangerous currents. Ronaldo, our guide, has already told us that the mainland is still another 7 miles distant and contains dense jungle. No wonder that in a hundred years, there were only two successful escapees from the islands.

Back in the centre of the island we visit the small museum and later take a coffee in the hotel, once the mess for the prison officers, the day definitely a worthwhile interlude before reaching the mighty Amazon.

Two days later, we arrive in Belem, our initial taste of the Amazon, a large city at the mouth of the river. First stop is the Vero-o-Peso, "see the weight" – the market. It is a huge edifice selling an enormous range of exotic and often gruesome-looking fish, tropical fruits, herbs and catching the eye, an impressive array of locally made raffia basketry. We wander through the market, exiting by a door at the furthest end that brings us back into the bright sunlight and alongside the harbour. First impressions are of rotting fish smells and the squalor. The tide is out and large cruel-looking birds are scavenging on the mud flats and on the dockside, looking for discarded remnants of fish filleted by the fishermen. They, whose early-morning catch has already been dispatched to the market, are to be seen now busy repairing nets ready for the following morning's fishing.

Moving hurriedly along out of range of the putrid smells, the road ahead past the fort looks equally unattractive; decaying buildings and garbage abound, but it is the only way up the hill into the Praca Francisco Caetano Brandao to view the cathedral. It is Sunday morning and when we look in through the open doors, the cathedral is packed for morning Mass. The priest leading the service from an ornate pulpit looks suitably imposing in his gold and purple robes. The astonishing thing is that the congregation surely cannot hear him above the hubbub of noise emanating from the pews. This looks and sounds like a weekly social gathering rather than a time for quiet reflection.

With the service in progress, we are unable to view the interior of the cathedral, so we move on, strolling past the beautiful colonial buildings of the old town. Many of these buildings are sadly neglected, although beneath the grime and decrepitude, most are adorned with *azulejos,* the colourful ceramic tiles popular in Portuguese architecture. From the main square we take the Rua Siqueria Mendes, at the end of which the avenue opens onto another much smaller square where we come across dozens of roller skaters, most dressed in distinctive blue and white shirts. This the Belem version of the local cycling or ramblers' club that might gather in our own town centres or parks on a Sunday morning.

Further along in the spacious Praca Dom Pedro the Second is the Casa das Onze Janelas, or "House of Eleven Windows". Built as his residence during the rubber boom by a successful local businessman, it is now part of the State Museum, but being still early on a Sunday morning, our hopes of visiting are thwarted, the doors remaining firmly closed. Instead, we decide to seek out the city centre and head down Avenue Portugal, turning into Rua Jono Dejo past a strangely deserted fire station totally devoid of any appliances. The heart of the city is the Praca da Republica, and when we emerge from the side street into the square, we are not disappointed. The streets have been near deserted during our walk but here it is buzzing. The outer perimeter of the square is filled with market stalls and in the gardens beyond, families promenade in their Sunday best clothes. On one side of the square, the prominent building is the Teatro Paz and in front, everywhere we look are firemen and their firefighting equipment. At first, we think it is a strike, but soon it is apparent this is some major PR exercise, with kids climbing over the fire engines and with the help of the firemen, trying on the masks of breathing apparatus.

In the tiring heat, we buy an ice cream and then take ourselves down the Avenue Presidente Vargas into the air-conditioned relief of the Estacao das Docas, a converted warehouse complex on the waterfront, now home to restaurants, fast-food outlets and upmarket shops.

Given this stopover in Belem is just for a day, it seems sensible to make best use of our limited time in port to see as much of the area as possible. To this end, from the quayside we take a boat on a trip up into the river delta. Navigating narrow waterways between the expanse of jungle, we get an opportunity to take a walk. Our guide, Oswaldo, tells us that one third of the world's flora and fauna are to be found here, and it is easy to believe as we take a path, albeit well trodden, through the forest. Oswaldo stoops to pick up an ant and tells us that this is one of no less than 22,000 species of ant to be found here in Amazonas. Further along the path, Oswaldo picks fruit from a tree. Acai, a so-called superfood increasingly popular as an ingredient in health foods, here in its natural berry form. There are lemons and mango, neither indigenous, and Brazil nuts that definitely are a true native species. Back on the boat we continue our journey, threading our way through narrow channels, between small islets and amongst mangrove swamps, reaching another landing stage. Oswaldo once again leads us along a path through the jungle until we come to a clearing. Here, he collects leaves from various plants used by the natives living in the forest to treat many ailments. As he gives his lecture on the medicinal benefits of each of the leaves, a young native girl emerges from the jungle, diffident but determined. Encouraged by Oswaldo, she opens her palm to reveal a tarantula. Oswaldo, not to be outdone, disappears briefly into the trees and emerges momentarily to reveal in his palm what he claims is the world's largest ant.

Back on board our ship by early evening, the wind speed is increasing and by the time we sail at midnight, we are cruising the river in a near gale.

The abiding memory of this Amazon trip will be that for most of the time travelling up to Manaus, a city 1,000 kilometres from the Atlantic Ocean, you could still be in the middle of the ocean. The river is so wide it remains difficult if not impossible to see both banks of the river at any one time. At the mouth of the river lie two major cities, on the south bank Belem, to the north Macapa, several hundred miles between them, including Ilha de Marajo, one of the largest islands in the world.

Ours being a small ship, it is therefore with some pleasure that we spend most of the next day cruising through the Breves Narrows, which offers just a glimpse of life along the river.

The Narrows, as the name implies, is a cut some 60 miles long but only around a quarter of a mile wide running north to south and leading us, as we head in a northerly direction, into the main stream of the Amazon River.

The river banks are surprisingly densely populated, given the remoteness of the region, a sort of strange ribbon development. We pass only two small towns of note and, although poor, most households appear to have satellite television, and on the river itself a profusion of small boats with outboard motors. There is some evidence of logging but this apart, no indications of agriculture, the forest reaching down to the riverside in most places.

Further testimony to the sheer scale of the river and the long distances, it is another day before we reach Santarem, our next port of call. There is little positive to say about this place. Boom times have come and gone. In the past, rubber, forestry and minerals have brought prosperity but now a reliance on soybeans, thanks to the American conglomerate Cargill. The environmental cost of farming and harvesting this crop is evident, with huge forest clearances.

Santarem's long history – it was founded in 1661 by the Portuguese – is barely reflected in the modern city with its grid system of roads, small business units and heavily protected domestic properties.

The biggest attraction lies not in the town but actually out on the river, the "Meeting of the waters" where the Tapajos and Amazon Rivers conjoin. The waters of the Tapajos are blue, and where it joins the brown of the Amazon, the two are quite distinguishable for several miles downstream before eventually merging.

We take a trip out of town to visit the Santa Lucia Arboretum. Privately owned and protected from forest clearance, it is nevertheless completely surrounded by land allocated to outsiders who have come from other parts of Brazil to farm soybeans. Our guide, Raimondo, is informative, so the gentle stroll amongst the trees learning about cacao and Brazilian hardwoods is an interesting diversion for an afternoon.

Back in town with time in hand before our ship sails, we stroll along the busy waterfront. Evidence here of a constant movement of people and goods between Santarem and other major riverside cities like Macapa, Belem and Manaus. Most of this activity takes place thanks to the double-decker boats found throughout the Amazon. A long line of these boats is tied up along the quay. We see one that is deserted so climb aboard to envisage what a journey on the river on one of these boats rather than our luxury cruise ship might be like. Hot and steamy seems to be the answer. In more ways than one, as we have been told that separate men and women quarters apparently become indefinable after two days on the river, whilst the lack of air conditioning means, evidenced by the hammocks strung willy-nilly around the decks, that most passengers find the best chance of sleep comes by hunkering down on deck under the stars.

In a world where even the most remote and backward communities are able to welcome visitors and embrace the wonders of modern technology, we bring them some of the worst elements of our own culture. Top of my personal list of dislikes arising from this opening-up of tourism to remote communities is "dollar tourism", where small kids often as young as four or five accost strangers with a 'Mister, give me a dollar.' One such example is Boca da Valeria. A small and, until the arrival of cruise ships, remote Amazon village set on the banks of the river, as its name suggests at the mouth of a tributary called Valeria. There is a sad mutuality in the arrangement. Easy money for an impoverished community that just has the good fortune to find itself on a tourist route and good business for tour companies wanting to offer their clients an insight into native culture and way of life.

I fear the worst as our ship's tender approaches the rudimentary quay. The welcoming committee is comprised almost entirely of children; some wear native dress with lots of feathers but most, shabby T-shirts and shorts. Whilst groups of small children accost our fellow travellers as they come ashore, we slip past and head towards the village. Along the rough path, we encounter various "dollar photo opportunities", a man with an anaconda draped around his neck, a boy with a caiman, numerous kids with lizards and most popular of all, sloths. Some of the kids don't even pretend and simply ask for a dollar. In the village itself, the locals sit around in indolent groups, showing a distinct lack of interest in the hordes of visitors, save for a few who attempt to sell homemade wooden carvings and beads in necklace form.

The village itself is relatively poor with stilt houses, a small church and a school. Interestingly, though, most of the dwellings boast a satellite dish, and there are motorised canoes both at the dockside and again in the small stream that runs through the centre of the village. The people are a surprising mixture, given the remoteness of the village; pure native, mestizo and some very black African faces, testimony to Brazil's incredibly diverse ethnicity.

Adjacent to the village, an area where a manioc crop is growing and beyond some cattle grazing in the scrubby grass.

Returning to our ship, it is with an uncomfortable feeling of intrusion and exploitation.

Our next stop is Manaus. A city of more than two million people set in the Amazon rainforest without any direct road access to the rest of Brazil. A starting point for the more adventurous tourist wishing to go further upriver into the jungle and set on the confluence of the Solimoes (Amazon) and the Rio Negro.

On our first morning, we take a tour with a local guide, Marco. He is an indigenous native and tells us he has taken a Christian name out of convenience. His real name would be unpronounceable to our ear and in his native language means, "huntsman" (a deadly snake found in these parts) and "bark of the tree". Marco took his new name from an Italian missionary who came to his village and who encouraged him to leave his home and come to Manaus to receive an education. He considers himself very fortunate, hailing from a remote village where he was one of five brothers and fifteen sisters, to have had that opportunity to get a proper education.

Our first excursion with Marco is to leave the city and take a boat across the river to a small island called Terra Nova. En route, we again encounter the phenomenon of the "meeting of the waters". The effect, although strange, is simply explained as the heavily silted and, in this place, milky-coloured waters of the colder Solimoes meet the faster-flowing dark and warmer waters of the Negro.

On Terra Nova, the villagers are friendly and have set up demonstrations of rubber making and manioc preparation. We try to converse with a little girl of about ten who tells us her name is Analena. She has an exotic tropical bird perched on her shoulder, a pet taken from its mother at birth. Although it is common here to have such pets, birds like this apparently do fly back to nature once they reach adulthood.

The following day, we have an organised tour of the city with another guide named Paul. Unlike Marco the previous day, he is pure Afro-Brazilian. Despite Brazil's broad ethnicity, he is one of the few people of African descent that we come across in Manaus. Paul has a charming manner and speaks cut-glass English with no semblance of an accent.

First stop is the market. The original built by the British in 1906 is under renovation, and the stallholders have been dispersed around the streets adjoining the market and in nearby old disused warehouses. The market despite its temporary form is large and impressive. Most notably the array of fish. The Amazon, given its size, spawns fittingly large fish: *tambaqui*, cod, bass, catfish, *mahi mahi* and many more. Stallholders are friendly and disposed towards photo opportunities; uninvited, one holds aloft a particularly fearsome-looking catfish. Eating seafood is clearly more popular here than eating meat, even though many crustaceans, like prawns and shrimps, evident in huge quantities, are imported from other parts of the country.

Fruit and vegetables are even more abundant, and stalls have been crammed into a particularly cavernous old warehouse. Here, there are to be found endless rows of stalls set together between narrow alleys where it is difficult to pass people coming in the opposite direction. Some stalls confine themselves to a single product – sacks of manioc, oddly shaped gourds or watermelons – whilst others present a range of fruit and vegetables beautifully laid out in neat rows and piles. Other stands sell spices and herbs, assorted chillies, hot and sweet and in every shape and size imaginable. There are familiar sights – potatoes, onions and tomatoes – plus more exotic fruits. Mangoes in many different varieties typically sell for the equivalent of 2p each. We emerge from this building to an even more staggering sight: a huge area devoted to the selling of bananas. If not in every conceivable shape, then certainly an almost infinite variety, of different sizes and shades of yellow.

The highlight of the city is of course its famed Opera House. Built between 1885 and 1896 at the height of the rubber boom, it saw its first performance on January 7 1897: the Italian opera *La Giaconda*. Constructed and fitted with the finest materials then available from all parts of Europe, it is indeed a splendid edifice and well worth a visit. Our timing is impeccable; we are allowed to slip into a box seat, suitably crafted from locally sourced *jacaranda*, to watch the conclusion of a rehearsal for the evening's performance. The theatre boasts many features from the beautiful parquet floors in light and dark brown woods made exclusively from Amazon rainforest trees and depicting the "meeting of the waters" to the incredible cupola of 35,000 ceramic tiles in the yellow, green and blue colours of the Brazilian flag. We are allowed onto the balcony to view the plaza below, and it is easy to imagine ourselves shoulder to shoulder with the bejewelled glitterati enjoying an interval champagne during that first performance, featuring none other than the famed Italian tenor Enrico Caruso.

Later in the day, we set out by ourselves to explore more of the city, ostensibly to find a post office. In most cities, this rarely proves difficult, but Manaus is to prove an exception. We find ourselves in the main square, centrepiece of which is the cathedral, the simple neo-classical style Igreja Matriz, more formally the Cathedral of Our Lady of Immaculate Conception. Everywhere in the grounds, around the plaza, up side streets, are crowds of people, small shops and stalls. We stop passersby to enquire as to the whereabouts of the post office but fail to communicate until a smartly dressed middle-aged man approaches us to ask if he can help. He is quickly able to respond to our problem with precise instructions that take us up a road adjoining the square. We reach the place he has described but cannot see a post office until it dawns upon us that we are standing outside the front door; only problem is the door is firmly locked and from the accumulated dust and grime on the windows, it is apparent that this once was, but has long since ceased to be, the post office. Thinking younger people may speak English, we approach two girls working in a small fashion shop. Limited success, they don't speak English but they manage to communicate that we should try at the bookshop a few doors along. Here, success, an English-speaking shop assistant, who points us in the right direction, and at last postage stamps are purchased and postcards sent. With football World Cup matches to be held in the city the following year, we wish our fellow Brits better luck in communicating with the locals.

Our ship is short of fresh water and to replenish supplies, it needs to remain in Manaus Port for two more days instead of travelling further upstream as indicated in our itinerary. An alternative trip is hastily arranged for us, involving travelling some 100 kilometres or so further west along the Rio Negro by high-speed boat. It proves to be an exhilarating experience. After an hour or so, we leave the main river and enter a tributary called the Acajatuba. Eventually, we dock at a small village where we are greeted by a family group dressed in tribal finery and performing native dances. This is quite an affluent village. There are a few traditionally built houses of mud but mostly modern brick constructions together with a tidy little Catholic church at its centre. A small craft shop has been opened for tourists like ourselves, but it feels as though this village has embraced a degree of tourism whilst not compromising day-to-day village life. A way of life which is very much about living on and from the river.

Although racing up the river at great speed has been fun, we are now in a designated bio-diversity reserve, so it would be good to see what this means in reality. In this respect, our next stop is a disappointment. We are to see the feeding of pink river dolphins. For the dolphins, the price of being fed is a heavy one: captivity. They are confined in large tanks set on the riverbed. There is the chance to swim with these beautiful and very pink creatures, but even in this remote location, this is a little too exploitative for my taste. A shame as this family business developed by chance when the two young daughters of the property owner started feeding the dolphins from the jetty at the bottom of their garden.

Back on our boat, it has to slow down to enter a narrow *igarape*, or canoe passage, where soon we see wildlife. Torpid caiman snoozing on the banks of the creek and birds aplenty; herons, skimmers, cormorants enjoying the rich fish-filled waters.

We have reached as far upriver as we are going to go and from here we turn to head back to Manaus at some speed. Back on board our ship, news that now with adequate supplies of water she is ready to head back downriver.

Next stop is Parintins. Another jungle town where the focus of activity, like all the river towns we have visited, is along its waterfront. Although it is Sunday morning, there is much frenetic activity with ferries arriving and leaving. A handscrawled notice in the terminal building lists ten departures today to Manaus, Santarem and a host of other destinations with Catholic-sounding place, names none of which I have ever heard but most prefixed with a "Saint".

The dock is another floating one typical here and a necessity, given the wide differences in the river level between seasons. Today, the river level is low and it is a steep climb up from our ship to the dockside. A clear pattern is emerging with these jungle towns: an attempt to present an impressive frontage to the arriving but one block back, a mass of garbage and broken pavements. Tiny Chinese-manufactured motorbikes buzz around the streets, usually ridden by young kids barely old enough to ride a bicycle. Sometimes an exception. Here an indigenous woman with a heavily lined face, two young children on the pillion, is anxious to give us a cheery wave.

From the dock, we can see the spire of the town church and head in that direction, but when we reach it we find that it has seemingly been abandoned, with doors padlocked and with political graffiti covering the walls. We have strayed a few blocks back from the waterfront and obviously stand out, but the locals are friendly and want to exchange greetings. A group of kids are waiting outside a large iron gate and they call across. Rosie as usual tries to engage them in conversation. They are aged around eleven or twelve. The boldest comes forward and says his name is Tony and tells us he and his friends are waiting to go swimming, and as if to prove it, he proudly shows us his pair of goggles.

We decide to try and locate the cathedral and along the way come across a stadium. It hosts not football but, seating 40,000, it is the home of Boi Bumba, an annual folklore festival second in Brazil only to the famed Rio Carnaval. Amazing that a stadium should be constructed for the sole purpose of hosting a single annual event, albeit an important one celebrating as it does the distinctive music and dances of Amazonas. The whole occasion is unique, embracing, we are told; not only incredible sights and sounds but a fiercely fought competition between the Reds and Blues. Sadly, we are here in February; Boi Bumba takes place in June.

Next day and our final stop along the Amazon. A sandy spit exposed in the dry season has turned Alter da Chao into something of a minor tourist mecca. Fine sandy beaches, a lagoon and now a small town with hotels and touristy shops. We set out along the waterfront but first impressions soon dissipate, thanks to the customary poor workmanship, crumbling pavements and gathering mounds of garbage.

We come across a group of Japanese tourists outside a Japanese hotel. Europeans too. Intent on taking a photograph without looking where he is going, a Frenchman bumps into me and expels an apologetic 'Pardon.'

A small hill overlooking the town offers a *mirador* with good viewing, but to make the climb requires paddling ankle-deep across the small stream linking the Lago Verde to the Amazon. It looks a good hike and given the tropical heat, we decide to take the easy option and double back into the town.

Apart from a few parrots spotted in Belem and sightings along the river during our trip to Anivalhanis, we have seen surprisingly few birds on this trip. Here, many more; an attractive little bird with a red head, parrots galore and in the street, rummaging through the garbage, vultures, fearsome-looking and intimidating.

Heading back to our ship in the centre of this small town, a *pousada*, cafés, restaurants and a couple of grocery stores. We come across a large emporium, roughly constructed with walls of woven tree branches. Inside, artisan handicrafts for sale, some of the best quality workmanship we have seen in Brazil. Lays (she pronounces it lay-is but spells it out for us) speaks a little English. She is a big-boned girl with native features. She explains that the handicrafts come from many different tribes, some living deep in the jungle. One tribe make wicker work, whilst another the elaborately painted discs that are worn in the earlobes or lower lip. There is a huge range of decorated masks, spears, boat paddles and arrows with feathered quivers from exotic birds. Also, attractive basketry, ceramics and what prove to be fertility symbols, the purpose of which is obvious once this has been explained.

This is a fascinating end to our sojourn up the greatest river on the planet. As we return to our ship, it is perhaps inevitable that we are accosted by street vendors. These selling whistles, flutes and blowpipes, the like of which we have seen pretty well everywhere in the Amazon region. Although it is time to say goodbye to this, the world's greatest waterway, the river continues to gently remind us of its sheer scale; it will be another one and a half days of hard sailing before we sight the city of Macapa off our portside and beyond the Atlantic Ocean.

Ten

The Guyanas: In the Land of Rivers

Guyana: Multi-ethnic country with a population of less than 1 million. Variously controlled by the Dutch, French and British. The British ruled from 1813 until independence in 1966. Language – English.

Suriname: With a population of half a million. Dutch ruled from 1667 until 1975 when, on being granted independence, some one-third of the people opted to leave for the Netherlands. A record of political instability since independence. Language – Dutch.

It wasn't meant to happen like this. Meandering reflections on travels in Latin America then after that brief visit to Devil's Island, I realised that we had visited all but two of the countries of South America. What was left were the only non-Latin countries: Guyana and Suriname. Needless to say, here we are in Georgetown, capital of Guyana, the "land of rivers".

Little do we realise when Dennis, our latest guide, meets us at the tiny city centre Ogle Airport that on this brief visit to Guyana, we will have guides queueing to be our escorts. The reason soon becomes clear, as on the short journey to our hotel he has time to tell us that Guyana has only 10,000 tourists a year, placing it firmly in the category of countries rarely visited. This by any standard is a pitifully small number, a shame, as we are to discover Guyana has much to offer the discerning visitor, not least the world's highest single drop waterfall. But first Georgetown.

We begin with a minor crisis. We have to obtain a visa for our subsequent visit to Suriname, but with the Suriname Embassy about to close for the weekend, time is short and I do not have the requisite photographs. This is singularly annoying, as we usually travel with spare photos for this type of contingency but were assured by our travel company in the UK that they were not necessary. Dennis is unfazed and although the first photo shop we call at is closed, we are successful at the second. The photographs secured, we hurry along to the nearby Suriname Embassy where with minutes to spare Dennis does the necessary and emerges triumphantly waving our passports in the air.

Guyana has been held back by the political fault lines on racial differences created by its history. A large country, the same size as the whole of the UK, but thinly populated due to its climate and harsh terrain. Its indigenous population is small, so when settlers came from Europe, the Portuguese, Dutch, French and British to establish a colonial presence and later sugar plantations, they naturally looked towards Africa for labour and so began a particularly harsh and brutal form of slavery, probably worse than in other parts of the Americas.

In a country so devoid of tourism, our itinerary looks suitably unpromising, and it is with some degree of scepticism that the following morning we are met in the hotel lobby by Zaman to be told that we will travel south that morning, ostensibly to visit one of the few remaining operating sugar plantations. Hardly the most exciting prospect for the visitor. Dennis, our guide from yesterday, has been demoted to the role of driver for the day.

Leaving Georgetown behind, the road leads towards the border with Suriname and is unremarkable insofar as it is straight, metalled and passes through few towns of any note. The most interesting feature is that at irregular intervals, a place name at the roadside. Sometimes every few hundred yards, at other times maybe two miles between the signs. These markers signify the boundaries between plantations back in the day. When lands were allocated in the eighteenth century for the purpose of cultivating the land, primarily to grow sugar cane, the plots were divided into rectangular blocks stretching from the coast for maybe two miles into the then virgin forest. Would-be plantation owners variously purchased one or more adjoining blocks.

As a result, plantation sizes varied, hence the different widths between the signs. In the ensuing years, many of these estates struggled to become economically viable, leading to a further consolidation. In their heyday, there were some 2,000 plantations along the coastal strip. Owners ranged from those choosing to start a new life in the Colonies to rich absentee landlords who appointed overseers to run the plantations on their behalf and who rarely, if ever, were to visit. An example was Sir John Gladstone, the father of the future Liberal Prime Minister William Ewart Gladstone.

Although very few of the plantations survive today, as we drive the fifty miles or so down to New Amsterdam, everywhere, evidence of the past. Not just the plantation names but also the canal network constructed by the Dutch. This is Guyana's history along the roadside. Whereas elsewhere in the West Indies it was customary to name a plantation after the owner, no such protocol here.

The colonial powers were in turn the Dutch, French and British. Along the road are names reflecting each nationality. The British names dominate, the most recent colonists. I manage to scribble some of these down as we drive along. Names that reflect where the plantation owner came from: a Dundee, a Litchfield and an Enfield, but also Amsterdam, Haarlem and Rotterdam. Some have a grander appendage, like Yorkshire Hall. Another favourite nomenclature, the Christian names of wife or child; an Ann, a Katherine, a Sophia. More intriguing, Rebecca's Lust and close by, Bachelor's Conquest.

Other names were clearly based on hopes and expectations but these were harsh conditions, and despite slave labour, many financial problems beset the typical plantation owner. An author in 1911 in an article on *Our plantation names* wrote:

...no doubt they thought a good name might bring good fortune; possibly they invoked the goddess in such names as Lucky Hit, Lucky Spot and Good Fortune. Unfortunately, however, their hopes were often disappointed and the estates went to rack and ruin, today most of them are taken over by the forest. Successes proved failures, Good Hopes ended in despair, Freedom meant slavery a century ago; Paradise and Garden of Eden were hardly abodes of happiness; even Arcadia has lost its ideal position as a coffee plantation. Eldorado did not bring the owner gold.

We spot Paradise and Good Hope and in the same vein, Prospect, Perseverance and almost forlornly, Now or Never.

As long ago as 1860, a survey revealed only seven hundred or so of the original two thousand plus estates remained, and many of those had been abandoned, others identified as "negro villages". With emancipation from slavery, many former slaves established their own communities, often on abandoned plantations where they turned to subsistence farming. The lack of sufficient labourers and the perceived poor work ethic of those from Africa led to a new input of labour in the second half of the nineteenth century, this time from the Indian subcontinent. This labour was cheap but not slave labour, distinguished from the latter by the use of an indenture system that guaranteed a contract of service, usually for five years, and the promise of repatriation to the home country, if requested, at the end of the contract. Most chose to stay, and today, the largest ethnic group in Guyana is those of Indian descent.

The demographics arising from the end of slavery are felt today. In 1830, there were 100,000 slaves with African origins, by 1848, after the abolition of slavery, only 20,000 of African descent still worked on plantations. By contrast, between 1838 and 1917, when the indenture system ended, some 240,000 workers had come to Guyana from India and other parts of Asia. Today, only 30% of the population is of African descent and a further 17% mixed race, whilst 43% are Indian and 10% indigenous Amerindian. Black and brown have not integrated, leaving deep divides in the socio-political structure of society here.

Reading the road signs occupies the time, but soon we reach the entrance to Blairmont, one of the oldest of the few remaining operational plantations in Guyana.

Once owned by James Blair MP, he in the early part of the nineteenth century was one to oppose abolition. He twice bought "rotten boroughs" to enter Parliament to defend the interests of plantation owners in the Indies. However, he could not stop the eventual passing in 1833 of the Slavery Abolition Act. It did not serve him badly, as being compelled to free his 1,598 slaves at Blairmont led to him receiving a compensation payment worth some £7M in today's money. Blairmont remained in the Blair family for several more generations and was more recently to be owned by the famous British sugar company Tate and Lyle before being nationalised by the Guyana Government in 1975.

Today, as we make our way up the driveway, many of the buildings still standing are those that were occupied by managers and overseers back in the days of slavery.

We pull up outside one such building, now the site office, and Zaman goes in search of a latter-day manager. Presently, we are piled into an ancient mini-bus for the short journey across the yard to the nearby factory. Samjaram, the Shift Manager, has been given the dubious task of escorting us around, and it is obvious that visitors such as ourselves are not part of normal life here.

Our first challenge is to clamber up a rickety metal stair to view the initial part of the process of turning sugar cane into sugar. From this high but precarious viewpoint, we can see below a canal system with small barges containing raw cane cut in the nearby fields being unloaded onto a conveyor belt and from there by hand into a huge hopper. The workers give us a cheery wave as we take photographs. They must rarely have had such attention. What is for sure, the work is hard and is exactly as it has been for the last 200 years. The cane is being crushed and from here we move down into the factory itself for a closer view.

The factory is unbelievably Dickensian, with steam emerging from cracks in the floor and ancient and noisy machinery adding to a somewhat chaotic atmosphere. We clamber up narrow metal stairs and stand on broken platforms. As we go along, I note the machine manufacturers:

Fletcher and Stewart of Glasgow and Derby. These were two competitors, sugar processing machine manufacturers both founded in the first half of the nineteenth century and eventually merging in 1964.

Clarke Chapman-John Thompson Limited of Wolverhampton. Another company with a history that can be traced back over 150 years, boilermakers.

Herbert Morris Limited of Loughborough. Cranemakers, founded 1857.

A microcosm of British industrial history here on one site in faraway Guyana.

Molasses are separated from cane, a liquid formed and subject to centrifugal force. The end product is a light brown crystallised sugar that Samjaram takes off a conveyor belt in his palm and offers to us to sample. Samjaram is rightly proud of his product, branded "Demerara Gold". Although most of the process we have seen, I'll admit, is still something of a mystery. What I do understand is that demerara, unlike brown sugar, is a natural product. It is only with further processing using the additional application of centrifugal force that it can become a refined white sugar. Demerara in contrast retains some molasses and its golden colour and caramel taste. Ordinary brown sugar is white sugar with some molasses added back for taste and colour. A well-known British sugar wholesaler describes the product on its website as "natural unrefined sugar cane", although, having seen the process that leads to the end product, this is of course not strictly true.

After leaving the factory, our subsequent visit to the nearby and supposedly historical town of New Amsterdam is frankly an anti-climax, given that the plantation visit has been so fascinating.

Day three finds us back in Georgetown. Zaman is joined by Kenneth, a bright young man with an infectious enthusiasm. The old colonial centre still retains many buildings of infinite charm. The Bishop's House on Main Street being a fine example; and opposite, the so-called Red House, once residence of the former firebrand Prime Minister Cheddi Jagan and now a small research centre; next door, the Walter Roth Museum. He, a British anthropologist, has donated an interesting collection of artefacts from Guyana's nine Amerindian tribes, and the museum is well worth the visit.

The city centre is only a block away. Here, St George's Anglican Cathedral, a construction reputed to be the world's highest unsupported wooden building. The present building, consecrated in 1894, is full of interest, including a chandelier presented by Queen Victoria. At the time of our visit, much-needed efforts are underway to renovate parts of the interior. We walk along North Road to the National Museum but find it closed on this a Saturday. Just across the road, we slip into a shop to check out the local crafts and buy a small basket and some postcards. The proprietor, Carol, lets us off the full price, as we only have some large-bill US dollars but Rosie, embarrassed by this situation, insists on finding the post office, where we buy postage stamps and manage to get some Guyanan currency, returning to the shop to repay Carol.

Further downtown, lots more interesting buildings from the colonial period; the Town Hall, Parliament Building, Courts of Justice and Staebroek Market. There really are some very fine buildings in this old part of town.

We head down Brickdam, one of the oldest streets in town, past the Catholic cathedral, schools and the offices of numerous NGOs. At the top of the street is the Independence Arch and beyond, at the gates of the Botanical Gardens, is the 1763 Monument.

What may not be appreciated is that slaves were not always subservient and resigned to their fate. There were numerous and often quite bloody slave uprisings. That was particularly true in Guyana, where settler numbers were relatively small, the climate harsh and the working conditions even harsher. The monument represents Cuffy, slave leader of a rebellion that took place in 1763. At the time, the whites were outnumbered by more than ten to one and under the leadership of Cuffy, the slaves took over plantation after plantation, forcing the then Dutch colonists into a small area to the north of the country, until help eventually came from the British and French. The rebellion lasted for more than a year and is celebrated each year with a national holiday.

Much later, another significant slave rebellion took place, in 1823, by which time what is now Guyana was a British colony. Now the whites were outnumbered by some thirty to one but, despite being so heavily outnumbered, the rebellion proved short-lived and the plantation owners were soon back in control, thanks to the intervention of a battalion of troops posted to the colony. Some 250 slaves were killed but not entirely in vain. In Britain, the Anti-Slavery Society was active and events in Guyana helped swing public opinion in favour of abolition. In actuality, as we have seen from the example of James Blair at Blairmont, the plantation owners did not fare badly from abolition, enjoying generous compensation payments granted to them in return for freeing their slaves.

The Botanical Gardens give the impression of unfinished business, but they do contain a system of canals dating back to the Dutch period of colonisation, and Zaman is keen to show us something in the water. He tears a branch from a bush and starts gently agitating the surface of the water. The result is a few ripples and nothing more. He bids us to be patient but after a few minutes his own patience is exhausted and he tries again from another spot. Meanwhile, Kenneth, his young apprentice, leads us across a bridge, and when he tries to tickle the surface of the water he is immediately rewarded when out pops the head of a large manatee. Not the most attractive of creatures but an interesting find. A herbivore, it readily munches on the leaves from the branch Kenneth is dangling in the water. Poor old Zaman is a little miffed and we leave him to sulk and, although not something we normally do, at Kenneth's suggestion we pay a short visit to the adjacent zoo. We are seeking the elusive jaguar that we have never managed to see in the wild in all our visits to South America, although almost everywhere we are assured of their presence. Not any surprise. Here in the zoo, with a cage barely the size of a small backyard, the jaguar still manages to preserve his anonymity.

Our guides here cannot do enough to satisfy our interests in their country and knowing of my interest in cricket, Kenneth and Zaman have arranged a little detour from our planned itinerary. Our next stop is Bourda, Georgetown's famed cricket ground. We find it in a sad, derelict state, neglected since the country invested in a new ground at Providence on the outskirts of the city to host the 2007 Cricket World Cup. Bourda is one of the oldest cricket grounds in the Caribbean, dating from 1884 and hosting its first test match in 1930, the opponents, the "mother country" England.

Kenneth leads us up the back steps into the pavilion. First shock is that on the outfield, a large American with an even bigger voice is instructing some local lads in the art of baseball. They all sport the caps and striped shirts associated with that sport. A case of out-and-out bribery must have led to this sacrilege on such hallowed turf. He must surely have given them free shirts and caps.

Kenneth treats me to a cold beer from the bar and I take the chance to stroll around. The honours boards are still in place. Great names who have performed feats here. This was the home ground for West Indies stars of the recent past like Rohan Kanhai, Clive Lloyd, Lance Gibbs and most recently Shiv Chanderpaul. The last test match staged here was in 2005. For the record: the highest test match innings on this ground was by Glenn Turner of New Zealand and the best match bowling by Imran Khan from Pakistan. Sadly, records unlikely to ever be broken. Being situated below sea level, the ground has always been susceptible to flooding and over the years, too many days' play have been lost to the elements for the ground to continue to be economically viable.

Either side of the bar area, the dressing rooms; one for the home team, one for the visitors – both dark and careworn – bare wooden benches and metal hooks. Nothing like the modern elite sportsman will expect. I sit on a bench in the home dressing room and soak up the atmosphere. To think it is probably just as it was on that famous day in 1930 when the West Indies recorded their first-ever victory against England. What joy there must have been, and a new power in cricket was emerging with their first huge stars George Headley and Learie Constantine.

Our city tour is coming to a conclusion, but the day is not over.

The evening is another first. We are to dine at the house of legendary steel pan band leader Roy Geddes. All I knew about steel bands until this encounter was that they were more associated with Trinidad than Guyana, due in part to the former island having an oil industry, and that they have been part of popular Caribbean culture since the 1940s. In fact, steel band music seems to have first developed in the 1930s when a popular percussion instrument, the tamboo bamboo, was banned. The steel drum as an instrument was refined in the ensuing years and first became popular in the UK after the Trinidad All-Steel Pan Percussion Orchestra performed at the 1951 Festival of Britain.

We have been driven by Zaman from our city centre hotel to one of the more affluent but still modest suburbs of South Ruimveldt. The Geddes house is a small detached two-storey property with a quirky garden decorated with gnomes and steel band paraphernalia. Important to say that the neighbours' properties are feet rather than yards away. Roy comes to greet us at his front gate and immediately leads us down the garden path and into the downstairs of the house that he has turned into a small museum in celebration of panning. Roy is an affable man in his mid-seventies, who is quick to tell us that he has been a pannist since the age of fourteen. One thing is immediately clear: Roy sees himself more of a teacher than a musician and has a strong work ethic that I am sure he instils in all of his students. *Discipline is love* is displayed on the notice at the garden gate and is a popular track on one of Roy's many albums.

I am keen to understand Roy's history and role in the history of panning, and he is equally anxious to give us hands-on experience of playing a steel drum. The first thing is to understand that unlike a normal drum, this is not simply about hitting the surface of the instrument with a stick. The surface of the pan has been carefully hammered into a bowl shape, and areas of the surface are further refined and tuned to form notes. Roy has kindly marked numbers on each of the notes and he shouts out numbers so we can play some semblance of a recognisable tune. Rosie proves quite adept and receives praise from teacher. I prove a little slower on the uptake, but Roy is patient and the tune eventually emerges, to ironic applause. Roy in his twilight years is now noted more as a drum maker and tuner, but his early career as a pannist was in the '50s, joining local bands and making his name as a particularly capable musician.

In the '60s, Roy's career really took off, thanks to a friendship with the then Prime Minister Cheddi Jagan. He was encouraged by Jagan to form the Guyana National Steel Band and later the Guyana National Steel Orchestra, having the ultimate honour for a pannist when he was invited to take the band to play at Trinidad's independence celebrations in 1962. In 1964, he formed The Silvertones and began recording and later that year they were chosen to play for the Queen during a royal visit to the country. In 2004, Roy's contribution to steel band music was recognised in the UK when the British Association of Steelbands and its magazine *Pan Podium* recognised his lifelong contribution to the now worldwide Steel Pan movement.

We are led upstairs to Roy's living room and meet his wife, Pamela. Roy, it has to be said, is something of a hoarder, and the room is stuffed full of memorabilia; much, but not all, pan-related. Posters adorn the walls and there are photographs and knick-knacks collected from his tours overseas and meetings with politicians and celebrities. We of course take some photographs and purchase a copy of the CD playing in the background. Roy remains an enthusiast for his craft and insists on us listening to another Silvertones production. He is keen to show off the versatility of the steel pan as a musical instrument, and this CD contains tracks of very recognisable classical music. I ask if the neighbours mind: the music is loud, the windows open and the next door house only feet away. Roy assures me they love to hear his music. Then it is back downstairs to the small patio, where we enjoy the meal of traditional Caribbean fare prepared by Pamela. Guyana is certainly providing some out-of-the-ordinary experiences.

Our busy schedule shows no sign of relenting. Another early start and we are back to the airport. Our party is gathered together in the departure lounge and we are introduced to our guide for the day, Carlos. A mixed bag of passengers; four locals, a middle-aged Swiss couple, a Barbadian lady visiting relatives, a young woman from Trinidad who is a staff trainer, taking time off in the middle of the course she is running, two American men working in their embassy and ourselves. Carlos is in the middle of giving us his life history when our pilot pops her head around the door and says we are ready to go. She is the daughter of the founder of this small local airline and quickly we are ushered aboard our Cessna aircraft.

We are soon at our flying altitude of 9,000 feet from which height it is possible to see that below is virgin jungle, no roads, only the Demerara River to access the interior and nothing but trees, save for the occasional mining camp. It is over an hour before we approach our first destination, the Kaieteur Falls, the highest single drop waterfall in the world at 942 feet. To put that into perspective, that is four times the height of Niagara Falls and twice the height of the Victoria Falls.

We pass low over the falls for photos. Earlier in our flight, the pilot had reported rain over the falls, putting our landing there in doubt, but the gods have been kind, the clouds have cleared, and we have perfect visibility as we circle before landing on the strip close to the falls.

At the small visitor centre adjacent to the airstrip, we meet the Park Rangers who will guide us the short distance down to the falls. One of the rangers tells us that en route we should look out for two rare sightings: the poison dart frog and the cock of the rock. The latter we are told is a bright orange-coloured bird that nests in the rockface below the falls. In the event, we are not fortunate enough to have a sighting.

The poison dart frog, so named because of its highly toxic secretions, was traditionally used by the Amerindians to create poison tips for their arrows. As the ranger leads us down the path towards the falls, he calls to us to look at a large bromeliad. Peering inside, barely visible, the tiny yellowish figure of a frog. Given its name, I had expected something larger. It is about the size of my fingernail.

We are taken to Boy Scout's View. Some distance beyond the falls but from here a good aspect to watch the water tumbling down into the valley below. The view is slightly obscured by a ledge jutting out from terra firma and seemingly suspended in mid-air above the raging torrent far below. This is Rainbow Ledge, offering a fantastic photo opportunity if one's partner climbs on it and stands precariously somewhere close, but not too close, to the edge. We take turns to indulge this photo opportunity before making our way down to the actual point where the river disappears into the gorge below. Not being the height of the wet season, there is a modest amount of water in the river and we are actually able to make our way from boulder to boulder to stand in the middle of the falls, looking first upriver and then down into the valley far below.

Back at the visitor centre, we are served a picnic lunch before boarding our aircraft for the thirty-minute flight to the Orinduik Falls on the border with Brazil. The surprise is that soon after take-off, the jungle below begins to give way to open savannah and we land on an airstrip set in low rolling hills, covered in grass.

It is about a ten-minute walk down to the falls from the airstrip and on the way, we meet two young native children: a little boy of about five and his sister, a little older, aged maybe eight. We try to engage them in conversation but, although not fazed by our presence, they are not to be drawn. Later, as we are about to reboard for our flight back to Georgetown, they reappear beside the aircraft and are happy to take the remains of our lunch, including some packets of sweets, before heading home. We watch them make their way down towards the river above the falls, and using rocks in the shallow waters, they cross. Home for them is a small village on the far side of the river in Brazil.

The Orinduik Falls themselves are in stark contrast to Kaieteur, stretching across the width of the Ireng River, a tributary of the Amazon, having no depth, dropping down only some 80 feet but comprising a series of cascades. Tumbling over rocks of red jasper and with the Pakaraima Mountains for a backdrop. I found it quite a pleasing way to fill out the remainder of our day.

Back to Georgetown, we have only a short time to prepare for tomorrow's journey to our next destination, Suriname.

The flight from Georgetown heads due south and is interesting insofar as for the first half of the journey, we are tracking our earlier road trip down to New Amsterdam, this time from 10,000 feet above. From this height, the layout of the traditional plantation structure is clearly apparent, even though the plantations by and large no longer exist. After half an hour's flying time, far below we can clearly see the Berbice River and close by the Blairmont Estate. Beyond the town of New Amsterdam, where we were a few days ago, and further on, the coast begins to bend inland at the mouth of the Courantyne River, forming the border between Guyana and Suriname. Once our flight passes across the river estuary, we are looking down on Suriname.

Minutes later, we are in Paramaribo, capital of Suriname, the thirteenth and final South American country we have visited. We have landed at Zorg en Hoop Airport in the heart of the city, which hosts Gum Air flights from Guyana, one of the world's lesser-known airlines but a routing which saves us the one-hour plus drive in from the Johan Adolf Pengel International Airport. The facilities at Zorg en Hoop are rudimentary and the formalities cursory, so within minutes of alighting from the ten-seater aircraft that has brought us this far, we are in the safe hands of Desmond, our guide for the next four days who is awaiting our arrival at the gate.

We soon warm to Desmond, a sentiment not entirely influenced by the fact that he has thoughtfully brought refreshments in the form of a brown paper bag containing a selection of Danish pastries and a local delicacy, Bojo cake, made from cassava. The secret to good guiding, which Desmond has worked out, is to tell a lot but not too much and to reflect your clients' interests rather than your own. In this cosmopolitan country, it is difficult to work out Desmond's ethnic origins but we guess Indian. What is for sure is that he is highly personable and we are going to get along famously.

We are straight into a tour of the city. Diversity is to be the theme of our short visit and our first stop is at the Arya Dewaker Hindu Temple. Although relatively new, it is undergoing renovation so we are unable to look inside. It is nevertheless an impressive and unusual construction. We learn from Desmond two interesting facts, firstly that the architect came not from India but from the Netherlands and was not a Hindu and that worshippers are part of a sect outside the mainstream Hindu religion. From here into the city centre and our next stop is the Catholic St Peter and Paul Cathedral. It is made entirely of wood, and although the cathedral in Georgetown claimed to be the highest wooden structure in the world, this building is said to be the largest wooden building in the Western Hemisphere. Around the corner, our next visit is to the Dutch Reformed Church in Kerkplein in the very heart of the city, established here by the Dutch in the seventeenth century. This building, octagonal in shape, was built in 1837.

Close by in Keizerstraat, the mosque and synagogue occupy adjacent sites. The diversity here is already apparent. Hindu, Protestant, Roman Catholic and Muslims co-exist in roughly equal numbers. We walk back into the city centre and down Post Straat, where Desmond leads us into one of the fine old colonial-style buildings, this housing the Numismatic Museum. We are not coin collectors but the museum is surprisingly well presented and amongst the exhibits a rare parrot coin dating back to 1679.

Already you will have a sense of the unique cultural mix contained within one small city. The Dutch reform colonisers, the black African slaves converted to Catholicism by missionary influences, the post-slavery indentured labourers from the subcontinent, largely Hindu but also Moslems brought from Java, another former Dutch colony. Throw in eight separate tribes of indigenous Amerindians and a smattering of Jews escaping persecution in Europe and you have Suriname, a unique potpourri of races and religions.

Continuing our walk from here further along Post Straat, we enter what is now Independence Square, formerly known as Orange Square in the Dutch period before independence. The square itself is a large open greensward, to our left three fine buildings, across the square the presidential palace and in our eyeline the substantial statue of Johan Adolf Pengel. The prominent local pre-independence politician died in 1970 so didn't live to see his vision of full freedom from Dutch rule. The statue may be accurate but is not flattering. Adolf was, to say the least, a portly man.

The three buildings on our left are in turn the Ministry of Finance, the Court of Justice and the "du Plessis House". All are examples of the Colonial Louisiana-style buildings, as the name suggests, an architectural style normally to be found in the southern states of the USA.

Looking across the square to the du Plessis House, Desmond recounts the story of Susanna du Plessis. Daughter of a lawyer employed by the Dutch West India Company. At an early age, she was married here in Suriname to a wealthy plantation owner. He died prematurely leaving her his estate. She subsequently married a younger man, also the son of a wealthy plantation owner. However, it is her reputation as a particularly harsh if not sadistic slave owner that has led to her name being handed down in the annals of Suriname history.

The story that Desmond relates is that Susanna felt her husband was showing a too manly interest in a young mulatto maid named Alida. Susanna ordered that her breasts be cut off and she had them served to him at her dinner table with the words, 'You admired these so much, now enjoy.' The maid subsequently died of her wounds and is something of a national heroine.

Another Susanna story tells how a slave's baby annoyed her with its crying. She had the child drowned in the river and when the mother went to recover the baby's body, she was subjected to 300 lashes.

These stories were recounted back to Europe by John Gabriel Stedman, a Scottish Army officer, in his book *Voyage into Surinam,* about his experiences in the country, although in fairness he did not attribute these cruel acts to her by name. Susanna eventually divorced her second husband on grounds of his cruelty to her and went to live in the house on the corner of the square. She died in 1795 and is buried in the city. She wrote her own epitaph: *Finally, I calmed down.*

The presidential palace is a pleasant white colonial-style building, not overly ostentatious, and was for most of its existence home of the Dutch Governor. Desmond leads us beyond the square behind the palace to the

Palmentuin, the Palm Gardens, a feature of the city since the time of the first governor and opened in 1685.

With time running short, we just have time to visit the site of Fort Zeelandia and admire the restored officers' houses just outside its walls. Here we have a strange encounter. A smartly dressed and elderly black lady approaches us and in perfect English and without any prompting or encouragement, launches a diatribe accusing the Dutch Government of anti-Semitic acts. She says the holocaust continues and then cites the case of her granddaughter, who she claims was taken from her family and shipped to Holland, where she was subjected to medical experiments. The woman, given her colour, was not obviously Jewish, her demeanour not overtly suggesting mental issues, and we unlikely targets for her story.

This is just a minor interlude in a fascinating tour of a small but historically interesting city, one well worthy of its UNESCO World Heritage status.

Next day, we take a drive out of the city and head some 70km south to Jodensavanne. The Chinese-built road makes it an easy drive. We pass the Amerindian village of Parakka but it has few traditional buildings; most of the houses are pre-fabricated, with a family car parked outside.

After crossing the Suriname River on a newly constructed bridge, we enter the site of Jodensavanne, a Jewish community established here way back in 1652. We park the vehicle in a small car park in a heavily wooded area and set out on foot. A Jewish foundation has been established to excavate the site and they have provided some useful signage but, this apart, we find few other indications of any serious efforts to excavate and restore this historical location.

In 1652, the community comprised some 150 Sephardic Jews fleeing persecution in Portugal and Spain. They had settled in what is now Brazil, but when the Portuguese arrived there, they fled again, encouraged by the British to take residence in what is now Suriname. Granted semi-autonomy and freedom to practise their religion, the settlement grew to some 600 Jewish people, aided by a slave workforce of 1,400.

Sugar being a valued commodity, the immigrants laid the foundations of the idea of sugar plantations. Employing slave labour, the settlement was economically successful for several generations, exporting to Europe and surviving until 1832. After some halcyon years, Jodensavanne was by then in decline with more and more competition from plantations in the West

Indies and the increasing use of sugar beet in Europe to source sugar. A fire and slave revolt led to the settlement finally being abandoned, the few remaining Jewish families moving to Paramaribo.

Given most of the buildings would have been constructed of wood, little physical evidence remains to be found today, only the cemetery, paradoxically in Hebrew the "House of Life", and the foundation walls of the stone-built synagogue. The cemetery has been subject to some limited archaeological excavation, and the gravestones are in a remarkable state of preservation largely because they are in a marble imported from Europe. The inscriptions in Hebrew or Portuguese can readily be read. Jewish researchers have catalogued the graves and recorded both inscriptions and iconography. Quite a lot of the family names are apparently still common in Suriname.

As we return through the woods, Desmond becomes quite animated, as he has spotted two tiny mating and apparently rare blue nunbirds. One of the delights of travelling is that one cultural experience can be followed so immediately by one from the natural world; history, politics, architecture, wildlife each with its own fascination.

Back in the city, Desmond suggests lunch. I have to say that Rosie can be a little conservative when it comes to Asian cuisine and she is almost vegetarian, so eating out in strange foreign climes can become problematic. Desmond suggests Indian on this occasion, not something with which either of us is overly familiar. Desmond's favoured place to eat proves more café than restaurant. Greeting mine host suggests Desmond is a regular customer. Rather than Indian restaurant, it is a roti house. Roti is a wheat flatbread into which various ingredients are folded, and is best eaten from the hands. None of these requirements will naturally appeal to Rosie, but she bravely battles through a vegetable roti whilst I happily demolish a chicken version.

Next day, we meet up with Desmond again and take a trip across the bridge over the Suriname River to Commewijne. Our first stop is at Peperpot, site of a sugar plantation started sometime in the 1650s. Later, a succession of Dutch absentee landlords saw the lands turned over to both sugar and cocoa production. After the emancipation of slaves, Chinese and then Hindu and Javanese indentured labourers were used. Although many of the buildings remain, Peperpot, like all the other plantations in Suriname, no longer operates as a business and what is left has fallen into disrepair.

More recently acquired by new owners, the old plantation house has been fully restored but is not open to the public, although Desmond tells us that there are plans to renovate some of the outbuildings, the storehouse and factory, as a museum.

Desmond seems to think that the plantation ceased operating around thirty years ago and interestingly when we walk to the back of the factory we come across a *kampong*, a village where the indentured Javanese labourers and their families lived, and indeed still live. Back at the main site we look around the factory, where rusting old items of machinery and creaky floorboards reinforce the feeling of a time gone by. We meet up with a group of elderly tourists and chat with their tour manager, a middle-aged German lady who tells us that her guests are from Munich. They are travelling north from here in a mini-bus, crossing the border into Guyana by ferry across the Courantyne River. Having decided ourselves not to take this route because of potential border delays, we wish her well.

Close by the old estate buildings is the entrance to the Peperpot Nature Park, and Desmond suggests we take a hike to see if we can spot any interesting wildlife. The park has a reputation for attracting a wide diversity of birds. The path through the forest, I suspect, is an old track through the plantation that has been there for hundreds of years so is well trodden and easy walking. We spot various birds and an amazing array of colourful dragonflies. On the way back, we hear activity high in the trees and a troupe of capuchin monkeys make their way down onto the ground on our right and cross the path in front of us before disappearing high into the trees on our left, then almost immediately we espy a family of smaller squirrel monkeys.

From Peperpot we head up to Nieuw Amsterdam, situated at the confluence of the Suriname and Commewijne Rivers and a natural place to build a fort to command views over the Atlantic Ocean beyond and to offer early warning of any potential intruders. The fort on this site was built by the Dutch in 1747, the likely invaders at the time being French buccaneers, although later it twice fell without a fight to the British. At the entrance, Desmond spots something in a large tree and points out a *great potoo*. A very large and fluffy bird, extraordinary-looking, bearing some similarity to an owl, with a big head and flat beak.

The fort itself is well preserved, with the Kruithaus (powder store) and a Coach House displaying a number of well-preserved old carriages, buildings dating back to the original mid-eighteenth-century construction. From 1872 until 1982, the fort was used as a prison, and there are a number of other buildings relating to this period. Finally, we inspect the wooden Commanders Building, one of the oldest surviving buildings in Suriname.

We move on to Marienburg. Another old plantation site, one with a typical and in this case a particularly unhappy history. The original plantation dates from 1745, although the site was subsequently purchased in 1882 by a Dutch company wanting to build a sugar factory. Javanese labourers were brought from the Dutch East Indies to provide the workforce, but harsh working conditions and low pay led to industrial unrest. In July 1902, a strike broke out, and a few days later the factory manager was chased by a group of strikers and beaten to death. Troops were called, arrests made and then as the workers protested, shots were fired and twenty-four strikers died. The factory finally closed in 1986. A memorial to the dead is the centrepiece of the now derelict site, the factory building itself now too dangerous to visit other than from a distance.

By now, it is time for a late lunch. Given Suriname's ethnic diversity and having eaten Indian cuisine the previous day, Desmond takes us to a *warung*. This is a small family-run Javanese restaurant. Although not particularly familiar with Indonesian cuisine, I had some years before been taken with the Malay dish *nasi goreng*. Apparently meaning "fried rice", it comes in many forms and my favoured version, one served with various meats and prawns and topped with a fried egg. Delicious. I ordered a local version, with chicken the main ingredient. Rosie somehow struggled through something vegetarian recommended by Desmond.

That evening, we say our farewells to Desmond as he takes us to a suburb of Paramaribo, the diplomatic district of the city, from where we are to take a small boat to cruise the Suriname and Commewijne Rivers in search of dolphins.

As an aside, it has been remiss of me not to mention Suriname's national sport. Whilst we await the arrival of our boat, a small local ferry arrives and an old man alights carrying a birdcage in hand with a tiny bird in residence. Our first evidence of the bird-singing phenomenon surely unique to Suriname.

Our sunset boat trip takes us across the confluence of the two rivers, apparently a feeding ground for dolphins, but this evening they make but a cursory appearance. The boat takes us to the far bank of the river to the village of Johan and Margaretha and, as the name suggests, it is on the site of another former plantation. Seems like a regulation trip for tourists and at the wooden dock, a small ramshackle café with a few gnarled old men sitting drinking and puffing away on roll-your-own cigarettes. They appear unperturbed by our sudden arrival. We take a stroll through the village. The Dutch-made canals from a former time define the village layout and a lock gate is still in place and beautifully preserved. With the sun going down, the light is perfect for photography and the whole place has a serene quality. At first it seems that the locals are of Javanese extraction like the old men at the quayside café, but then we come across some Indian families taking an evening stroll. Once again, evidence of Suriname's unique ethnic mix. We return across the river and the sun sets under a clear blue sky; a perfect end to an excellent day, despite the lack of dolphin sightings.

Our final day in Suriname sees us left to our own devices and we take a mini-bus from our hotel and return to the city centre. We have decided to visit Fort Zeelandia, and the bus drops us at one corner of Independence Square.

When first constructed in 1650 by the British, the fort was known as Fort Willoughby. When the Dutch became the colonial power, the name was changed and this was the centre for their control over what became known as Surinam. Much of the original fort is still intact and forms what is now the National Museum, although it has variously been an army barracks and prison.

By chance, as we arrive in the square, across at the presidential palace some activity. A large limousine drives up and we wait to see what is going on and there, emerging from the front door, the bearded figure of Dési Bouterse, the president no less, together with the first lady, saying his goodbyes to some foreign dignitary. Minutes later, the president reappears, climbs into his own limo and escorted by police outriders, sirens screaming, is driven out and up Gravenstraat.

Bouterse is a man with a colourful back story. Soon after being granted independence by the Dutch in 1975, Suriname was gripped by political discontent and accusations of corruption against the new government. Many people fled to the Netherlands and in an atmosphere of instability, in 1980, a coup d'état led to the overthrow of the government and installation of a military dictatorship. In the days that followed, many opponents of the military takeover were rounded up and imprisoned in Fort Zeelandia. A few days later and fifteen critics of the military were tortured and shot in the fort complex in what became known as the "December murders". Leader of the coup? None other than the current President Dési Bouterse.

Bouterse had served in the Dutch Army before returning to Suriname at independence and at the time of the coup held the rank of sergeant in the new Suriname Army. He was leader of what became known as the "Sergeants' Coup".

From the time of the coup in 1980 until 1988, Bouterse was the de facto president. Democracy returned but Bouterse laid down the condition that he remained head of the army. Soon, dissatisfied with the newly elected government, it wasn't long before he led another coup, the "Telephone Coup", in 1990. Fresh elections were held in 1991 with a government more acceptable to Bouterse, who continued to hold various positions of state. His popularity and power thereafter waned and he largely disappeared from public view until being finally dismissed from public office by the then president, a former colleague in 1999. That same year, "in absentia", he was found guilty in the Netherlands of smuggling huge quantities of cocaine into that country and was sentenced to eleven years in prison.

In the intervening years following Bouterse's demise, Suriname returned to full democracy but continued to suffer from severe financial problems. Yet amazingly in this new democratic era, Bouterse was to return to the political scene. He stood in the election of 2005, then in 2010, in free and fair elections, he was elected president, and his party, the Mega Combination, took the majority of seats in parliament. Until then, politics in Suriname had been defined on ethnic lines, each major party representing a particular ethnic group, but Bouterse had cleverly put together a coalition, crossing the racial divide.

Although he is the undisputed and legitimate leader of his country, three significant events hang heavy over the figure of Bouterse.

Firstly, was he present and responsible for the "December murders"? A lengthy trial took place, culminating in 2012 when one of his fellow conspirators, Ronnie Rozendaal, suffering from an incurable disease, claimed he wanted the truth to be told before he died. At the trial, he gave evidence that Bouterse was personally responsible for two of the fifteen killings, a claim which Bouterse denied. However, before the trial could play out to a conclusion, hurried legislation brought before parliament gave the conspirators a pardon, making the trial irrelevant, and it was halted, despite some of the accused wanting it to continue.

Secondly: the Moiwana massacre. In 1986, troops loyal to Bouterse massacred thirty-nine villagers, mainly women and children, in a Maroon (mixed race) village and burned the houses to the ground. The village was the home of Ronnie Brunswijk. Brunswijk was a former bodyguard of Bouterse who, unhappy with the excesses of Bouterse's regime, had left that role and formed a rebel group called Jungle Commando to oppose the Bouterse regime. Did Bouterse personally give orders for the massacre?

Thirdly, claims that Bouterse led a drugs cartel in the 1990s (according to Wikileaks, an activity that continued up to 2006). This being the point in time when he revived his interest in politics. The drug-running charges that let to that prosecution in the Netherlands.

Nevertheless, despite his controversial past, Bouterse has introduced social change and clearly still retains support amongst the poorer sections of society.

After our pleasant experience in this charming yet diverse little country, it is hard to believe we are watching the day-to-day comings and goings of such a controversial figure.

Three days before, we had stood outside Fort Zeelandia with Desmond and admired the restored officers' houses and viewed the statue of Queen Wilhelmina at the fort entrance. Today we are taking a look inside. The museum is an eclectic mix of artefacts from the indigenous cultures, from items such as tribal masks to colonial era photographs and exhibits illustrating the use of slaves, with some natural history thrown in. Apart from a group of excited schoolchildren, we are the only visitors.

From the fort we walk along the waterfront past the modest parliament building. A small group has gathered outside, we guess journalists and photographers, so expecting some more action we loiter for a few minutes but nothing of note happens and we continue our walk into the city. The buildings along Waterkant are without exception splendid examples of the colonial style, the best exemplar The Cornerhouse, one of the finest preserved residential properties in the city.

Further along the waterfront we see a few older men hanging around a quayside café drinking coffee and then lo and behold, coming towards us two burly young men carrying birds in cages. I have alluded previously to the unusual sport of bird singing and here an example of prime contestants in training.

Contests in the Suriname Bird Whistling League actually take place only yards away every Sunday morning on the green facing the presidential palace. The origins are unclear. Some say it was Chinese immigrants who brought the practice here around one hundred years ago, whilst others claim that it was commonplace in jungle villages in Suriname to cage birds and teach them to sing. Certainly, the competitive nature of bird singing appears to have been around here for more than fifty years.

Birds are of various species, small and some colourful, although for the tropics, more often frankly bland, in browns and blacks like the picolet or a finch, locally known as a *twa twa*. Training does genuinely involve walking the birds in their cages and teaching them songs, a process on which the most serious protagonists spend two hours a day. The competition is a knockout, with birds going head-to-head (not literally), with a winner determined by judges scoring against clear but complex rules. Cages are hung only feet apart and the clock starts. Songs are counted and the judge adjudicates, making a chalk stroke on a board every time he hears a different song.

We stop the young men to ask about their birds. One is yellow, although the young man holding the cage is unable to give us an English name. The other, chocolate brown and black, I believe is a picolet.

Subsequent research suggests that the bird-whistling phenomenon is not after all confined exclusively to Suriname but also occurs in neighbouring Guyana and in Trinidad, and immigrants from these countries have exported the practice and birds variously to Belgium, Holland, Canada and the United States. The Olympics next?

We find ourselves back in Kerkplein, where the centrepiece is the Dutch Reformed Church. We take another look inside to fathom its odd design and lack of a centre aisle but semi-circle of pews around the main altar. The original church was destroyed in a major fire in 1821 that decimated much of the city. The great and the good from Dutch colonial society were buried here, and when the church was rebuilt and consecrated in 1835, the gravestones of the notables were laid in the floors. One of these was the notorious Susanna du Plessis.

It is a particularly hot and humid day so finding a post office close to the church, we content ourselves buying some postcards and stamps, scribbling some messages to those back home and retreating back to our hotel.

We take a late flight out that afternoon, returning briefly to Georgetown, where Zaman the ever faithful is there to greet us. Our short but rewarding visit to the Guyanas is coming to a close.

Eleven

Guatemala: Mayan magic

Guatemala: Straddling Central America from the Pacific to the Caribbean. A population of 15 million. Ruled by Spain for 300 years until independence in 1821. Thereafter a turbulent history, including a 36-year civil war ending in 1996. Spanish speaking.

'*Hemos perdido las maletas.*' It was the end of our final Spanish lesson with Rosa in the cramped sitting room of her small end-of-terrace house in Ipswich. Days later, we were heading west across the Atlantic once again, this time to Central America, and instead of the usual lessons conjugating our verbs, she was anxious to leave us with some phrases that might be helpful on our travels. We joked that this phrase might indeed be useful, as although our travels had taken us around the world, our luggage had never yet gone missing. How prophetic these words seem as we stand beside the empty and now motionless luggage carousel at Mexico City Airport.

Since that first visit to Argentina some twenty years ago, we have become fascinated by the cultures, natural wonders and sheer diversity of countries that, perhaps because of their Spanish rather than British colonial periods, seemed somehow strangely exotic and mystical. This then is our umpteenth visit to Latin America but our first serious attempt to discover something about those countries between the continents of North and South America: Central America.

When Rosie and I finally retired to spend more time travelling, our fascination for Latin America led us, despite our dotage, me then in my sixties, to start learning Spanish. Rosa is our third teacher. A young mother struggling to pay the mortgage and the other household bills, she makes a few useful pounds giving lessons from her front room, where we spend an hour a week with her and her small menagerie of cats. Rosa has several advantages for us. One, she is Spanish but has lived in the UK since her teenage years, and this means that whilst she knows her mother tongue, she is also grounded in English humour and the nuances of our language. Secondly, in an earlier life she worked as a sales manager for a UK company with business interests in many Latin American countries. This means that she has travelled to some places we have been to or intend to go to and understands the way in which Latin American Spanish varies in the same way that English as used by Brits differs from that of people from the United States. Perhaps learning the conjugation of all those verbs will prove useful sometime.

We have to give up on our quest to find our luggage with assurances that it will be at the gate when we check in for our next flight in the morning. As we make our way through the now near-deserted airport terminal to our adjacent airport hotel, we are aware that outside there is torrential rain that we later discover is to cause severe flooding in and around Mexico City.

Despite those promises that our luggage will be at the gate when we board our aircraft early the following morning, it is nowhere to be seen, and nobody seems interested enough to locate it for us, so in desperation we make a call to our travel company in London and move on to our next destination, Guatemala, with only our hand luggage.

It doesn't matter how much research you do in advance or how many guidebooks you read, there are always places that will shock, dismay, disappoint and, if you are very lucky, pleasantly surprise. In the latter category is Guatemala. Small in world terms, unimportant, and until relatively recently riven by civil war but from our tourist perspective a gem of a place.

What had whetted our interest was a brief visit to the country a few years before when our cruise ship had called at the port town of Santo Tomas de Castilla. From here we take a tourist bus with a young and rather intense guide, Armando Escobar, a self-described Ladino. That is, of European descent in this country where the vast majority are either ethnic Mayan or Mestizo (mixed race). We are heading south-west through the countryside to the site of the important Mayan city of Quirigua.

Although a civil war, now mercifully ended, has raged for some forty years, Armando is a young man barely impacted by those troubled times and is something of a romantic. Untarnished by his country's turbulent past, he is able to look positively at the future, and that is no bad thing. As we make our way, he describes Guatemala as a land of trees.

He has brought with him a packed lunch and as he ferociously attacks the meal as only hungry young men can, he describes the contents and the typical diet of his country. At this point, I knew little of Central American cuisine beyond a very limited exposure to Tex-Mex cooking in the southern United States. This experience had come years before, when I worked for a large British food company. Our Chairman, affectionately known as JC, returned from a holiday in the United States to announce that we were now the proud owners of a chain of restaurants in Texas. As the company had no similar businesses across its fairly substantial empire, this came as something of a surprise to us poor souls in middle management but it has to be said as an even bigger shock to members of the Board. Anyway, as a consequence, I was to enjoy the occasional business trip to the States and to sample the menus served up in our restaurants.

I digress. Back to Armando's lunch. This is to prove insightful for future reference on trips to come. The *tamale* is the staple of the Guatemalan diet. There are almost infinite varieties but in essence it is a dough, usually corn but maybe rice or potatoes, with added ingredients, sweet or savoury, and wrapped in banana or plantain leaves or in corn husks. Today, Armando produces a red *tamale* with tomato and beef, swilled down with a drink of mango milk. He is also something of a chocoholic and extols the virtues of Guatemalan chocolate. An interesting addiction insofar as it is quite possible that the ancient Mayans actually invented chocolate.

We arrive at what remains of the ancient city of Quirigua. It was the place where Eighteen Rabbit met his comeuppance. The strangely named Mayan ruler had commanded respect throughout the Mayan world from his impressive capital at Copan. An empire which stretched from modern-day Yucatan in Mexico through large parts of Central America. Quirigua was small by comparison with Copan but a strategically important staging post on the route between Copan and the other major Mayan city of Tikal. Equally, by comparison to Copan, this was but a minor fiefdom, nonetheless also ruled by an ambitious overlord, with the equally improbable name of Two Legged Sky. When Two Legged Sky invited Eighteen Rabbit to visit, it was not, as the VIP supposed, for those at Quirigua to pay homage to his wisdom and influence but to become the scene of his assassination, underwritten by powerful influences, possibly opposed to the axis between Tikal and Copan. Such intrigue is of course largely supposition. These events happened in the eighth century AD and are part of the mythology of this impressive and long-established culture.

Only a couple of days before, we had visited another Mayan site at Altun Ha in Belize and gradually the Mayan world was beginning to make sense. Here at Quirigua, the 10-metre high-stelae with carved figures and hieroglyphics tell a story that few have been able to decipher with any sense of certainty. Strange that years before, on another Caribbean cruise, we had visited the Mayan site at Chichén Itzá in Mexico, clambered up its huge pyramid, taken in the views, but had not as now become fascinated by these people and the sheer scale and complexity of what they had created so long ago.

Whilst the Mayans still occupy these lands, it is odd that it was not until 1841 that the outside world discovered in the midst of thick Guatemalan jungle the remains of this lost city. Yet as Armando describes these events to us on a steamy hot day in October and we admire our first stelae, my gaze extends beyond the wide-open expanse within which the remains of the city have been painstakingly excavated to the thick near impenetrable jungle beyond. At this moment, I am set about learning more of Mayan civilisation and its apparent sudden demise.

Rio Dulce, the sweet river, proves sweet indeed. The Caribbean Sea is not only about islands, because its waves lap the shores of Central America too. The Dulce River flows into the Caribbean Sea at the interesting town of Livingston, but our journey starts upriver at the town named after the river, Rio Dulce. The river here is something of a surprise. At this point, it is some 300 metres wide and spanned by the longest bridge in Guatemala.

After that morning spent in dense rainforest at the only partially yet impressively excavated ruins of Quirigua, we took our leave of Armando and made our way by bus to a rendezvous with another guide for a trip down the river and back to Santo Tomas de Castillo. Antonio proves to be an interesting character. Unlike Armando, he is a mestizo with a dark complexion and sports a bushy beard. Dressed in khakis with ample pockets, a matching baseball cap and a stout pair of walking boots that have seen plenty of action. He is carrying a pair of binoculars on a strap around his neck and in his arms a formidable photographer's tripod upon which, not a camera but a large telescope.

I soon warm to him. Unlike many guides, he is not at all circumspect about expressing his personal views to clients he is meeting for the first time. Enthusiastic, committed to his cause of protecting the environment and overtly anti-establishment. It is easy to speculate that unlike young Armando, his background would have involved a more active participation in the civil war now consigned to history.

We greet Antonio on the bank of the river, where he points out our transport: a handsome-looking speedboat with a young man at the tiller who Antonio says is Richard. Richard gives us a cheery wave whilst Antonio gives us a briefing on the plan for the afternoon ahead. There are other tourist boats but unlike us, they all seem to be headed upriver to the Castillo de San Felipe, a fort built by the Spanish to ward off intrusions by British pirates and privateers.

Richard's first task is to ferry us across from the riverbank to a nearby island in the middle of the river. Here, a local hotel where we are to lunch. It is an eco-hotel, fairly rustic, and after a meal of black bean soup and grilled snook, we stroll through the attractive tropical gardens. The island is small and it is not long before we reach the far side and here in contrast to the modest nature of the hotel, a small marina where moored are a number of seriously expensive ocean-going yachts. Most are registered in various ports in Florida but a fair number are locally owned. An illustration of the chasm between the haves and have-nots in this relatively poor country, differences soon to be reinforced as we make our way back to the ocean.

Shortly, we rejoin Antonio at the jetty, climb aboard the speedboat and begin to make our way downriver. Antonio stands in the bow and with a nod to his helmsman, Richard, the throttle is opened wide on the powerful outboard motor. Above the sound of the engine and wind, Antonio is soon into his stride and pours scorn on the large imposing riverside retreats of the monied elite that line one side of the river. The boat scuds across the surface of the water and despite the high humidity and ambient temperature in the high 80s, it feels cool and exhilarating.

After about fifteen minutes of high-speed cruising, Antonio signals to Richard with a hand across his throat and we slow to approach a small wooded islet known locally as Bird Island, and for good reason as Antonio points out nesting cormorants, white and brown pelicans, egrets and bitterns. With his keen eye, he also points out a tree-climbing iguana, completely camouflaged to the untrained eye.

We continue our journey and the river widens into a lake, and Antonio again signals to Richard, who steers our boat into a narrow creek and up along a small tributary. Almost immediately we come across a village. It looks idyllic, with a pool of lilies and water hyacinth in front of small jetties and boats with outboard motors and sturdy houses with corrugated roofs. The waterway narrows through a mangrove swamp and soon five small kids come alongside in a dugout canoe. They offer open cupped hands; a sure sign we are not the first visitors around here. Shortly, we come upon the village where they live, visibly poorer than the one we passed earlier. Here, traditional mud houses with heavily thatched roofs that almost reach the ground, so you have to stoop low to enter. Antonio leads us ashore. The village is occupied by indigenous people living by fishing and foraging in the forest. These things are relative; most of the villagers have small boats or dugouts, and some even have outboard motors.

Antonio, obviously a familiar figure here, greets the village headman, who invites us to take a peek in one of the huts, but this apart we are largely ignored by the villagers. Antonio then takes us on a short nature walk on a well-trodden path through the dense jungle, studiously avoiding ant armies that are crossing the path at regular intervals, and in all seriousness, he informs us that their bite can have dire consequences. His passion for this environment is evident as he points out different plants, some with medicinal value, others an unlikely food source, and those poisonous to eat or in some cases even to the touch.

Back in the village, Richard is awaiting our return and soon we are back on the Rio Dulce and heading down to the mouth of the river, past the small town of Livingston. Linked to the outside world only by water, the town is a unique part of Caribbean culture and history, being the home of Garifuna people. This community is a strange anachronism. Back in 1635, two Spanish slave ships were shipwrecked near the Caribbean island of St Vincent. The slaves made their way ashore, where they were welcomed by the indigenous Carib people. Subsequent inter-marriage led to this unique civilisation. Later, when the British colonised St Vincent, they forcibly relocated the Garifuna to Roatan, an island in what is now Honduras. A group of Garifuna later moved down the coast and settled here, a location so remote that it is accessible only by sea, and so isolated that they retain very much their own distinct culture and language. Sadly, time prevents us from going ashore, but we go close to the shore and receive cheery waves from the locals.

It had been an interesting day, a small appetiser that encourages this return to Guatemala for a longer stay.

So it is that some years later, and free from the encumbrance of luggage lost at Mexico City Airport, we arrive at Guatemala's international airport. At the airport, one piece of good news: our luggage lost in transit has been located and will arrive at our hotel, if not later today, then tomorrow.

The airport is in Guatemala City, the capital, but from the little we see as we drive through, it doesn't seem to have much to offer the traveller, and we are reassured in the sense that we plan not to stay here but to journey west to the old Spanish colonial city of Antigua.

In Antigua, we check into the impressive Santo Domingo, a former monastery beautifully converted to offer high-class hotel facilities whilst retaining the integrity of a historical building, a living museum.

Time to explore. We are walking down the narrow cobbled streets of the old city of Antigua, along the Calle Tercera Oriente. Refreshed by a shower embellished by the few remaining drops of eau de toilette from an airline amenity kit, I am anxious to find a change of clothes, or at the very least a new shirt. The city has a good feeling. It is well preserved and has not been allowed to grow willy-nilly with the influx of modern buildings that afflict so many Latin American cities that notionally date from the Spanish colonial period. This we later discover has occurred more by luck than by foresight or plan. A series of earthquakes in the eighteenth century culminated with a decision by the King of Spain in 1773 to move his capital from here to a new safer location, the modern-day capital, Guatemala City. For two centuries, Antigua lay largely ignored, if not totally abandoned, and as a consequence little has changed since those colonial times.

Thanks to the grid system and numbered streets designated north, south, east and west, we readily find our way from the Casa Domingo at the top end of Tercera Calle Oriente to the main square, Parque Central, the hub of the city. It is a large open plaza with gardens, at one end of the square the cathedral, at one side the Palacio de Ayuntamiento and opposite the Palacio de Capitanes, now looking a little sad, the grand building from where the Spanish ruled not only this city but the colony of Guatemala. We climb the town hall steps onto a balcony to take a few photos across the square and then seek out our first cup of Guatemalan coffee. In the corner of the square, a coffee shop, empty apart from a couple of giggly teenage girls in smart school uniforms. The coffee is as we take it, strong and sweet.

There is little time to enjoy the street scenes. I am a man on a mission, on the lookout for that new shirt. In the adjacent Calle Cinco Norte, a whole row of clothing stores. I am drawn to one and select a shirt of ethnic design. It seemed right at the time but I have to confess out of place once I returned home, and has subsequently rarely seen the light of day.

We have hired a local guide to show us around the city, so it is something of a surprise the following morning to be met by Jane; British and with a distinct Brummie accent. She is married to a Guatemalan and proves well versed in local history.

We had both been inexplicably woken from a deep sleep following the tiring journey from London at about 5 am that morning. Now from the roof of the Capuchinas Convent, we are blessed with the sight of Mount Fuego actively expelling large amounts of smoke and fire. It is a rare sight for the locals, as the mountain peak it seems is almost always shrouded by cloud. We enquire of Jane the level of volcanic activity and she replies that here on the San Andreas Fault Line, it is common. In fact, only this morning, tremors were felt in the city. A ready explanation for our early-morning awakening.

After a morning walking tour of the old city, Jane leaves us at the Serrano restaurant where I am seated on a chair with a plaque commemorating a previous luncheon guest, President Bill Clinton. Later, replete from a fine meal, we return to the hotel to be reunited with our baggage, much to Rosie's relief.

Next morning, we are on the move again, travelling further south and west towards Lake Atitlan.

As the prow of the boat cuts through the increasingly choppy waters of the lake, I am feeling just a little nauseous. To distract myself from the unpleasant prospect of vomiting over the side, I decide it is time for quiet reflection. The most interesting days when travelling are usually the ones that start with little promise and a low level of expectation. This has been such a day. The morning had been grey and the journey uneventful as we had been driven down from Antigua. As we arrived at Lake Atitlan in late morning, occasional shafts of sunlight appeared through broken cloud, and across the lake to the south we were aware of the ubiquitous and brooding presence of volcanoes. Here, from left to right, Atitlan, Toliman and San Pedro.

Now to the rhythmic chug of the outboard motor in the background, a little time to try and take in events and, in particular, Dolores' story. We had been first introduced that morning in the hotel lobby. We had just checked in when we were approached by this small native lady who introduced herself as our guide. This is Dolores and she informs us that as soon as we are ready, we will leave by boat to cross the lake to a small town on the far bank called Santiago Atitlan. Dolores says to take our time, but we have a sense that the real message is, 'Hurry, we are behind schedule.' We respond by depositing our bags unopened in our room and soon we are on our way.

By now, the skies are clearing and it is a pleasant trip across the lake. Dolores seems a little detached and barely engaged, even though Rosie in inimitable fashion seeks to converse with her with a compliment about her dress, the multi-coloured skirt and white embroidered blouse traditional to this area. At the far side of the lake, we climb from the boat onto a pathway up a steep cliff, eventually emerging breathless in front of a small hotel where Dolores says we are to take lunch. The conversation continues to feel a little stilted, but over lunch, Dolores points out a grey-haired man in the corner of the restaurant dining with a local family. She says he is Father Tom, once the parish priest, who has returned to the village from his home in the United States to take a holiday here to renew old acquaintances.

After this rather pedestrian start to our visit to Santiago Atitlan, things begin to move on at some pace. Lunch over, Dolores leads us onto the road that passes by the hotel, and miraculously, within seconds, a tuk-tuk, a vehicle we are accustomed to seeing in the Far East but not here in Central America, draws up and we are ushered aboard, even though the initiated will appreciate these tiny three-wheeled motorcycle taxis are designed to take, at best, two passengers.

It is a mercifully short journey to the edge of the town. Like most experiences of this nature, one is taken with the moment and it is only later with time and the wonders of the internet that it is possible to research and understand the events that followed. On this day, our journey takes only a few minutes before our driver pulls off the road and we alight, to be led by Dolores up a short uneven path to the doorway of a small hut. Dolores ushers us inside and here we are introduced to Maximon.

Maximon is dressed in a suit and wears a tie, on his head a trilby hat. He has sharp features and is puffing away on a cigarette. We take a seat on a pile of cushions and begin to absorb the scene. In the hut, there are already four other people. One sits in front of Maximon and between puffs on his own cigarette addresses him frequently, referring to some notes scribbled on a scrap of paper held in his hand. From his dress, it is impossible to distinguish this man from the others sat in more peripheral positions around the hut. They appear to be, and Dolores later confirms, local villagers. The hut is decorated with coloured streamers and is cluttered with a wide array of items of food, packets of cigarettes, beads and other trinkets. The hut is filled not only with cigarette smoke but a sweet and frankly unfamiliar and to our untutored nostrils not particularly pleasant smell.

Later, a couple of young backpackers arrive and present Maximon with some small gifts; a cigarette and some sweets. We take this interlude as an opportunity to leave. Not to escape the acrid smell but rather to ask more about Maximon. Why was he here and what ceremony have we witnessed? Outside, Dolores begins to respond to our questions and explain the significance of Maximon, and it is perhaps at this point when our interest has been aroused that her attitude towards us begins to change.

The answer to the first question is not at all clear-cut. Dolores describes him as a figure from Mayan legend, although whether he is for good or bad is not easy to establish. However, the explanation is not entirely satisfactory, given Maximon is dressed in Western clothes. Somewhere there must have been a crossover with Catholicism, and my thoughts on the subject are reinforced when I later discover that in some villages he is called Saint Simon. His bad habits, smoking and accepting gifts, also it seems accurately reflect a darker side, as many think that his deity has developed from Maam, the ancient Mayan god of the underworld. On the second question of why Maximon is residing in this hut at this time, it appears that he has a rota and families vie to have him resident in their house for a year before he moves on with great ceremony to another house within the village.

We had unwittingly encountered Maximon two days earlier whilst in Antigua, where we had entered an enormous bazaar to find ourselves surrounded by carved figures and masks in various forms that we could now recognise as Maximon. Our man is of course an effigy.

As to what was going on in the hut. This was to have some significance as our day unfolded. Dolores explained that the man addressing Maximon, although not particularly distinguishable from any other villager, was actually the local shaman, or witchdoctor. He was not, as we thought, pleading on his own behalf with this "god" figure but making representations for a fellow villager encountering marital problems.

There are many more questions to ask as Dolores shepherds us back towards the road, and minutes later, she waves down another tuk-tuk heading from the direction of town. It is being driven by a youth of seventeen or eighteen, and his friend, another youth of similar age, sits in the passenger seat. An animated discussion in the local dialect ensues and eventually, it seems with some reluctance, the young man agrees to turn around and head back to town with us on board. A tuk-tuk with three passengers is an unlikely load, but before we clamber on board, the second youth, hedgehog-like, shrinks himself into a ball-like shape on the tiny shelf behind the passenger seat, the three of us on a seat designed for two small oriental people and off we set, a tuk-tuk with five on board!

The town Santiago Atitlan proves to be a deprived place. Unmade roads and rows of small adobe brick houses. In the plaza, or town centre, in our experience an often very attractive part of even the poorest Latin American town, there is little of note. Even the church with its broken and uneven steps looks shabby. This nevertheless is our next destination. Dolores leads the way. On entering, we are immediately struck by the impression that this is not a typical Catholic church. In the alcoves along each side of the interior are highly decorated effigies. It is an interesting mix of representations of Catholic saints and other figures with a remarkable resemblance to Maximon. Dolores explains that this parish was presided over by an American priest who rather than compete with local beliefs embraced the indigenous deities into the church. This priest was Stanley Rother, so even more interesting is a large brass plaque in Spanish apparently dedicated to him that we read in some haste. Next to this, a stone shrine; this one in English and Spanish is dedicated to the Martyrs of Atitlan.

We begin to piece together the story. Father Stanley was here for many years through the 1970s. His approach of integrating rather than rejecting these traditional ideas of worship is not universally accepted by many locals, who have foresworn such rituals to fully embrace Catholicism and so, popular with many of his parishioners, he also had his enemies. The civil war is raging and Santiago Atitlan becomes a garrison town for the Army. Local citizens begin to disappear and Father Stanley becomes the spokesman of the poor and oppressed. In 1981, after thirteen years in Guatemala, Stanley is identified as being on a hit list for assassination and is recalled by his bishop to the United States. Nevertheless, within a few weeks, he decides to return to his parish, and only weeks later in his rectory, he is beaten and then shot dead by three assailants.

It is an interesting story but soon Dolores begins to relate her own involvement. She talks of a mysterious young native American. He arrives in the village to be met by an old man who tells him, much to his surprise, that he has been awaiting his arrival. The old man is the much-revered local shaman. The young man falls under the influence of the old man, who over time teaches him the secret powers of healing that he possesses. At the very culmination of the learning process to become a shaman, the young man falls ill, probably due to a narcotic-induced trance. The young American has taken a room in the house next to where Dolores, a teenage girl, lives, and during his sickness, she takes him food and tends to him. They fall in love and marry.

We leave the church and Dolores asks if we would like to visit her family home. We agree and as we stroll through the streets of Santiago Atitlan, she reveals more of her story. As a foreigner, her husband, like Father Stanley, comes to the attention of the military and with Dolores heavily pregnant with their first child, they decide they must leave. A plan of escape is hatched and at dead of night her husband, Martin, leaves and aided by friends is taken to a safe house in Antigua. Dolores follows and eventually, narrowly avoiding arrest, they escape to the United States. Here, Dolores gives birth to her first child, a son, and another child follows. In due course, the marriage breaks down and Dolores returns alone here to her home village, leaving her husband and sons in the US.

A particularly large wave slaps the side of the boat and I look up. The shoreline, perhaps now only a quarter of a mile away, is increasingly shrouded from view by low cloud and the air is full of a fine drizzle. The engine rhythm changes, a definite time gap between each phut and then with one final gasp, it expires. We are drifting. The young helmsman reassuringly doesn't seem panicked by this development. I look across to

Rosie. 'Bloody marvellous, I had an inkling this would happen,' I shout through the cries of the wind, now whipping up white horses on the crest of the waves. Worst-case scenarios flood my mind but as the young man tries to restart the engine, perhaps we need to take strength from his apparent lack of concern. The engine springs briefly into life before dying once again. Then I realise there is a second motor. The cord is pulled and the engine reluctantly responds with a sickly sound. It beats exceeding slow, but there is life, and slowly, slowly, me hanging on to every slow and reluctant chug, we move forward inexorably towards our safe harbour.

Months later, I finally put in place the last piece in the jigsaw. After the visit to her parents' house, Dolores escorted us to the harbour at Santiago Atitlan where our small boat was waiting to take us back across the lake. As we said our goodbyes, Rosie told Dolores that her story was amazing and that as I am a writer, she may appear in this book. Then before finally bidding us farewell, almost in passing, Dolores said, 'My ex-husband has also written a book. It is called *Secrets of the Talking Jaguar* and contains much of what I have told you.'

We have returned home and I have now read the book by Martin Prechtel, and things at last make sense. Although the book tells little of how Martin and his family escaped to the States, it is nonetheless fascinating. It is his story of how he, a half-American Indian, arrives as a young man and a stranger in Atitlan to be welcomed by the local witch doctor, Chiviliu, who over many years teaches him the amazing ways and skills handed down over generations that will enable him to become the village shaman when the old man eventually dies. Skills that bring man and nature together in quite staggering ways.

It is the following morning and in the hotel lobby we meet up with Daniel, a young Mayan guide who is going to take us over the mountains to see the colourful and famous market in the small town of Chichicastenango. The journey on narrow winding mountain roads is to say the least "hairy", thanks mainly to the former American school buses that hurtle past in both directions on even the narrowest and steepest parts of the road. These buses, many still in their traditional yellow livery, others beautifully decorated in lurid colours in the fashion found throughout Central America, all have one thing in common: they are driven by men with a death wish. Daniel says they are called "chicken buses", as it is the habit of locals to bring on board live chickens to take to market. He confirms, no surprise here, a high rate of accidents and deaths but tells us that this is in part a consequence of the system under which local drivers rent the vehicles, and their ability to pay the rent and earn themselves a reasonable income is determined exclusively by how many trips they can make in a day.

The twice-weekly market in Chichi has become something of a Mecca for tourists, although they remain heavily outnumbered by the locals and for good reason. This is probably the largest, noisiest, most colourful and vibrant native market in the region, if not the whole of Latin America. We are immediately into the throng, but standing head and shoulders amongst the majority of locals with their tiny stature, this provides us a view of the sheer numbers of people gathered in this one small town. The scene is not only colourful with the traditional costumes of peoples from different regions of the country but is an attack on all the senses with the smells and noise. I am startled by a loud bang feet away, which Daniel explains is a *bombas,* or firecracker, that the local people like to fire off through the day, to what purpose I am not sure.

We make our way through the masses to the steps of Iglesia St Tomas. This, the focal place in village life, is also the centre of commercial activity, with literally dozens of flower sellers conducting their business in front of the doors to the church. Here, a strong smell of incense in the air. Despite the initial impression of mayhem, it soon becomes apparent that there is an underlying sense of order here, developed over decades. Like the flower sellers on the steps of the church, there are parts of the market for fruit and vegetable sellers, another area for selling pigs and chickens, alive rather than dead, and an area where you will find sellers of traditional medicines and herbs. There is a section for farm implements and tools, another bread, here candles, there pottery. The list goes on. You name it, you will find a row of stalls selling that product. Daniel points out the dresses, or *traje,* worn by the women. To our eyes, they are traditional and colourful; to the well informed, the region or even the village where the women have come from can be identified. Often from distant parts of the country.

Leading us through the throng, Daniel wants to show us something that he thinks is special and will be of interest. We arrive at the cemetery. Not an obvious tourist spot, but his reasoning soon becomes apparent. The tombstones, crosses and sarcophaguses containing the dead are colourfully painted, apparently in the favourite colours of the late lamented therein. Daniel explains the local practice that each year on All Saints' Day the villagers visit the cemetery to clean up and repaint, ensuring this remains a spectacle worth seeing, if a little macabre. On that day, the villagers themselves dress up in their most colourful clothes, and when their work is complete, they adorn the graves with flowers, say prayers for the dead relatives and then have a picnic in the graveyard.

The following day we are back on the road, initially to Guatemala City and from there a short flight north to Flores. En route, our driver stops at a roadhouse for refreshments and a comfort stop. Typical of most such establishments, the fare is poor and overpriced. The place is nearly empty but for a few locals supping bowls of a seemingly popular but sickly-looking local stew. That is until a bus draws up outside and empties its occupants. The bus is adorned with slogans, the largest of which is *Jesus saves*. No one has scrawled any addition, but it reminds me of the famous graffiti from home where some wag had added, *but Greaves scores from the rebound*. A contemporary version of which would doubtless attribute the goalscoring to Kane.

The bus passengers come in and purchase some items. Noticeably avoiding local delicacies, almost all choose a Cola and packets of potato chips (or what we call crisps). This is a group of American Evangelical Christians conducting missionary work. In the heartland of active Catholicism, this seems a little odd, but these missionary buses are by no means an unusual sight throughout Central America. It is a mixed group, predominantly twenty- or thirty-somethings but also some older adults and surprisingly school-age youngsters, clearly part of family groups.

Having decided not to include Guatemala City in our itinerary, passing through the outskirts again, heading for the airport, this seems a wholly justified decision, particularly as our Guatemala experience has been essentially positive.

Although the flight to Flores takes barely an hour, ours is a late-afternoon arrival and the sun is already low on the horizon, yet the first impression exiting the aircraft door is of a stifling heat quite unlike anything previously encountered on this trip.

Flores is situated on the southern shore of Lake Peten Itza, but the purpose of our journey here lies on the northern bank of the lake: the remains of the ancient Mayan city of Tikal.

When travelling, it is a moot point whether or not to use the services of a local guide. We are not purists in this regard and should you choose to call us tourists rather than travellers so be it, but invariably the guide will ensure that when time-constrained, you do not miss the essentials. Equally, we travel always believing that you cannot see everything.

Guides come in all shapes and sizes, with their own personal interests and prejudices. Eric is typical of this unpredictability. We are visiting perhaps the greatest of all the Mayan sites, Tikal. Whereas at Quirigua, Armando had whetted our appetite with stories of Mayan history and mythology, Eric, with delightful good humour, wants to reveal the secrets of the Tikal natural history, flora and fauna.

It is an hour or so's drive around the lake, and by the time we reach our hotel it is dark, and we have an early start the following morning. However, the drive is long enough for us to find out a little about this our latest guide. Our first impression is of a pure blood Mayan, short, stocky and very dark-skinned, so it is some surprise when he introduces himself as Enrique Garcia, about as common a Spanish name as you are likely to come across. Enrique says to call him Eric, his Anglicised name, a practice familiar with guides around the world.

As you travel, you are bound to meet other travellers, some interesting, some less so. That evening in the hotel, we fall into conversation with Victor. As with most Americans, he introduces himself by name and home town. He is from North Judson, Indiana. This really must be small-town America. Victor runs a hardware store and is venturing outside of the US for the first time and is oddly, given all the places in the world, on a whistle-stop tour of Central America, but that said, he has a strange fascination with Britain and spends the evening quizzing us about good old Blighty. To give you just a flavour, his questions include: What is tombola, what are trainspotters, what is Blackpool? Not wanting to be judgemental, but we often come across Victors and say to each other, 'They really shouldn't let them loose on the world,' but Victor is charming and his naivete is somehow beguiling. We hope that someday he made it to our sceptred isle.

Our early start next morning is rewarded and we find ourselves amongst just a handful of visitors at the entrance to the ancient Mayan city of Tikal, although in fairness visitor numbers here are miniscule in comparison with other famous historical sites in Latin America such as Machu Picchu. Eric points out a murky pool close to the entrance gate with a *Mind the Alligators* sign, but is then on his hands and knees, closely inspecting a tiny flower. Almost as an afterthought, he suggests we might like to climb Pyramid 1 followed by Pyramid 4. Eric points out the relevant edifices and says he will meet us in two hours. This is certainly a new take on the role of guide, and we suspect that he will spend the free time we have afforded him engaged in further close inspection of the local flora.

Tikal was the power centre of Mayan civilisation in the Classic period around AD 250 under the leadership of Great Jaguar Paw and his general, Smoking Frog. Pyramid 1, also known as the Temple of Giant Jaguar, is in fact the tomb of a later great leader of Tikal named Lord Chocolate and dates from around AD 730. We embark upon our quest with some enthusiasm but Eric has set us a tough task. By now, the sun is higher in the clear morning sky, and temperature and humidity have shot up to uncomfortable levels.

As we climb Temple 4, improbably the only other visitors we meet are an English couple; a man in his fifties and his twenty-something daughter, who volunteers to take our photograph, us all smiles and dripping in sweat.

Finally, we reach the pinnacle of the pyramid and look across the site. Above the treeline and looking down, only now do we realise this is the tallest structure. Despite the dense surrounding forest, many buildings are evident almost as far as the eye can see in what is a huge complex. Some 3,000 structures have been identified in an area covering more than 6 square miles. In its heyday, it must have been a truly impressive sight. Even today, 1,000 years since it was abandoned, we are still in awe. A suitable climax to our visit to Guatemala.

Twelve

Belize and Honduras:
More of the Mayans

Belize – the former British colony of British Honduras achieved independence in 1981. A diverse population of only a third of a million. The only English-speaking country in Central America, although most locals speak Creole, combining English, Spanish and native languages.

Honduras – a Spanish-speaking country of 10 million people, almost all of whom are mestizo (mixed race European/indigenous). One of the poorest countries in the Americas. An uneasy relationship with its neighbour El Salvador led to the so-called "football war" in 1969.

Our fascination for the Maya continues. Our trip to Guatemala offered us a far greater insight into Mayan culture and with this new-found knowledge, today we are on the Yucatan Peninsula in Mexico. The whole coastline dotted with resorts has become a magnet for tourists, but rather than seek out the beach, we head for one of the lesser-known Mayan sites at a place called Uxmal. As I recalled earlier, our first Mayan encounter had come many years before, close to here at Chichén Itzá, but then we had no concept of Mayan civilisation.

We make our way from the town of Progreso across a flat limestone plain before coming to Uxmal, set in low hills, some two hours' drive. In contrast to Chichén Itzá, the site is relatively small as is the number of visitors, but it is of significant enough size to warrant UNESCO World Heritage status. As we enter the site, we are confronted by the Magician's Pyramid. Most Mayan sites have the buildings bearing fanciful names given by the Spanish colonialists, although the purpose of the buildings is usually the subject of conjecture. The purpose of the pyramid however is in no doubt, as it is clearly a burial mound. Comparable in size to the Pyramids of Giza in Egypt and not dissimilar in appearance.

The Mayans occupied this site in the period from the seventh to tenth centuries AD. Archaeologists are convinced that the structure evident today comprises up to five buildings constructed one upon another. Local myth says that it was the work of a dwarf over the course of one night, but in practice it would have taken hundreds of years, following the Mayan custom of adding to such shrines every fifty-two years.

Beyond the pyramid is the Nunnery Quadrangle, so-called because it reminded the Spanish of a building from their own culture: a convent. More recent archaeological research suggests that it may have housed a school for scholars studying mathematics and astronomy. In the corner of the site, an enormous iguana attracts much attention, but it is a sideshow for what is still a splendid example of an architecture that demonstrates the sophistication of the Mayans. Such constructions would not have been possible without the ability to measure. We know they could count using a system of dots and dashes to base 20. They also studied astronomy, enabling them to have a calendar of 365 days, albeit with eighteen months of twenty days.

We climb to the back of the site onto the roof of the Governor's Palace, possibly an accurate description, from where one gets a magnificent panoramic view of the whole city. A lesser-known UNESCO World Heritage site but one worthy of the accolade.

Two days after leaving Mexico and we have made our way down the coast of Central America and are in Belize, visiting a small and less significant Mayan ruin at the mildly discouragingly named Cahel Pech, or "place of ticks". Mercifully, we are not to personally encounter any of the little critters on this occasion.

The site is located some two hours' drive from Belize City at the end of a bumpy road, surrounded by mangrove swamps and close to the small town of San Ignacio.

Pedro is our local guide and his personal story brings to life what we are seeing as we stand here viewing what has been named the Courtyard, the main excavated area of a still only partially unearthed Mayan settlement:

'We were about twelve or thirteen at the time, Carlos, Juan, Enrique and myself. We had decided the day before we would 'bunk off' school, so we made our way through the town as usual, as if we were heading for school, but then took a path towards the edge of the town and into the jungle beyond. The town of San Ignacio was of course much smaller then, and beyond the last house, the jungle started almost immediately, so we were out of sight of prying eyes, parents or teachers. We were so excited and in high spirits as we climbed up to here on to what we now call the Plaza. Then the undergrowth was thick, but of course there were paths, as men from the town came up here hunting.

After an hour or so, we stopped to rest. Carlos wandered off and minutes later we heard a strangled cry from the direction that he had disappeared. We rushed over, but Carlos was nowhere to be seen. Only then did we realise that the sounds were coming from beneath our feet. Carlos had fallen into a deep hole. At first, we three fell about laughing, until we realised Carlos was in some distress. We had a box of matches and used several in unsuccessful attempts to peer into the abyss to see our friend. He was naturally afraid but assured us that he was unhurt. Nevertheless, despite his efforts, he was unable to climb from his prison in the ground. We decided that a better form of illumination was to set fire to a dry tree branch. In hindsight, a dangerous but in the event successful strategy, as when we shone it down into the hole, we could make out our friend perhaps three or four metres below, standing amongst a lot of debris on the floor. We looked around and eventually we decided to pull some vines from around a large nearby tree. This was our rope and it proved to be long enough and strong enough. We lowered the vine into the hole and were able to pull poor Carlos back up to ground level. This was turning out to be more of an adventure than we had anticipated.

We decided it was time to take some lunch and clean ourselves off. We came across a small stream and rested. Whilst in his hole in the ground, Carlos had the presence of mind to stuff some things into his pockets before his rescue and now he spread them out on the riverbank as we opened our school bags to take out the bits of food we had secreted before leaving home that morning. We were of course in high spirits and our laughter must have attracted a hunter, because to our amazement, a figure emerged from the forest. He was friendly enough and seeing our booty strewn along the ground picked up one particular item and asked us if he could have it. Only later did we discover it was a jade bracelet. Fortunately, we refused and he went on his way.

Eventually, when we judged it must be about the time that we should have been leaving school, we made our way back to town, anticipating returning to our homes as if we had been at school as usual. Just as we had returned to the safety of the town, we turned a corner to be met by the figure of a policeman standing by his vehicle. It was as though he had been expecting us. We were too scared to run and frankly unprepared to try and talk ourselves out of trouble, so we told him our story, reluctantly handing over the bits and pieces Carlos had retrieved from the hole.

Next morning, we made our way to school expecting to receive our punishment and sure enough at the end of our first lesson we were sent to the headmaster's office. He leads us outside to where there is the police Land Rover, our policeman from the previous day and two strangers, *jipatos*, or white men, smartly dressed in tropical suits. They offer us sweets and Cola and ask us to tell them the story of our adventure into the forest. When we have related our story, they ask us to lead them to the place where Carlos had fallen the previous day. Once this was over, we were returned home and nothing more was said, no retribution, no punishment. Much later, of course, I am able to make sense of the whole thing. The two men are archaeologists from an American university and what we have stumbled upon is a major find of Mayan burial artefacts. Gradually, over the intervening years, this site has been excavated to what you can see today, not one of the most important but nevertheless a significant part of our Mayan heritage.'

Pedro has related his story as he has surely done hundreds of times, but paradoxically, his life has remained very much influenced by that one day in childhood.

Pedro spent ten years as a young man working for the British Army and tells us about a little-known skirmish here in the late 1980s, when neighbouring Guatemala was sufficiently emboldened to consider invading Belize. Pedro acted in a liaison role, assisting SAS operations in the border region, and recalled the presence of the aircraft carrier *HMS Ark Royal* and its squadron of Harrier jets that in a matter of days deterred the Guatemalans from pursuing their claims on Belize militarily.

Pedro tells us that his brother Fernando Cruz is a noted and controversial artist who has lived and exhibited in the UK, but more interestingly, when he leads us to the small onsite Museum and Visitor Centre, we discover that Pedro is quite an accomplished artist himself. His murals adorn the walls of the building.

Although the whereabouts of a Mayan site at Cahel Pech have been known since the 1930s, excavations have only been undertaken since the 1950s and then in a modest and dilatory manner, and pillaging of the site has taken place, undoubtedly leading to the removal of many valuable and possibly significant historical artefacts. With this in mind, although the site was relatively unimpressive in comparison with, say, Tikal, it was interesting to hear Pedro's story of his first encounter with a place that now provides his "bread and butter" income.

Another day, another place, and we are headed for the last of the great centres of Mayan civilisation that we have yet to visit: Copan. With a history extending over 2,000 years, this is truly a major historical site, its location in the west of Honduras close to its border with Guatemala. We have travelled for over four hours by road from the port town of Puerto Cortes, passing through the large city of San Pedro de Sula, before climbing some 1,000 metres to the suitably named modern town of Las Ruinas.

Saul is a music teacher, jazz guitarist and part-time guide. The deeply furrowed lines on his face testimony to many long nights in night clubs throughout Central America. He tells us he was classically trained as a musician in El Salvador, but as civil unrest spread across the region in the '80s, he returned here to his native Honduras. Saul is the latest of our "character" guides of Mayan sites.

In truth, Copan is a little disappointing. Unlike other Mayan sites that have lain undisturbed in the jungle for centuries, Copan was known to even the earliest Spanish colonists. As a consequence, the site has been periodically stripped of valued artefacts by both local inhabitants and visiting archaeologists over the intervening centuries. Yet this was one of, if not *the* greatest, Mayan city.

It is believed that a Mayan warrior king, Shining Quetzal Macaw, travelling south with his army in the fifth century AD, established Copan, and over the ensuing four centuries, it was to be a dominant force within the lands under Mayan influence.

Unlike that of the Incas, the Mayan empire was not united under one emperor/god but consisted of a number of autonomous city states competing, trading and often warring. Copan grew into one of the strongest, and the dynasty begun in the fifth century went through sixteen kings and held sway over much of the surrounding area, not least over the smaller city of Quirigua, a vassal state constantly having to pay homage to the dominant Copan through the imposition of taxes. Ultimately, this uneven relationship was to contribute to the downfall of Copan, although in the intervening centuries, it became larger and grander, pursuing the Mayan practice of building bigger and better structures on top of existing temples and pyramids.

You will recall our earlier visit to Quirigua, and now in Copan we have come full circle in relating how the smaller and less significant city state influenced the ultimate downfall of the latter. By AD 738, Quirigua, weary of its subservience to Copan, managed a military success, ensnaring and then executing the Copan king, Eighteen Rabbit. Although this single act did not in itself signal the end of Copan, with the demise of this powerful and influential leader it gradually went into decline. Poor land management leading to insufficient food production to sustain a growing urban population, malnutrition and disease were becoming endemic to Mayan civilisation, and by AD 822, Copan was abandoned. The remaining population dispersed, some moving to the more prosperous north, others returning to the countryside and to subsistence farming.

The jungle reclaimed Copan, helped in part by natural disasters, like earthquakes, although its existence remained known to local people and with the arrival of Europeans, it is mentioned in dispatches from Diego Garcia del Palacio to the king of Spain in 1576. However, it was only after an expedition by American explorer John Lloyd Stephens in 1838 that the secrets of Copan began to be uncovered by archaeologists. Since then, Copan has become the best known and most researched of all the great Mayan cities.

So what did we find on our brief visit? Firstly, the site is extensive, some 10 square miles. Secondly, unlike Tikal, no huge pyramid structures remain, rather many stelae, inscribed stones relating the story of the ancient city. Fascinating to the archaeologist but less impressive to the casual visitor.

Centrepiece of the site and now carefully protected from the elements by a canopy structure is a giant petroglyph staircase. Presumed to tell the whole story of Copan and its sixteen kings, it was in such a state of disrepair when first discovered by nineteenth-century archaeologists that in their ignorance, attempts to reassemble the structure were both crude and misguided, such that today much of its story remains untold and incomprehensible.

Only snapshots, but from that brief insight at Quirigua to our Copan visit, we are beginning to have at least some elementary understanding of that first millennium AD civilisation and the history, beliefs and superstitions that still pervade the Mayan culture that continues to exist up until this day.

Finally, before ending this chapter on the Mayans, as an avid sports buff I should mention the ball game. The Greeks had running and throwing competitions, the Romans gladiatorial contests and chariot races, so sport is by no means a modern concept, but the Mayans devised what was probably the first sport to use a court.

The ball game in some form was popular throughout the Mayan world, and courts have been discovered at pretty well all the sites we visited. The scoring system appears a little uncertain and the rules varied between cities, but broadly speaking, the game was played out like this. A court in the shape of a capital "I". Two teams. Set high on a wall to one side of the court, a stone ring. Purpose of the game: to manipulate a large rubber ball through the hoop without it touching the ground. Use of head or hands was not permitted, only knees, elbows and hips, which, we know from hieroglyphs that have survived, were heavily padded. Passing the ball through the stone hoop must have been fiendishly difficult, so one can conclude that a 0-0 draw was common. The consequences of losing could, it seems, be dire. Not being dropped for the next match, the fate befalling the modern sportsman, but being ritually sacrificed to the gods.

Thirteen

Nicaragua: Face-to-face with a Filibuster

Nicaragua: Population 6 million. Spanish speaking. Best known for the civil war between the Sandinistas and American-backed Contras in the years following the overthrow of the Somoza family, who ruled the country from 1934 until 1979.

We have checked into our hotel in Granada, Nicaragua. My eyesight is not what it once was, so lying on the enormous wooden-framed double bedstead, supported by two bolsters and writing my notes, I can barely see my own writing. The room is large and imposing with a high ceiling from which is suspended a single 60 watt bulb. The room is probably the best the hotel can offer, but it is located immediately over the hotel entrance and facing the Calle La Calzada, the city's busiest thoroughfare. In the absence of air conditioning, the shuttered window is wide open and even now, still only late afternoon, the noise from the street below cuts through the thick humid air. We are too tired to bother, but tomorrow we will ask to be moved to a quieter room at the rear of the building's inner courtyard.

Apart from the incessant rhythm of marimba music, Rosie reports news from a vantage point looking out from the window. She calls me across to view some street theatre below. The troupe comprises a whirling cloaked figure fully 3 metres high, a small figure with a huge head, a conductor dressed in white shirt, bow tie and tails, and a drummer. The "tall" person is elaborately dressed in a beautiful orange and red dress and has a wig of long red hair. We are watching *La Gigantona,* a centuries-old play in which the supposedly "stupid" mestizos (mixed race) people, represented by the smaller figure, poke fun at their "superior" Spanish masters. Or in this case, mistresses, as the tall figure represents a Spanish lady. It is going to be a long, hot night.

We had arrived mid-afternoon in Nicaragua at Managua Airport to be met by our guide, Harry. Nicaragua is a relatively poor country with an underdeveloped tourist industry so it should have come as no surprise that outside the airport, Harry piled our bags into the back of his pick-up truck and with the three of us sitting abreast up front, we set off for the journey down here to Granada. Harry dropped us off at the hotel, but before leaving us to enjoy the evening exploring the city, he sternly warned us not to walk in the lower part of the Calle la Calzada near the lake after dark.

With dusk approaching, we set out to make an initial recce of the city, heading firstly down towards the lake. The street is one of stylish Spanish colonial architecture with many small shops and restaurants. We take a few photographs and soak up the atmosphere. A few blocks beyond the Iglesia Guadalupe, even now some dodgy-looking people on the street, and feeling uncomfortable after Harry's warning, we turn sharp left and head back towards the city centre on the Calle el Arsenal. In gathering gloom, we enter the Parque Central, the main city square. My guidebook implies a vibrant part of the city and a good place to get a feel for what makes this city tick. However, this evening, apart from a couple of stalls selling local delicacies and a bunch of kids kicking a football, the square is remarkably quiet. Having been in Antigua, Guatemala only a few days before, it has, in comparison, little to offer and is frankly untidy and unattractive. Most of the plaza is unpaved and a small garden area is poorly maintained. In one corner the town hall and at the top of the Calle la Calzada the cathedral, built in the neo-classical style and the only place showing signs of any significant activity, with people coming and going to and from evening mass. The only other building of architectural note within the square is the Bishop's Palace, across the street from the cathedral.

Back at the hotel, we dine early and alone in the restaurant, no doubt more used to customers who eat late Spanish-style, before retiring to our room. It has been another long and weary day in debilitating heat and humidity.

The street hubbub quietened surprisingly early and with the reassuring whir of the large propeller fan high in the ceiling, aided by the fatigue of the long day's travel, we sleep reasonably well.

Next morning, after breakfast, we are shown to a smaller and even darker room at the rear of the property facing out towards a fountain, the centrepiece of a pleasant courtyard garden. The receptionist seems surprised when we accept this alternative accommodation for the remainder of our stay.

Harry arrives soon after and we set off to explore as much of the area as possible, given we are to remain in Nicaragua for only four days. First, we are to visit Volcan Mombacho. Once out of the city, we soon pick up a gravel track and begin to climb and shortly on the lower slopes of the mountain Harry parks the pick-up. We have told him we enjoy a good coffee and he announces that, 'You are going to visit a small family-run coffee plantation and I guarantee you will love their coffee.' The methods employed are basic: from the verandah of the family hacienda, we look down to see the coffee beans spread around the roof of a low adjacent building where they are drying in the hot sun. The product, however, as Harry has promised, is excellent, and sufficiently pumped with a rapid caffeine rush, we transfer to the back of an old truck for the climb the rest of the way to the mountaintop.

At the summit, we clamber out and begin a trek on the so-called "Crater Trail" through the rainforest. Soon we begin to learn the first of Harry's two great passions – nature. He has an infinite knowledge of the flora and fauna found here, and the only distraction from this fascinating insight is that dressed in shirt sleeves I am ill-equipped for the cold and dank atmosphere. We are quite literally walking in the cloud that shrouds the mountain. Eventually, we emerge into sunlight. In a matter of seconds, the temperature has gone up about 20 degrees and the views across Lake Nicaragua, the largest in Central America at over 8,000 square kilometres, are spectacular.

Then it is back to the city where we get to know about Harry's other passion – history. "Filibuster" appears frequently in his conversation and initially I am confused. I am familiar with the term in the context of delaying tactics in a legislature, but Harry keeps referring to the Filibuster William Walker. We clamber up a rickety wooden ladder, each rung precariously secured by a length of rope, and squeeze through a narrow trapdoor onto the roof of La Polvera Fortress at one end of the Calle Real. Despite the grand title, this building was a gunpowder store, a product that readily became unstable in the high humidity and too volatile to keep in the main fort situated outside of the city at a strategic point on the San Juan River. From the rooftop with views across the city, Harry explains that much of what we can see postdates 1857, when the city was burned down by William Walker and his men.

Thanks to Harry and a little bit of subsequent research, I can tell you something of filibustering and of William Walker in particular. By the middle of the nineteenth century, the Spanish had departed Latin America, leaving behind independent but largely ill-defined and chaotic states, whilst to the north the United States was belligerently seeking to expand its sphere of influence over its closest neighbours. Filibusters were in modern parlance mercenaries, often Americans, whose nefarious activities the US chose to turn a blind eye to when they coincided with the US expansionist policies. Not unlike the British and their attitude towards pirates in an earlier time.

Amongst these filibusters, William Walker stands out as a quite amazing larger-than-life figure, although paradoxically physically a man of small stature. Something of a child genius, he had completed his first degree by the age of fourteen, adding further academic achievements, degrees in law and medicine. He worked as a journalist travelling widely in the United States and Europe before embarking upon his first filibustering escapade, taking with him a small group of armed men across the US border into northern Mexico where he declared himself President of Sonora. He was still not thirty. He was eventually ousted by troops sent by the Mexican Government and returned to the US, where he was tried but acquitted. Within months, Walker had set his sights upon a new venture, this time in Nicaragua.

In the days before the construction of the Panama Canal, the land that is now Nicaragua was strategically important, providing the shortest land route connecting the Atlantic and Pacific and hence the main trade route between the Eastern seaboard of the United States and the flourishing West Coast states like California.

With this in mind, supported by a small group of mercenaries, Walker marched on Granada in October 1855, captured the city and declared himself President of Nicaragua. Walker however overstepped himself by making an enemy of Cornelius Vanderbilt, a US shipping tycoon who controlled much of the trade passing through Nicaragua. With neighbouring countries fearful of Walker's destabilising influence on the region, Vanderbilt was soon able to finance a counter-coup and Walker was unseated, but not before he and his men had fired the city.

To complete this tale, Walker was not done and planned his return to Nicaragua. However, before he could embark upon this new adventure, he was captured by the British Navy and turned over to the authorities in Honduras, where he met a premature end before a firing squad. At thirty-six years of age, his had been a short but eventful and colourful life.

By now, our stroll through the streets of Granada had brought us to Guadalupe Church. As Harry's story reached its conclusion, this was an entirely appropriate place to end. On the outside of the church, a small plaque on the wall records the fact that this was Walker's last bastion; he was holed up here for eighteen days before he finally fled the city.

The following day and another busy programme in prospect as Harry arrives at the hotel in the pick-up truck. We are to visit the city of Masaya, but first we will stop en route in San Juan de Oriente, one of Los Pueblos Blancos or "white towns" at the heart of local craftsmanship, dating back hundreds of years to pre-Colombian times.

As we have discovered in other parts of Latin America, towns or villages tend to specialise in a particular craft or commercial activity. In San Juan de Oriente, it is the production of hand-shaped and beautifully painted ceramics, plates, pots and other articles. Other nearby villages produce furniture, baskets, leatherware. For example, on our way, we take a detour to Diria, a village specialising in cut flowers, to view from an elevated position the crater lake Lago de Apoyo. From here, we continue through Diriomo, which produces a local confectionery called *cajetas*.

Many of the artisans in San Juan de Oriente sell their work through a Co-operative, but Harry takes us to a small family-run business. Here, we are shown the processes involved in making, baking and finally painting the ceramic pots, and finally a foray into the small shed, providing the opportunity for some retail therapy for visitors like ourselves just passing through.

Continuing our journey down to Masaya, we pass through yet another village. This one, called Catarina, specialises in an eclectic mix: houseplants and the manufacture of bamboo furniture.

Along the way we have been chatting to Harry, and the conversation turns to politics.

After many years in opposition, Daniel Ortega has once again become president. In the 1970s, one of the longest-lasting political dictatorships in Latin America drew to its close. Since 1936, the Somoza family had run the country. Attempted coups had been put down with ease and an iron fist. In the early '60s, a new opposition group, the Frente Sandinista de Liberacion Nacional (FSLN), now commonly known simply as the Sandinistas, was formed. Riven by factionalism and opposed by a repressive regime, it seemed destined to go the way of previous opponents of the Somozas but popular resentment against the regime was rising. The final straw was after a severe earthquake that decimated the capital, Managua, in 1972. Foreign donations to rebuild the country almost all found their way into Somoza bank accounts. In 1977, Ortega emerges as the outright leader of an increasingly popular Sandinista movement.

1978 saw the beginning of the end for Somoza. Paradoxically, the assassination of the Conservative Party activist and newspaper editor Pedro Joaquim Chamorro led to public protests which enabled the Sandinistas to markedly increase their military activities, supported by spontaneous uprisings in mainly indigenous towns and villages. In July 1979, Somoza fled to exile and a Committee of National Reconstruction was installed in power. Sadly, peace was short-lived and within months the CIA-backed Contras had begun an anti-FSLN civil war. The war continued throughout the '80s until a Peace Agreement reached in 1990. In subsequent democratic elections, Ortega lost to Violeta Chamorro, widow of the assassinated Conservative leader, and much to the surprise of many foreign observers, Ortega accepted the result and went into opposition.

To arrive in Nicaragua twenty years later to find Ortega back in power was something of a surprise. It was interesting to hear from Harry that in the old days he was a staunch Sandinista, and in his teens he had enrolled in the Sandinista Army. Knowing from Harry that he was forty-two, I made a quick mental calculation and deduced that he had enlisted in the middle of the Contra War sometime in the mid-'80s. I ask him whether he had seen much action. He laughs and replies that although the war had been bloody, he personally had spent too many long nights guarding installations like electricity substations from attack. Never to fire a shot in anger.

By the end of her period in office, Violeta Chamorro was unpopular. Perhaps the people expected too much from their leaders in the aftermath of dictatorship and civil war, so in 1996 they elected a Liberal President (a misnomer in our terms, as the Liberals were the traditional Party of privilege and of Somoza). The winner took 51% of the vote ahead of Ortega's 37%. Despite opinion polls to the contrary, Ortega failed again at the next election in 2001, but with a highly corrupt Liberal Party split at the following election in 2007, still polling only 38% and after twenty years out of office, Daniel Ortega once again became president of Nicaragua. As for Harry, he like many of his countrymen had clearly become disenchanted with his country's politics but described Ortega as still the best of a bad bunch. He shared my view that Ortega's resilience and commitment to democracy is quite amazing for a one-time Marxist revolutionary.

In Masaya, Harry leaves us on our own to spend some time strolling around the famous El Mercado Viejo, now known as the artisans' market. Here, an array of local crafts geared to the tourist trade. Pots, masks, leather goods, wooden toys, clothing, but rather too many T-shirts for our liking. Intriguing are the multi-coloured hammocks; unlike anything we have seen on our travels. The word hammock derives from the language of the Arawak, early inhabitants of the Caribbean, and they are common around this part of the world. The early European explorers were suitably impressed by the simplicity and practicality of the hammock, and they were adopted by the Royal Navy as early as 1590. The Nicaraguan version, once made of sisal, is now nylon or cotton but still amongst the finest and certainly most beautiful found in Central America. They are not however easily transported by travellers like ourselves and instead of making a purchase, we find ourselves in conversation with a stallholder selling a rather smaller item. Beautifully hand-painted birds' feathers. A little gentle bargaining and a purchase is made.

From Masaya, we head out of town towards the brooding presence of the Volcan Masaya. Ever-active, it has to be remembered that this is a country perpetually under threat of seismic activity. I first became aware of this in 1972 when the capital, Managua, was flattened by a devastating earthquake. Volcan Masaya kind of reinforces this with an endless stream of smoke that has been expelled from deep down in the earth on this spot not occasionally but daily, not for a few or even a hundred but for thousands of years.

As we drive up past the Visitor Centre to a small car park constructed on the rim of one of the volcano's three main craters, Harry offers another reminder of the Somoza regime. 'It was a favoured option of the security forces in those times to tie opponents of the regime below a helicopter and drop them into the crater, a sure way of destroying any evidence.'

At the parking place, a small notice advises spending only a short time here in the sulphurous smoke and then suggests that you park your vehicle so that it faces down the mountain in case of the need for a speedy evacuation. When we ask Harry what to do if the volcano blows, he replies, 'Run like hell.'

Another day and our short visit to Nicaragua is coming to an end. This morning, Harry is driving us down to the border with Costa Rica. We have become quite attached to our driver guide. He has revealed that after a turbulent marriage he divorced but has found happiness with a much younger woman, and they have a son on whom he clearly dotes. The road south has little of note, apart from a short break to take photographs of the island of Ometepe out in the middle of Lake Nicaragua.

As we approach the border, the volume of traffic increases. Thousands of locals cross the border daily in search of work in their more prosperous neighbouring country. Short of the frontier we stop at a roadside booth. Harry pays a dollar. The enterprising locals charge every vehicle that passes through their village. Good business, as this is the only road to the border.

Soon we come upon a seemingly endless line of parked trucks and soon we are in the midst of a chaotic scene, with literally hundreds of people milling around trying to get an exit stamp in their passports. Although not initially apparent, the people are queueing in front of a small building where behind protective iron grilles, officials are processing the formalities that will enable a departure into Costa Rica. Unfortunately, only two of the six work stations appear to have an "on duty" official. We join what seems to be the back of the line. Some sharp operators, no doubt in cahoots with the immigration officers, are touting for business. US$10 to get you to the front of the queue. Rosie is ready to oblige but somehow Harry has persuaded an official sat in his booth behind a sign that says *Closed* to process our papers and importantly to issue the tiny piece of paper confirming payment of our exit tax.

We have had to leave the bags in the open on the back of the pick-up truck, but Harry has paid someone to keep them safe, so we hurry back to the truck, drag them off and make our way through the melee to the fence marking the border. We say a genuinely fond farewell to Harry, before heaving our bags through the gate and across the no man's land into Costa Rica.

Costa Rica is immediately in stark contrast to what we have just left behind. A certain order and serenity reigns, with well-tended gardens in front of a plush modern customs and immigration building and a row of shops. In the adjacent car park, we locate our next guide, Pedro, and he takes us to meet our driver, Gustavo, seated in an air-conditioned mini-bus. We pile the bags in the rear compartment and board, ready for the off. Pedro asks for our passports to check that our entry stamp is in order as he tells us that we will encounter frequent road blocks along the way. It is then and only then, looking across towards the buildings, that we realise our formalities are not complete. There is an orderly but nevertheless still very long queue of people waiting to be processed through Costa Rican Immigration. The length of the queue suggests we are faced with another tedious wait until Gustavo, a man mountain of Welsh rugby forward proportions, grabs our passports and disappears towards the official buildings. He re-emerges barely five minutes later triumphantly waving our passports, which on closer inspection we see have been duly stamped with our entry visa. We ask no questions as we drive away from the border and into the Costa Rican countryside.

Fourteen

Panama: Two tribes

Panama: Strategically important, with the narrow isthmus between the Pacific and Atlantic leading to the eventual building of the Panama Canal to link the two oceans. Given its strategic position, a country long subject to United States control and influence. The USA eventually ceded direct management of the Canal in 1999. Population 4 million. Language – Spanish.

The floppy brimmed tropical hat periodically hoves into view, about 100 metres from the shore. Rosie is adding to her range of life skills, venturing out into the Pacific Ocean in a kayak. Being faint-hearted and unable to swim, I am content to watch from the safety of the beach. We are on Coiba, the main island of a little-known UNESCO World Heritage site that is part of Panama.

Having already traversed the Panama Canal three times aboard cruise ships without ever stepping ashore, we are hoping that this trip will provide opportunities to get to know the country of Panama a little better. Together with about forty other passengers, we have picked up a small American-owned expedition ship at Port Leona on Costa Rica's Pacific Coast, making our way down the shoreline and visiting two national parks before heading out into the ocean.

We have already spent a week in Costa Rica following our border crossing from Nicaragua, but to be frank there is little to report, it being a country with a highly developed tourist industry, and we pretty well confined ourselves to the normal tourist sights around the Arenal Volcano before taking a pleasant drive down to the coast and resting up for a couple of days in a comfortable beach hotel at Port Leona, before boarding our ship. The only thing of note was that Rosie seemed to have formed a fatal attraction for the local wildlife. On the first evening at dinner, like all meals at the hotel, taken alfresco, she suddenly screamed and sent her dinner plate flying. A passing raccoon had brushed past her legs. Then next morning whilst momentarily leaving the table to get something from the buffet, she had her breakfast stolen by a troupe of marauding monkeys.

Expedition cruising is a market segment very oriented towards our interest in finding the slightly more obscure destinations. They are usually on smaller ships with up to 200 passengers. They typically have a support team of specialists, a naturalist, ornithologist, geologist, historian and other experts and rarely tie up in a port but transport passengers ashore in zodiacs, heavy-duty rubber inflatables. This is one such trip.

During our first two days on board, we have visited two remote national parks along Costa Rica's Pacific coast: the Manuel Antonio and Corcovado.

On day one, the expedition team immediately test our metal with morning and afternoon hikes in the Manuel Antonio Park. We make our way out to Cathedral Point on a narrow path, with clear instructions not to grab foliage for fear of disturbing snakes. Neither of us is very partial to reptiles, so we are thankful that on these outings there are no snake sightings, only squirrel monkeys, sloths and *coatimundi*, a long-tailed member of the raccoon family quite commonplace in Central America.

Later, we visit botanical gardens owned and run by an American couple. After walking the grounds, admiring the plants and flowers, we are welcomed to the verandah of their house for drinks and refreshments. A fellow passenger casually asks us if we had seen the snake. Pointing to a nearby tree, where almost totally disguised is a vivid green, and we are told, extremely venomous snake.

Rosie slept badly that night after the close encounter with the snake, but the next morning, we find ourselves back in the jungle in the even more remote Corcovado NP, inaccessible by road. Two hours later, we emerge back onto the beach, incredibly hot in the high temperature and humidity and none the worse for wear. We have sighted toucans and scarlet macaws and no snakes. From the beach, the sight of whales circling our small ship anchored in the bay.

Now leaving Costa Rica behind, we have reached Coiba, the largest of thirty-eight islands in the archipelago and uninhabited but for the occupants of a Ranger Station and some unusual species of wildlife. Until relatively recently, it was also a penal colony, housing many more inhabitants than it does now. Since the closure of the prison, the island has been allowed to return to nature.

We wade ashore from our zodiac onto a pristine beach. There is a yacht anchored out in the bay and some, it has to be said "illegal", fishing boats are moored against an old dilapidated jetty. The rangers have obviously decided to turn a blind eye to the activities of their fellow countrymen. The first thing that catches my eye is a warning notice: *Beware of the crocodiles*. I hadn't seen that coming. The sign is next to a pool of dark green, foul-smelling and frankly uninviting water, so there is no temptation to inspect any closer.

The morning activity organised by the expedition team is kayaking. Rosie is up for this new experience but after a near-death drowning experience at the age of six, I am not attracted to any watersport; hence, you find me taking a leisurely view of the action from the beach.

In the afternoon, the expedition team organise another hike, on this occasion to the highest part of the island. Rosie, after her morning exertions, is one of those choosing to remain on the beach, but our intrepid expedition leader takes about twenty of us on the relatively short but steep climb on the Gambute Peak Trail.

From the beach, we pass by the back of the ranger station where some very large iguana are basking in the sun. I suspect that they are being regularly fed by the rangers and are enjoying a rather easy lifestyle. As we climb, we pass a weather station with some rudimentary equipment to measure temperature and precipitation and then the path gets steeper, passing through thick undergrowth to the summit of Cerro Gambute. On the way, we are rewarded with the sighting of a crested eagle nesting and on the return journey back to the beach we come across a Coiban agouti, a short-tailed version of the animal we had seen a few days earlier on the mainland. At the top of the climb, an impressive viewpoint looking down to the beach below and across the archipelago to many other islands and islets in the Coiba group.

Back on the beach, I relax on a hammock conveniently strung between two large trees. I exchange greetings with one of the crew of the splendid-looking sailing boat we had spotted earlier anchored in the bay. He is English and he tells me that he and his three colleagues, who are American, are Bahamas-based bankers taking a short vacation. They have rented the boat on the mainland and are looking forward to an idyllic break sailing around these islands. However, they have discovered the boat is not what it seems to the untutored eye. Shortly after leaving port, the auxiliary motor that powers the boat when not under sail as well as the cooker and an air-conditioning unit have all failed. The men have spent two uncomfortable days at sea and nights on deck. Seeking relief from the tropical heat, they spent last night ashore at the island's ranger station, sleeping in the spartan visitors' quarters. Now facing the sail back to the mainland, he appears less than enamoured at the prospect.

Overnight, we sail due east towards the mainland coast of South America to the edge of the Darien jungle, still in Panama, albeit close to the border with Colombia. Here in the village of Playa de Muerto, or Beach of the Dead, we are to meet people from the Embera tribe.

We are on deck early, eager to view our landing place. The skies are heavy and with visibility poor, it is difficult to make out the village from our vantage point barely half a mile offshore. Some boys from the village arrive alongside in dugout canoes, interested in us but too shy to engage or to ask for money or gifts. We make it ashore sometime later and are met by an official reception party on the beach. A village elder, some younger men and crowds of kids. Nearby, a group of women who are sitting talking, showing a marked disinterest in our presence. I cannot help but notice several uniformed and heavily armed men that we later establish are a police contingent, permanently stationed here to protect the villagers and intercept drug smugglers coming across the nearby Colombian border.

One immediate thing of note is that all the Embera – men, women and even small children – have heavily painted bodies, not brightly coloured but black on their brown skins and in elaborate geometric shapes. This is apparently a dye extracted from the berry of a tree called *genip* and apart from decoration is thought to keep insects at bay. The men are wearing nothing but a loin cloth, the favoured colour being a bright red. The women, bare-breasted, wear brightly coloured and patterned skirts around their waist. Both men and women also wear elaborate necklaces, either made of metal (my guess being silver) or coloured beads. Their hair is dark black and straight and largely unadorned, except for narrow bead headbands favoured by many of the men and colourful headdresses, which remind me of Polynesians, worn by some of the older women.

A short ceremony of welcome takes place and we are escorted through the village. Most Embera live close to rivers but at Playa Muerto, as the name implies, the village is literally on a beach. The houses are well-spaced wooden constructions and upon stilts, raising floor level to some 8 or 10 feet above the ground. The sides are open and the roofs thatched.

The villagers are friendly. Outside one house, a mother is showing her young daughter how to grind rice with a pestle in a large wooden bowl. Some other pre-pubescent girls gather around and laugh shyly as Rosie takes a video of the activities. They are fascinated when she plays back the footage. This is invariably a good gambit with peoples unaccustomed to mass tourism. The oldest girl is about thirteen and she tells Rosie that her name is Marienetta. At another dwelling, we are invited to mount the steps that lead up into the house, where some of the ladies of the village have gathered to give us a demonstration of weaving. Later, in the centre of the village, we are invited to assemble whilst the villagers present to us a show of dancing, singing and music.

At the end of the show, the chief, who speaks some English, explains that he is democratically elected. Unlike in many cultures where the chief is from a "royal" family and is a village elder, this chief is a young man, I would guess in his thirties. He tells us that the Embera are still primarily hunters, even though they live adjacent to the sea. Their staples are monkeys and birds that are hunted using blowpipes with arrows tipped in a poison obtained from yellow-eyed frogs. He concludes his speech with an invitation for we passengers to come and watch the clearly highly anticipated annual football match between the villagers and the ship's crew. In a classic case of pulling rank, the ship's captain, a short, overweight middle-aged man, leads his team onto the pitch and at kick-off promptly takes up the position of centre-forward. More Madonna than Maradona, he loiters around the opposition penalty area in the vain hope of goalscoring glory, but his chance of one minute of fame doesn't come today.

Some of us accept an invitation from the villagers to take an escorted jungle walk. Two men from the village are to be our guides. A path takes us through the forest and after wading knee-deep across a small stream, we come to a banana plantation that our guides are clearly proud to show us. The jungle has much in the way of birdlife and we spot *motmot*, toucan, *tanager* and scarlet macaw. On the way back to the village, we are fortunate. Our guide at the front stops and points to a large tree. Poking its head out of a hole in the trunk is a night or owl monkey. Lucky because they are the only nocturnal monkey and therefore rarely seen during the day. This one we see has clearly emerged from its home in a hole on the fork of the tree trunk and seems of an inquisitive disposition, as interested in us as we are to see it. Its distinctive features are its large eyes and small ears.

Late afternoon, it is time to return to the ship. The expedition staff have related an earlier visit when one of the zodiacs was flipped over by the Pacific breakers hitting the shore. Frankly, in the morning, this had seemed an unlikely scenario; although the skies then had been grey, the sea was relatively calm. Now the tropical sun is high in a clear blue sky, humidity is steamy and our clothes soaked through with the effort of traipsing through the jungle. Returning to the beach, it is a whole new scenario. The sea has taken on some of the characteristics that led to this being named Playa Muerto. Huge rollers make this maybe an ideal spot for surfers but not so attractive for oldies looking forward to afternoon tea on board ship. The zodiacs reach the shore easily enough, but heading back out to sea is more of a challenge. The expedition crew are seriously tested. We pile into the boats, but getting them away from the beach into the oncoming tide proves challenging. Instead of sweat from our earlier exertions, now all we can do is hang on. Getting thoroughly soaked with the sea spray and enduring a hairy few minutes seems a small price to pay when we are thankfully all back on board our ship.

From here, we will turn north-east and make a transit of the Panama Canal. Our ship will pay many thousands of dollars in fees, but being small, we are low priority compared with one of the larger cruise ships paying literally hundreds of thousands of dollars. A consequence is that we make a night transit of the Canal, leaving the Pacific to emerge around dawn into the Caribbean, heading to Portobelo.

Portobelo is a small town, originally Puerto Bello or "Beautiful Port", with an interesting history. Sir Francis Drake is reputed to have been buried at sea in a lead coffin in the bay after he died here in 1596, suffering from dysentery.

Founded by the Spanish, Portobelo was one of the exit routes for ships carrying Peruvian silver back to Europe and as such was heavily fortified. For obvious reasons, it attracted the attention of pirates. Some of the most notorious of that ilk attempted to capture the town. Perhaps the most famous and in the event successful attacker was Captain Henry Morgan, who with some 450 men captured and stripped the town of its wealth in 1668. In 1739, a rather more official British attack was successfully led by Admiral Edward Vernon, and it is in commemoration of this victory that we still come across the name Portobello in British cities, most notably in London with its famous market and Edinburgh, where a whole district bears the name.

The old fort San Lorenzo has been designated a UNESCO World Heritage site and it is our first stop on coming ashore, but in reality there are scant remains, only some crumbling fortifications overlooking the bay.

Leaving the fort, we walk down the road into the centre of the town. The streets are quiet and the only locals we see are people of African descent; however, on reaching the town centre, we come across a different ethnic group. These are Kuna people.

In contrast to the Embera with their friendly disposition and laughter and near naked bodies, the Kuna Indians are little people with colourful clothes and sad, pinched faces.

Their presence here appears as aliens in a strange land, in the community but not of it. Retaining their own culture and with no desire to integrate. Their existence in Portobelo is entirely commercial, to sell their wares, colourful *molas*, hand-sewn blouses using an unusual layering technique.

A group of the Kuna perform a traditional dance for us in desultory fashion in the square. I notice a young albino man is leading the dancers. Albinism amongst the Kuna is statistically higher than in almost any other race, but whereas in many cultures albinos are commonly subject to prejudice, in Kuna culture they are to the contrary regarded as something special. After the performance concludes, we find a small market with stalls where some Kuna women are selling *molas*. We make a purchase and take a photograph of the stallholder, with her permission, holding the garment. I have it in front of me as a reminder. The face of the downcast. The Kuna have had a history of oppression and it shows in their demeanour.

After a day at sea today, we are on another journey and are scheduled to encounter the Kuna again in the place they have made their home, the San Blas islands, an archipelago of no less than 378 small islands off the east coast of Panama.

From here on the deck of our ship, I can see many of the isles and islets that form this island group, a ribbon of low sandy dots set in the azure blue ocean, some so tiny as to be dwarfed by a small number of ocean-going yachts anchored off, no doubt attracted by the opportunity of visiting these little-known islands and their people.

The Kuna are not the indigenous people and have found refuge here after a turbulent history on the mainland. It is believed that their homeland before the sixteenth century when the Spanish began to colonise the South American continent was in an area that is now part of Colombia. Here, they were probably neighbours to the Embera people. However, being an essentially peaceful people, they avoided conflict with other more warlike neighbouring tribes, gradually migrating further east into the Darien jungle and then by the mid-1800s towards the coast and the Gulf of Mexico. It was then that the first Kuna began to move onto these islands.

When Panama became independent in 1903, the new government sought to impose a "national culture" on all of its people, challenging the Kuna tribe's very particular way of life. A repressed minority in perpetual conflict with its government, difficult years followed, culminating in a rebellion in 1925. Thanks to US intervention, the outcome was to prove positive, with the Kuna being granted semi-autonomous status with guarantees over the territory that is the San Blas islands.

The Kuna now live a relatively peaceful existence on the islands, although like the Kuna we came across in Portobelo, many more still live for economic reasons in mainland Panama.

We are ferried ashore in small boats onto the island of Porvenir, distinguishable from the many neighbouring islands only by virtue of it being bisected by an airstrip.

Our boat runs up onto a shallow beach and we clamber ashore. There are palm trees, a few buildings and diagonally across the length of the island a scar, the runway providing a link to the mainland. Almost immediately as we walk up from the beach, we encounter the Kuna. As in Portobelo, it is mainly the women selling their wares. The only male we meet is an old man sheltering from the sun under a large tree. Some of the women are displaying their *molas* on crude wooden frames, whilst others have hung their wares on the wire fence that separates the rest of the island from the airstrip. The less fortunate who have missed out on the best pitches have laid their goods out on the sandy ground. The women are not to be drawn into casual conversation and are as dour as their kin on the mainland. My first observations are confirmed. Small of stature, dark-skinned with sharp, pinched faces and always wearing the traditional blouses, skirts and headscarves.

I guess one of the few advantages of finding a permanent home on these remote islands is that the Kuna, or Tule as they call themselves, can maintain their traditional customs relatively free from the incursions of the modern world. This includes maintaining their language, Dulegaya, handed down by speech, the Kuna not having any written alphabet.

As we wander along admiring the goods for sale, the Kuna we meet, like those on the mainland, are not very engaging beyond the selling of their wares, which once again embrace the intricate *molas* with their geometric designs and abstract depictions of fish, animals and flowers. Apparently, these were traditional body paintings, and only after the Kuna came into contact with Europeans less than 200 years ago did they begin to weave their patterns onto cotton cloth and begin to cover their bodies. Although the full costume involves ear and nose rings, a patterned wraparound skirt – known as a *saburat* – and a coloured headscarf, it is the *mola* which holds the greatest significance in Kuna culture. The making of a *mola* is a complex process, involving up to seven layers of cloth sewn together. The patterns are formed by cutting away parts of each layer.

As Kuna is purely a spoken language, this carries over to an oral tradition where history is handed down through the *saila*, a community leader, both mayor and priest, whose responsibilities include memorising and relating the history of the tribe. A form of democracy exists through the Onmaked Nega, which like the role of the *saila* is both the parliament and synod.

Leaving the Kuna women to sell their wares to our fellow passengers, we decide to explore further. Beyond the end of the airstrip, a narrow peninsula stretches out into the ocean, forming a small bay, but this part of the island is deserted. We walk back past where the Kuna women have set up their market and try our luck at the other end of the island. Almost immediately we come to a homestead, a solid concrete construction with the detritus of modern living scattered around the rear door; fishing nets, an old outboard motor and garbage. Behind stands a more substantial building on two storeys. Above the porch flies the Kuna flag, yellow and orange with a swastika motif inverse to the one used by Nazi Germany. A notice indicates this is the office of the Kuna Government but it is closed for business today.

Further along, a crude wooden sign says *Museum*, with an arrow pointing to the next building, again one of two storeys. The ground floor is an open storage area so we climb the wooden staircase on the outside of the building to the upper floor. A large room, strewn around a collection of artefacts. It dawned on us both. Some government official or all-knowing NGO had decided that creating a museum was a good idea, but the Kuna either had failed to grasp the concept or had rejected it as contrary to their culture of an oral history. Some spears, fishing gear, a millstone lay on the floor, just gathering dust.

Walking back across the island, we come to where a large fishing boat is being hauled up onto the beach. About a dozen men busying themselves. It is as though we don't exist as they secure the vessel and begin unloading their catch.

We return to look again at the goods for sale and, despite our renewed efforts, the women are disinclined towards chit-chat. When it is time for us to leave, the Kuna begin to pack their goods into large bundles, and it becomes apparent that they themselves live not here but on adjacent islands. They have chosen to do business on this "neutral" territory rather than have us poking around their village. The contrast between the Kuna and their former neighbours the Embera could not be starker.

Fifteen

Mexico: In love with Rivera

Mexico: The largest and economically most highly developed country in Central America, with a population of 120 million. After finally ejecting the Spanish in 1821, the Mexican Empire was created but losing the Mexican-American War 1846–48, it was forced to cede California, New Mexico, Arizona, Nevada and Utah to the United States of America. The Mexican Revolution, in fact a civil war, raged across the country through most of the 1910s and featured two charismatic leaders, whose names live on in folklore: Emiliano Zapata and Pancho Villa. Language – Spanish.

I am dedicating this chapter to Rosie for reasons which will become apparent.

We like to think of ourselves as travellers but not in the mould of filling a backpack, heading to the nearest airport and taking a flight to who knows where. In some ways, I envy those who travel with that freedom, I once read a famous travel writer who said *…the real traveller travels alone unencumbered by the wishes and desires of another*. That is not to be my experience but, together with Rosie, ours will be experiences shared. In another life before retirement, Rosie was a project manager handling multi-million pound computer system installations, so our trips are both well researched and planned. This process tends to follow a pattern. You find us in Mexico City, yet this particular trip arose from a brief visit to Guatemala and a decision that it was a country we would like to see more of, not least to see the ruins of the Mayan city of Tikal.

So the planning began. Guatemala is adjacent to Nicaragua. Another country we had not visited. Sounds interesting, add on Nicaragua. Then we spotted an expedition cruise visiting some obscure parts of Costa Rica and Panama. The dates fit, Nicaragua and Costa Rica are neighbours, let's do it. Itinerary complete save for the question of how to reach Central America from the UK. No direct flights so it is via somewhere, Madrid, Miami or Mexico City? We choose Mexico City. Well, we wouldn't want to come all this way and simply pass through the airport. There is another reason very special to Rosie's heart as to why we need to take some time here at the end of our long trip.

Aged ten and still at primary school, she won a book prize. The book was *The Lands and Peoples of Central America*. Despite the daunting title and subject matter for one so young, she obviously read the book, because she often refers to the exotic and mystical mountain Popocatépetl. Surely this will be a chance to fulfil that childhood curiosity and see the mountain for herself.

So here we are in the centre of Mexico City, driving down the Paseo de la Reforma. Already as we pass the Museum of Anthropology on our right, situated in the huge park, the Bosque de Chapultepec, and the Monument of Independence, we have already concluded that this is one of the great cities of the world.

Our first foray into the city is under the guidance of Leo. For this role, I would describe him as old and battle-weary from a few thousand guided tours like this but both well informed and erudite. Leo has a full head of grey wavy hair, a lined face and is, shall we say, of stout stature, broad but not overtly fat.

Leo calls to the driver to pull over and we alight at "El Caballito", the Little Horse statue, bright yellow and modernistic, and begin a walking tour of the historic centre of the city.

Although we will return here in our own time, Leo is anxious that we get a good orientation, and we stroll down Avenida Juarez, the Alameda park on our left, and soon we come to the art nouveau-style Palacio de Bellas Artes and get a brief look inside to admire its impressive art deco interior.

The street names change; Juarez becomes Madero as we pass the Torre

Latinoamericana, the 1950s' skyscraper, and just a little further down we visit the "Casa de los Azulejos", or House of Tiles. The blue and white tiled exterior a reminder of Portugal, a former power in the very early days of European influence over the New World. Inside, we discover that this former palace is now an upmarket store and restaurant.

The sights come thick and fast and at the end of Madero, we enter "Zocalo", Constitution Square. To our left, the huge Catedral Metropolitana, the biggest church in Latin America, the construction of which took almost three centuries until its eventual completion in 1813.

By the time we reach the gates of the equally impressive Palacio Nacional, we have just missed the last entry time for members of the public, but undeterred, Leo ushers us inside, despite the protestations of the door attendant.

The Palacio Nacional stands on the site of an Aztec temple constructed sometime in the fourteenth century by Montezuma and was where some 200 years later, the Spanish conquistador Hernán Cortés chose to establish his quarters, so Mexico has effectively been run from this spot for 600 years. We are in the palace courtyard and turn to climb the main staircase, and there it is. The pictorial history of Mexico painted on a wall. It is our introduction to Diego Rivera.

This incredible piece of art was painted by Rivera between 1929 and 1935. Rivera was perhaps the greatest exponent of this art form, but not being an expert on the subject myself, my research suggests it would be remiss not to also refer to two of his contemporaries, David Alfaro Siqueiros and José Clemente Orozco.

Muralists in twentieth-century art are a strangely Mexican phenomenon, very much associated with a leftist view of taking art to the people, and although this painting adorns the walls of a palace, typically in the '20s and '30s, murals were created on the walls of public buildings throughout Mexico.

Unwittingly, we had already seen one of Orozco's most famous works, *Omniscience*, on the staircase of the Casa de los Azulejos and then years later we came across an unusual 360 degrees work by Sigueiros that resides in the Museo del Bicentenario in Buenos Aires.

By force of circumstance, it is a whistle-stop tour and soon we are outside the palace and making our way through the throngs of visitors watching street artists at work, dancers, acrobats, singers. We hurry through the crowds, as Leo is keen to show us the work underway to uncover previously undiscovered parts of that Aztec temple. Time is short, we move on.

Nightfall is closing in by the time we reach Mexico City's famous park the Bosque de Chapultepec, and lo and behold, we come to the Fuente de Tlaloc. This strange fountain is supposed to evoke traditional indigenous Mexican culture in the form of the "god of rain". The designer none other than Diego Rivera. Our whistle-stop tour is over, barely time to take breath, but we like what we see. Our kind of city.

We are staying at a rather upmarket boutique hotel in the Polanco district of the city, owned by an apparently famous Mexican TV personality Lolita Ayala. Each room is named after a Mexican cultural icon. I could claim that we are staying in the Diego Rivera room but that would be a little white lie. We are in fact in the room dedicated to Rufino Tamayo. Tamayo was also an artist and muralist, a contemporary of Rivera but not somebody sharing his revolutionary views and partially for this reason, a man who spent many years living in New York away from the political turmoil in his mother country. We know this because in the room a potted history of each of the people who have a room dedicated to them. Reading these brief biographies, our fascination for learning more about Diego is further heightened.

Enter Frida Kahlo stage right.

At this point, I had not seen the Oscar-winning movie nor read the biography written by Herman Herrera, both titled *Frida*, so she was something of a mystery, but reading the blurb in our hotel room and searching the internet, we are intrigued by both these characters, Diego and Frida.

Before we can continue our search for Diego, something of an interlude. We have arranged to spend the next two days visiting outside of the city.

To our surprise, next morning we are met not by Leo but his colleague Alfonso. Not someone we are going to lose in a crowd, the bulging eyes makes him a Marty Feldman lookalike... and that toupée. So old and moth-eaten that the hairpiece itself has bald patches. Another busy day ahead begins in the city with a visit to the Museo National de Antropogia. Mexico City boasts some 200 museums, and this has to be one of the most impressive with its vast collection of pre-Colombian artefacts.

The museum visit is for context, for we are heading to the site of one of the most impressive cities of the ancient world, Teotihuacán. Pre-dating the Aztecs and largely in a parallel period with the height of the Mayan empire, the history of this site remains subject to much speculation and few hard facts. What is certain is that this city was large by the standards of that period, with a population of perhaps 125,000, and that the inhabitants had some contact with the Mayans situated geographically to the south. The city achieved its zenith around 500 BC before going into decline, as did many of the great Mayan cities.

It being a Sunday, the site is heaving with visitors, and after some pushing, shoving and queueing we get sight of the Jaguar mural, the fragmentary remains of what must have been a colossal painting. As seems the habit amongst local guides, we are sent on a climb up the highest structure, the Pyramid of the Sun, whilst Alfonso remains firmly at ground level in the shade of the enormous structure. We make good progress to a platform about two-thirds of the way to the top. It is quieter here, most visitors wishing to claim they have climbed to the summit. We have no such ambition, and from our vantage point we are afforded excellent views across the whole complex.

We move on from Teotihuacán to another busy location. Here, in December 1531, a peasant, Juan Diego, came upon a vision of a woman, the place Tepayac Hill. She identified herself as the Virgin Mary and instructed that a church be built on the site. Juan Diego travelled to see the Bishop of Mexico City to relate the story, but the bishop was not convinced. The vision appeared before Juan Diego again with the same message and again Juan Diego went to the bishop to repeat his story. The bishop's response was that he needed a sign that this story had some truth. Juan Diego returned to Tepayac Hill and sure enough the vision appeared for a third time, and when Juan Diego related to her the bishop's request, she acceded and instructed Juan Diego to return the following day when she would give him a sign.

The following day, Juan Diego's uncle falls sick and Juan Diego tends to him at his sickbed. When his uncle's condition deteriorates, Juan Diego sets off to seek the local priest to administer the last rites, studiously avoiding Tepayac Hill, feeling guilt over his failure to rendezvous with the vision. Nonetheless, on his journey he is again confronted by the vision. He tells her why he failed to arrive the previous day and in reply she assures him that his uncle is now recovered and tells him to collect flowers from the top of the normally barren Tepayac Hill. Following her instructions, he climbs the hill, where to his amazement he finds roses, not native to Mexico, and gathers them in his cloak.

Once again, Juan Diego goes to see the bishop and on opening his cloak, the flowers fall to the ground and on the cloak is left an image of the Virgin Mary. Juan Diego then returns home to find his uncle indeed fully recovered, and the uncle tells of seeing a vision at his bedside.

The vision had said that she desired to be called Guadalupe and we are at the place where she first appeared in front of Juan Diego. Now this is the site of the Basilica of Our Lady of Guadalupe, the most visited shrine of the Catholic Church. A fact not hard to believe on this Sunday afternoon; the site, which contains not one but seven churches, is thronging with people.

The new basilica consecrated as recently as 1976 holds 10,000 worshippers and here the cloak worn by Juan Diego is on display. To view, we join a queue and edging forward eventually climb upon a moving travelator and pass by the icon at what I thought was a speed rather faster than "sedate". Then who am I to quibble? There are a lot of people wanting to pass through the basilica in a short time. Once outside, we explore the rest of the site. The gardens are beautifully laid out, but the first thing we notice is the music. Not the sombre organ music you might imagine but loud raucous pop music. Immediately adjacent, over a wooden fence, is a large funfair.

The next day, we head out of Mexico City in the opposite direction. We have told Alfonso about Rosie's interest in Popocatépetl and about an hour after leaving the city, Alfonso calls to the driver to pull over into a lay-by and we alight from the vehicle to the sight of the mountain in all its glory, the peak framed in a beautiful blue sky. Rosie has been blessed. A crystal-clear day, apparently quite rare as the mountain is invariably shrouded in cloud.

There are in fact two mountain peaks in view, not just one. The second is Iztaccihuatl. Legend has it that Popocatépetl was a great warrior who fell in love with Princess Iztaccihuatl and was promised her hand by her father if Popocatépetl was victorious in battle against the dominating Aztecs. A rival for Iztaccihuatl's hand told her Popocatépetl had died in battle, and overcome with grief, she died. It was a lie, and Popocatépetl returned in triumph only to receive the devastating news about his loved one. In dedication, he took her body and laid it on the top of one of the mountains, now dedicated to her name, and placed an eternal torch to look over her from the top of the adjacent mountain, what is now Popocatépetl, a still very active volcano.

Rosie is naturally delighted with our viewing, albeit from a distance, and we head on to Cholula.

We are going to climb the hill to the church of Nuestra Senora do los Remedios but first we visit the nearby Archaeological Zone where stood the tallest pyramid built in Mesoamerica. The site is not fully exposed, so the best impression of the overall site is by viewing a cutaway model exhibited in the museum built within the passage complex discovered inside the pyramid structure.

Emerging from the museum, we face the daunting prospect of climbing to the church. On a particularly hot day, it is a strenuous climb, albeit on a set of wide steps cut into the hill. Once we have reached the church, Alfonso is anxious to show us something. The figure of the Virgin Mary dominates the altar but Alfonso beckons us to follow him behind the altar, where we discover an image of baby Jesus in a cot. He is surrounded by huge amounts of toys, sweets and assorted other gifts left by visiting pilgrims. Before departing, we gather our breath for the descent down the hill and take the opportunity to admire the views of Cholula below and in the distance our next destination.

This is a busy schedule. From Cholula, we head on to Mexico's fourth largest city, Puebla. Time is the enemy so it is with some good fortune that we find a place to park in the main square adjacent to our first place to visit, the cathedral. It is worth making the point that although Mexico borders the United States to the north, where any edifice over 200 years old is regarded as seriously old, here lived sophisticated societies for hundreds of years, even before the Spanish arrived. Hernán Cortés landed on these shores in 1519 and by 1521, the Aztec Empire had fallen and centuries of Spanish influence and culture were to follow. With this in mind, I can confirm that this cathedral was consecrated in 1649. Alfonso is still clearly fatigued from the strenuous climb up to the church in Cholula, so after showing us around the cathedral, he excuses himself and suggests we explore the city on foot by ourselves.

We have heard of the *talavera* pottery unique to Puebla and head for the nearby El Parian market and the adjacent Barrio del Artista. Here, the proliferation of tiny shops sell many local artisan products; hats, basketry, textiles and the famed pottery, although not necessarily all to factory standards. The *talavera* pottery is an elaborate and unique fusion of influences from around the world. Spanish naturally, but also Moorish and Chinese and, significantly, Italian. The technique emanates from the town of Talavera de la Reina in Spain and is believed to have been brought to Mexico by Dominican monks. Puebla became the epicentre for making the pottery because of the suitability of local clays. The original designs have evolved over the years, hence the cosmopolitan nature of both the designs and the colours. Whilst we admired the merchandise, I will be honest; we did not make a purchase based on several factors: the risk of damage when travelling with ceramics, cost of the genuine article and frankly not actually liking the designs.

Back in Mexico City, and next morning, on our quest to find out more of Diego and Frida. We are heading for Coyoacan, the district of the city where Frida began and ended her life and to the house where she and Diego spent much of their turbulent marriage. The journey starts in some confusion. At the Metro station, the ticket office is deserted. We are perplexed, as there is no obvious alternative method of buying a ticket. After a few minutes, a man in a uniform, somewhat breathless, comes up behind us and apologising tells us that he has had to vacate his post as a matter of urgency. A pressing call of nature had led him to find relief using the facilities in the closest restaurant, apparently some distance from the station.

At the end of our Metro journey, we are back on the streets in an unfamiliar part of the city. Fortunately, given the reputation of Mexico City for being potentially unsafe for the unwary tourist, we find that Coyoacan is a well-established and fairly upscale part of the city. It takes us some time after leaving the Metro station walking the streets before we come to the intersection of Allende and Londres where we find the "Blue House". Here Frida was born in 1907 and lived for much of her life and where she died in 1954. Her story is well known so I will be brief in offering a synopsis.

At the age of six, Frida contracted polio, which left her with a limp but no significant other side effects and she led a normal life for a child of middle-class parents, her father, Wilhelm, being an accomplished photographer. She was one of few girls to attend the National Preparatory School, where she became active in politics. It was here that she first saw Diego Rivera, who had been commissioned to create a mural in the school lecture hall.

Born in 1886, Rivera was at this time, in 1922, already an acclaimed artist. His studies had taken him to the San Carlos Academy of Fine Arts in Mexico City and after graduation he had travelled to Europe. In Paris, he met Pablo Picasso and was influenced by late-impressionist painters like Matisse and Gaugin, establishing a reputation in his own right. Like Frida, he became interested in politics, in his case directly through the Mexican

Revolution of 1914–15 and subsequent events in Russia, and this began to influence his work. Later, travelling to Italy, he had been enthralled by the frescos of the Renaissance period and this spawned his unique contribution to muralism. Returning to Mexico, he was asked by the government to undertake a mission to decorate public buildings in an effort to take art to the people. It was one of his first commissions that saw him at Frida's school.

Several years were to pass before their paths were to cross again, but most significantly, it was a random event that occurred in the intervening years that was to influence both of their lives. At the age of seventeen, Frida was travelling the city in a wooden streetcar when it was hit by another vehicle, leaving Frida impaled upon a steel rail, which entered her hip and exited the other side of her body. Her serious injuries included a fractured hip and spine, injuries that were to leave her in pain for the rest of her life.

A long period of convalescence followed, during which Frida took up painting. She began the self-portraits for which she ultimately became famous. At first straightforward portraits copied from her image viewed via a large mirror placed at the foot of her bed, but gradually these images transmogrified to reveal her inner feelings and her permanent state of pain. In the following years, Frida began to build a reputation as both an artist and, after she joined the Communist Party, a political activist.

Through these common interests in art and radical politics, in 1928, Frida and Diego finally met. He encouraged her painting and soon the relationship developed. They became lovers and were married the following year. Whilst the Blue House remained the Kahlo family house, the couple actually lived elsewhere in the city and in the 1930s they moved to the United States. Here, Rivera had earned various commissions, including work on behalf of Nelson Rockefeller, the outcome a controversial piece called *Man at the Crossroads*. Whilst accompanying her husband through these years, Frida was able to mix in New York artistic circles, establishing a reputation in her own right. During this period, her works became more surrealistic, perhaps first evident in a work titled *Henry Ford Hospital,* painted in 1932.

The couple's relationship was turbulent, Diego being guilty of multiple infidelities. There was a separation and at the end of the decade a divorce.

Apart from the art, there was politics. Amongst their political friends was the Russian exile Leon Trotsky. Trotsky and his wife actually took up residence in the Blue House in 1937 and lived there for two years, although Trotsky was in constant fear of assassination by agents of Stalin, a fear ultimately proving accurate with his violent death in 1940. When the Trotskys vacated the Blue House, Frida returned and apart from a brief interlude living in Paris, this was to be home for the remaining years of her life.

The divorce followed shortly after Frida's return to the house. Yet, despite the tempestuous nature of their relationship, within two years, the couple were remarried and Diego also came to live in the Blue House. Here, he was responsible for alterations to the fabric of the building, still evident today, aimed at improving Frida's quality of life.

Frida's health began an inexorable if somewhat protracted decline, although she continued to work, producing a raft of even more controversial and insightful paintings. *The Suicide of Dorothy Hale,* commissioned by the dead woman's grieving mother in memory of her daughter. The result, it has to be said, was not what the heart-broken mother expected. Many of the later works were more personal, showing the extreme pain that Frida suffered on a daily basis. Typical examples were *The Two Fridas,* 1939; *The Broken Column,* painted in 1944, which followed more major surgery; *Self-Portrait with the Portrait of Doctor Farill,* 1951, after a long period of hospitalisation, and many more.

Despite being bedridden, Frida attended her first solo exhibition in Mexico City in 1953 but by now her health was in terminal decline and she died in the Blue House in July 1954 at the age of forty-seven.

Although he married again shortly after Frida died, Diego, suffering from cancer, outlived her by only three years and died himself in 1957. Rivera bequeathed the Blue House as a museum in memory of Frida.

So here we are at the Blue House, and stunningly blue it is; bright cobalt, angular and fortress-like. The unique feature of the museum is that it is in fact a home frozen in time. The furniture, the artefacts, the decorations and the Mexican cultural art, the paintings by Frida (including her last, *Viva la Vida*), Diego and other of their famous friends and contemporaries adorn the walls. Everything pretty well as it was up until Frida's death. Particularly moving, the extension to the main building that Rivera had constructed for Frida containing her bedroom and studio. Her bed and the mirrors she used to draw herself, a corset she was forced to wear to support her damaged spine, her wheelchair. Frida's ashes sit in an urn next to a funeral mask. It could be viewed as a little macabre but, knowing her story, it is very touching.

We decide to walk back to the city centre through the avant-garde artist area of Coyoacan, with its galleries and street artists. To complete our day of sightseeing, we find ourselves back in Alameda, and to round off a memorable day we decide to visit the Museo Mural Diego Rivera to admire one of Rivera's greatest masterpieces, *Dream of a Sunday Afternoon in Alameda Park.*

Sixteen

Cuba: Castro's legacy

Cuba: The large Caribbean island situated less than 100 miles from Key West Florida with a population of 11 million. Communist since the 1959 overthrow of Dictator Batista by forces led by Fidel Castro. Language – Spanish.

Why is it that the craziest people on the planet, those without concern for life or limb, either theirs or yours, short-sighted and insane, oblivious to other road users, particularly drivers in large trucks, have found themselves jobs as taxi drivers operating from outside the world's airports? As usual, we found one. The journey into Havana was quick but interspersed with frequent jolting stops at every traffic light and junction. Thus, with one eye on the road ahead, I digest the fact that this is a large, sprawling and distinctly down-at-heel city. The outer suburbs punctuated by ugly blocks of low-rise flats almost certainly funded and built in the '60s and '70s by the Russians or East Germans and already crumbling under the hot Caribbean sun. Traffic on the wide avenues leading to the city centre is light compared with most cities of comparable size, but almost immediately we are aware of the legendary American-built saloons from the '40s and '50s, Dodge, Plymouth, Lincoln, Cadillac, Oldsmobile and many, many more, usually painted in pastel shades and frequently to be seen beside the road with their bonnets up. Apparently, there are still 17,000 of these vintage cars registered in Havana alone. The poor relation in terms of age, style and condition are the many Lada dating from the Soviet period but also quite a lot of small modern cars, with Hyundai for some unaccountable reason having a significant market share. We also spot our first Camel. No, not the four-legged variety but a local bus into which as many as 300 people are crammed during the commuter periods. These are articulated lorries, the trailers of which the Cubans with some nifty metal bashing have converted. The Camel nomenclature derives from the appearance, with two humps; one behind the driver's cab and the other at the rear.

We usually like to try out the local transport system in a large city, be it bus or metro, but on this occasion we decide to give it a miss. Instead, our preferred form of transport is to be the yellow coco-taxis, loosely based on the tuk-tuks we had encountered in Bangkok, which is best described as a broken egg-shell moulded in glass fibre with three wheels and a two-stroke engine attached.

From our guidebooks, we establish that Havana proper divides into three major sections: Vedado, Centro and Vieja.

Vedado, or new city, is the downtown area to the west where our hotel, The Nacional, is situated. Here, wide avenues and some pleasing buildings from the '50s and later, interspersed by high-rise buildings, the tallest of which is the thirty-three storeys Edificio Focsa. Nearby, the Hotel Libre, the former Hilton Hotel, the post-revolution headquarters of Fidel Castro and his government. Despite being relatively new we soon discover that even Vedado is suffering from lack of maintenance and repair with many fine buildings, not to mention pavements and roads, desperately needing attention.

To the east of Vedado lies Centro, constructed over a period of time from around 1860 until the 1930s and originally built to house the overflow of population from the old city. Again, many fine buildings but the decay is even more advanced and most buildings have the appearance of not having seen a lick of paint since the day they were built. From the guidebook, it seems there are sights worth seeing here, but after a few blocks walking around manholes without covers and across garbage-strewn streets, we change tack and head for the Plaza de la Revolucion, the very heart of Castro's Cuba. This is the place where for well over forty years, crowds have gathered in huge numbers to hear El Comandante Fidel address them. To avoid any ambiguity, at the time of our first visit to Cuba, Castro was still

President, albeit soon to hand-over the reins of power to his brother Raul. The square is huge and its two main features are a celebration not of Castro but of the two true heroes from Cuban history: José Marti and Che Guevara.

Marti was the late-nineteenth-century patriot who led the fight against Spanish colonial rule and who was killed in battle in 1895, several years before Cuba eventually gained its independence. His life is celebrated by the impressive monument bearing his name that soars above the Havana skyline with his statue set at its foot. Che Guevara, the Argentinian-born intellectual and aesthete whose image complete with trademark beret has adorned the T-shirts of many thousands of young people around the world for five decades, is the epitome of the true revolutionary. One of the seventeen men who travelled with Fidel on the *Granma* from Mexico to Cuba in 1956 and who later became Minister for Industry in Castro's first government. He later left the island to continue his revolutionary activities in South America, dying in a CIA-inspired ambush in Bolivia in 1969 at the age of thirty-nine. Che is remembered on the side of the building that was his ministry in the '60s, where his features are replicated in copper.

This is just a diversion, given that our real interest is the third part of the city, Old Havana, Habana Viejo. Unlike Centro, which was such a disappointment, this is to please beyond expectations. We have been advised of the decaying and crumbling nature of the old city but it is nevertheless a treasure that thankfully as a UNESCO World Heritage site is now in the process of being lovingly restored to its former glory. A project at its current pace that will probably take the remainder of this century to complete, but one that will be worthwhile.

We start at one of the city's five squares, the Plaza de Armas. Here stands a *ceiba* tree reckoned to be located on the very spot where the city started in 1585. The square has been restored and around a pleasant garden are many fine buildings, of which the most impressive is the Palacio de los Capitanes, completed in 1792. To the left, the Calle Obispo, Bishop's Street, a main thoroughfare where the one major act of desecration of the old city has occurred but is now being redressed. Here, in the '50s, the dictator Batista ordered the university buildings be destroyed, to be replaced by a concrete monstrosity that became the Ministry for Education. Now most of this building has in turn been destroyed and in due course a replica of the original university will stand in its place.

Opposite at the junction of Calle Obispo and Calle Mercaderes is another restored building, the Hotel Ambos Mundos, home for many years in the 1930s of the Nobel Prize-winning author Ernest Hemingway. For $2 you can view Hemingway's bedroom (Room 511) on the fifth floor, where he is reputed to have written his best-selling novel, *For Whom the Bell Tolls*. We take the view that one hotel room is much like another, and as we are by now hot and very thirsty, we keep climbing the narrow staircase until we reach the roof garden bar, where we order a well-deserved *mojito*, a popular Cuban cocktail. Rosie has come across this local delight on our first night in the city. What we are to discover is that although the recipe is the same – sugar, lemon juice, crushed ice, white rum and copious amounts of mint – there are as many versions of this revitalising drink as there are barmen in Havana. For the record, this was quite the worst we encountered, a watered-down tourist version. Hemingway, a man noted for his drinking almost as much as for his literary skills, would surely not have been impressed. Surprisingly, the best we find is served in the café at the Hotel Nacional.

Refreshed, we walk along Calle Mercaderes and into Plaza Viejo, the old town square. Until recently, this was being used as a car park. Now with loving restoration work, the square will once again emerge as a must-see part of the city. The partial restoration sets into relief the contrast between what is and what might be. First laid out in 1559, the Plaza Viejo lies a little away from the main tourist area and with its decline, doubtless reference to it has disappeared from many guidebooks. The square is a cosmopolitan mixture of buildings constructed in four different centuries, including the Casa del Conde Jaruco, completed in 1737, now with its stained glass windows properly restored and its shiny light blue paintwork typical of Habana Viejo. The centrepiece of the square is the fountain designed in 1796; as testimony to the transformation taking place today it is hidden behind hoardings. Despite the fine restoration work already completed, the square is a quiet backwater, save for the school children doubtless freed from a nearby stuffy classroom for a period of organised energy release. Unlike the trend in the UK, here it seems that for Cuba's ruling Communist Party, team games are the order of the day for this group of excited four- and five-year-olds.

The calm serenity of Plaza Viejo contrasts with our next stop, the claustrophobic nearby compact and very crowded Plaza de la Catedral. Here in the tiny square, tourists jostle with locals trying to earn a dollar, from pretty girls in traditional dress to old crones smoking foot-long cigars, their faces plastered with cheap make-up. It is a relief to push on up the side streets, less crowded, where the real people of the city are eking out a harsh existence in near derelict and yet-to-be restored buildings, a family to a room. Soon past the old city wall we find ourselves back into Centro and outside the old presidential palace, now symbolically the Museo de la Revolucion, at its rear a motley collection of revolutionary memorabilia, including *Granma*, Fidel's famous boat on which he and his small band arrived back in Cuba in 1956 to start the campaign to oust Batista. Here too, relics of the Bay of Pigs, the unsuccessful American-backed bid to topple Castro.

We stroll up Zulueta and fall into conversation with a smartly dressed young couple. They tell us that whilst times are hard, they are reasonably contented but then proceed to talk about "The Change" speculating that the whole political and economic system is likely to change dramatically after Castro. We bid them farewell as we enter the Parque Central, the large open area which contains the Capitolio, styled on the building of the same name in Washington DC. We take a strong coffee at exorbitant dollar prices on the terrace of the Hotel Inglaterra, but confronted with the persistent approaches from cabbies and hawkers selling cigars, we decide to leave the bustling central area and turn down Paseo del Prado that runs from the Parque Central down to the Malecon. More baroque-style buildings alongside others of a Moorish appearance. All in various states of disrepair but with some initial signs of renovation. A central tree-lined and wide pavement still allows the Habaneros to promenade in all their finery as the aristocrats did when the Marquis de la Torre first laid out the Prado in 1772.

At the bottom of Prado, we turn right and stroll past the baroque building that houses the Spanish Embassy with its endless line of visa seekers, then we hail a coco-taxi along the Avenue del Puerto by the Castillo de la Real Fuerza and make our way back along the Malecon, the wide seafront promenade, to the Hotel Nacional.

We take a post-dinner stroll from the hotel. As we are walking self-consciously along the avenue, doing our best not to look conspicuous, a young guy sidles up to us. 'Hello, my name is Robert. What are yours?' We tell him but at the same time Rosie squeezes my hand. It is a sure sign that she is feeling very uncomfortable in these unfamiliar surroundings. She had been very unsure about this trip and I know it had been a big effort for her to say, 'Let's go.' I remember her having the same feelings of apprehension before our first visit to Argentina and that had worked out fine. I hoped that the same would happen here.

We are standing at the junction of La Rampa and Calle L. Maybe we look a little lost and too much like tourists in this our first venture onto the streets of downtown Havana. Certainly, this local had readily picked us out from the evening crowd, promenading along one of Havana's main thoroughfares. In one sense at least, I know Rosie and I are on the same wavelength, trying to work out his scam.

'Where are you from?' We start to move along, replying politely but without engaging, but Robert stays in close attendance. 'England, oh a very nice country', an observation we are to hear repeated many times in the coming days.

Robert is about twenty. He wears an open shirt and slacks. His appearance isn't smart but equally he is no scruffy street urchin. He seems very bright and open and I don't detect the little touch of slyness that tends to betray the streetwise kid committed to parting you from your money. We try not to be too gullible in these situations, guarded, without appearing too unfriendly. Robert produces a slightly dog-eared business card from his pocket and oddly, rather than handing it to me, he holds it up so I can read it in the poorly lit street. It advertises a local restaurant. Robert points across the street to a large yet careworn villa, typical in the area. On the tiny first-floor verandah a small number of tables, perhaps three or four at most, and some people eating. It seems quite pleasant. It was only later that we realised it was a *paladares*. One recent small concession in Cuba to capitalism, a small private family-owned but government-licensed restaurant allowed to offer a maximum of twelve covers. This not to be confused with *Palmares*, the government-owned chain of much larger restaurants.

On the street, Robert explains that he is a "promoter" for the restaurant. His terminology brings a smile to our faces. All is becoming clearer. Robert earns a small commission from the owners by bringing tourists along to their establishment. We explain that we have already eaten but that we will keep the place in mind. Robert doesn't seem too concerned with this brush-off and continues chatting, eventually leading us back to our hotel, the prestigious Nacional. Here, he delivers his coup de grâce. No, we are not going to be ambushed by his confederates, nor is he going to pick our pockets or grab our camera and run off. 'Do you have any soap or shampoo from the hotel bathroom for my mother and sister?' Of course we don't, but there and then Rosie decides from here on in she will be better prepared. Actually, Robert was too nice to be a street hustler and he was to prove typical of the people we meet in Cuba, poor but genuinely friendly. Most of them seem only interested in trying out their English, although most, like Robert, were happy to be offered a small gift like a bar of soap, apparently in short supply and of very poor quality in Cuban shops.

That is not to say there weren't a few more doubtful characters on the street, some beggars and a few touts peddling cigars, but usually a firm, 'No' was sufficient discouragement. However, I must admit that despite my vigilance, I was to be suckered.

It is the next day and we are ambling through the old city. Two old men approach me with a smile and a handshake, but once in their grip they begin to serenade me, one on flute the other on guitar. They can play all right, and the toothless smile at the end is beguiling. At this point, they extend an open palm. I hand one of them a dollar bill. They want one each, but I send them on their way with a cheery but firm no.

I nearly fall for the same trick again the following day. This time, the old boy doesn't even have a musical instrument. We are again wandering through one of the narrow streets in the old city when he catches my eye. He beckons me across to where he is standing in a shady spot; he draws me close and then whispers softly in my ear. We are well into the first verse of *When Irish Eyes Are Smiling* before I realise what he is up to. I quickly slip from his grip and keep walking. With old folk standing on every corner and many more sheltering from the hot sun in pretty well every doorway, it could have been an expensive stroll.

The hardest sell comes outside the Museum of the Revolution. A gnarled octogenarian member of "The Party" approaches, trying to persuade me to buy the English language version of *Granma*, the state-controlled newspaper. He asks for a dollar but I point to the cover price of 50 *pesos*. One dollar, he insists, so I keep my money in my pocket. I had actually seen the paper in the hotel that morning and as it didn't contain the English football results I wasn't really interested. In fact, it would be an exaggeration to call it a newspaper, there being little news, only diatribes railing against the American imperialists. Well, it might have had a point.

People who have not visited Cuba tend to ask whether there are the obvious trappings of a police state, with armed soldiers and police on the streets keeping a rebellious populace under control. Well, the answer from our experience is an emphatic no. In fact, we didn't actually see any military, and the only police were those on the roads stopping motorists for speeding infringements. That is not to say there isn't a lot of bureaucracy, and maybe the methods of control are more insidious, with spies and informers, but it is certainly the bureaucracy that marks this out as a Communist country. Our first encounter with this occurs as soon as we get off our plane at José Marti Airport. As is usual, incoming passengers form a line for immigration. We spot that there are a number of booths in operation and instead of falling like sheep into one line behind the other passengers, we start our own queue. Almost immediately, we are beckoned by the immigration officer and step forward to be processed. With hand gestures, the official signals one at a time, and Rosie reluctantly retreats back to the head of the queue that has now formed behind us. I hand my documents across the counter. I can't help it but my eyes are drawn to the immigration officer's thick black moustache. I have worn one myself for the last thirty years, but I have to admit that this luxuriant growth between nose and lips leaves mine looking little more than a nine o'clock shadow. I try to avert my gaze as we exchange some light banter. I am asked to remove my glasses to check whether in fact I am the person on the passport photograph. Satisfied, the immigration officer duly stamps and hands back my passport. I thank her and pass through the door into Cuba. Yes, a woman!

Our time in Havana is short but we manage to visit areas both to the east and west of the city. In Calle Mercadores, in the old town, we visited a small museum whose sole exhibit was a scale model of the city. It was only by seeing this that we appreciated why a great city had been built here. Through a narrow and easily fortified channel, there is a natural harbour. The fortress Castillo del Morro, designed and built in 1589, was constructed to protect access to the harbour from the sea beyond. The only problem until recently was that the fortress side of the harbour was accessible only by a very long journey around the harbour by boat. Fortunately, there is now a tunnel which has not only opened up access to the fortress but has enabled commuter satellite towns to be built along the coast to the east of the main city. The fortress has been impressively renovated to its former condition and offers splendid views back across the harbour mouth to the Plaza de la Revolucion and beyond.

Another short excursion takes us in the opposite direction, west to the suburb of Miramar. This has more of an affluent feel, wide tree-lined boulevards, large villas and a number of modern hotels. The area is home for the majority of the Diplomatic Corps. By far the most imposing building is the Russian Embassy. Once housing several thousand, it now appears deserted. Within a large compound stands the embassy building itself, a huge concrete monstrosity. It is surely no coincidence that it resembles a huge rocket sitting on its launch pad.

We are now mingling comfortably with the locals, conspicuous to them as outsiders but I can tell that Rosie is now at one with the ambience. 'There's so much more to see, we must come back.' Maybe, but for now that was Cuba... well, not quite.

It was only five minutes behind schedule as, just after nine in the evening, our Air Jamaica flight to London taxied towards the head of the runway. The captain came on the intercom to introduce himself. 'Minor delay, folks. A passenger who checked in was ill at the gate and unable to travel so we had to recover his bag from the hold. Only five minutes lost and we expect to make that up on our journey to London.' As the plane stuttered to a halt, paused, I had a perfect view through the cabin window. We were poised to turn onto the runway; in front of us the nightly Air France flight to Paris lumbered its way down the runway before lifting into the clear star-filled sky. Very soon, we would follow. Another plane landed and I felt us inch forward, the captain surely waiting for the tower to signal for him to depart. Minutes passed and nothing. Then on the PA, the captain announcing that there was a problem at the end of the runway. Perfectly placed to see, I shielded my eyes from the cabin lights and peered through the window to see what was happening. Sure enough, in the far distance, the dark outline of a plane and flashing lights. We sat and waited, then after about another thirty minutes the captain again. 'There is a security situation and the authorities have closed the airport until further notice. We have been asked to return to the terminal building and disembark.'

As we left the aircraft, I said to Rosie, 'Collect all your things. We won't be getting back on board for a long time.' She thought it was my natural pessimism coming to the fore but already "hijack" was in my mind. In the terminal building, we were told to hang around our departure gate, ready to reboard. At the next gate, a flight to Madrid was ready to board and the passengers had formed a long line. Rumour was rife amongst our fellow passengers and a hijacking was the favoured explanation, although nobody in authority was available to confirm or deny the rumours. Feet away, though, the Spaniards awaiting their flight seemed oblivious, waiting, waiting, waiting for the gate to open. After about two hours, they were at last becoming restless and an altercation broke out. They had been told that there was a technical fault but to be patient. In another part of the terminal, a group of Italians crowded around the information desk. Rosie went across to earwig. They were to be bused to Varadero, where their incoming flight from Milan had been diverted. They were grumbling. Many of them had travelled up from the resort that very afternoon. I rather suspected that they were in fact to be the lucky ones.

At around one in the morning, we were advised that our flight would not be leaving until four o'clock the following afternoon and we were to be taken to local hotels for the night. It was now that Cuban bureaucracy came to the fore. First, we had to navigate our way through Immigration, where hours before we had handed over our completed departure forms. No problem, an official appeared from a side office with a bundle in his hand wrapped in newspaper. He carefully opened the package to reveal some 300 departure forms. In a heavy Spanish accent, he then began calling out names. Three hundred people crowded around one little guy. I shuddered; this was going to take a long time.

I was tired and fed up. Rosemary nudged me. 'Listen out.'

Magically, they called her name and then mine. Numbers five and six. Thank God for that. 'How the hell did you know they were going to call our names?'

'Simple really; they just called out the two guys who checked in ahead of us'.

We exited into the arrivals lounge. Chaos. Officials were busily telephoning hotels to find us rooms, and more problematically trying to rouse bus drivers from their slumbers. It took another hour but eventually we were headed back towards the city. We struck lucky, a brand new western-style hotel. We were first off the bus. I went to the desk. One lone receptionist on duty.

'We are from the Air Jamaica flight.' Blank. 'Are you expecting us?' I feared the worst, but he nodded in the affirmative.

'Can I have your vouchers?'

'We don't have any vouchers.'

'No vouchers?'

'No.'

Bemused look. He goes to the telephone.

By now, there are fifty of us, all waiting to check in.

Eventually, he finishes his conversation.

'Okay. You must fill in these forms.'

Mad rush for forms. One pen. Scribble anything. Grab the room key. Let's go.

The receptionist tells us there are refreshments for us in the bar. Predicably they're not ready.

It's 2.30 am, we decide it's time for bed.

Early morning in England. Best phone home and say we won't be arriving today.

Mother-in-law. 'Hello, dears. Late. Oh, is it the hijack? I've just seen it on the news.' At least she is better informed than us.

Next day. I am faced with whiling the day away in the same clothes as I wore yesterday and hoping nobody notices. However, by pure chance at the airport on the previous evening, I made what I thought was a last-minute purchase, the obligatory T-shirt bearing a Che Guevara image. Today, it gets an early and unexpected outing.

We are bused back to the airport and eventually at around six o'clock we are airborne. Hurray. Don't cheer too soon. At Kingston, Jamaica, a scheduled stop. As we decamp to the transit lounge, I notice an identical plane to ours on the tarmac. No sooner have we arrived in the lounge than we are told to embark. We all about-face and head back to the plane. We are to board the second plane. It's identical so if we all go to the same seat, no problem. This plane was due to fly to London late tonight. All clean and tidy, spick and span. They have four hours to valet and service our original plane and that can fly later. At last, somebody is showing some common sense. But it is too good to be true. No sooner are we settled back into our seats than the pilot announces that we are heading to Montego Bay. It is only twenty minutes away. There we are to pick up passengers who were expecting to fly to Manchester. Instead, they are coming with us to Heathrow, and then by coach to Manchester. Ouch!

At Montego Bay, the cabin crew tell us to stay in our seats, we will be here only thirty minutes to load the Manchester passengers and then be on our way. On they come, moaning that they are going to London instead of Manchester. Given our trials and tribulations we are perhaps uncharacteristically not very sympathetic and tell them that if they think they are being flown from London to Manchester they are mistaken, they will be going by bus. At least they will arrive on the day they expected to get home.

There are about fifty boarding passengers but they have been allocated seats that are already occupied. Chaos and confusion reigns. It is an hour and a half later before we take off again. Eventually, we land at Heathrow twenty-two hours behind schedule.

Three years later and the lure has been too strong. We are back in Cuba. This time via a cruise ship, and our first stop is the city of Santiago de Cuba some 400 miles south-east of Havana. We grab a taxi near the port. It is a clapped-out old Lada, probably dating back to the '80s, when the Russians were much more in evidence here. The driver has introduced himself by the name of Beche and he makes a circular motion to indicate a tour around the city, but what we have in mind is a trip to Castillo del Morro, set on the headland that protects the natural bay in which the city is located. We agree on a fare of US $40 and set off. It is an official yellow cab but has seen better days, with all the wiring exposed beneath the dashboard, and Beche quickly demonstrates the air-conditioning system by leaning backwards to turn the handle to open the rear window. Despite his attention, it is barely ajar. It must be a persistent problem, as he gives the handle a turn at every opportunity, rather negating the need to pay attention to where he is going, but the window remains stubbornly just a few inches open.

From the outset, we fear some misunderstanding, because instead of heading out of the city we are driving up the hill towards Cespedes Square. We pass a group of schoolgirls in smart uniforms; they must be about eighteen, with ultra-short skirts and shapely figures redolent of St Trinian's. Beche and I exchange knowing looks, but I am immediately rebuked when a voice from the back seat says, 'Lecherous old man.' Our concerns about direction of travel are reinforced, but eventually we transit the square and head in what we perceive to be the right direction.

Beche cannot quite get his head around the idea that we don't understand Spanish, well, very few words, and he babbles away, obviously pointing out places of interest.

The castle is some 8 miles from the city centre but well worth the visit. When we arrive, Beche guides us along a path, past kiosks selling the usual tourist paraphernalia to the castle entrance. He tells us to wait and I correctly guess that he has gone in search of an English-speaking guide. Marta is a charming mulatto girl, smartly dressed in a white blouse and khaki skirt. From the ramparts, the strategic significance of the castle is only too obvious and Marta explains how the Spanish protected the city from the unruly elements that made life difficult here during the seventeenth through to the early nineteenth century.

These seemed to have been graded by degree of moral degradation; filibusters, corsairs, buccaneers and pirates. I had heard of these terms but would have been unable to explain the distinctions without this history lesson. Sir Francis Drake was perhaps the most famous filibuster. These were people undertaking military activities in foreign lands without the express permission of their own government. Drake of course caused so much discomfort to England's enemy, Spain, that Queen Elizabeth the First eventually gave him recognition in the form of a knighthood. Drake's activities led to the emergence of what in the Caribbean were often called Privateers although in the Mediterranean that had existed for some hundreds of years where they were known as Corsairs. Henry Morgan was one such, Captain of a vessel being outside the formal military structure but holding a writ to act on behalf of a Government against its enemies. The term Pirate refers to robbery committed at sea and the distinction between Pirates and Buccaneers being that the latter committed criminal acts on both sea and land. This period of lawlessness ended in the early nineteenth century at which time the colonial powers, particularly Britain and France, wanted to establish more formal governance over this part of the world.

I compliment Marta on her English. Although spoken with a slight accent, her prose and vocabulary are consummate. She says that she majored in English at the local university but has never travelled outside of Cuba.

We have moved on to the ramparts of the castle with views back over the city, but more importantly we look down on a narrow entrance to the harbour that made this such a significant strategic structure. Little wonder the marauding pirates had no success in penetrating the defences of the city.

Our tour takes us on to the arsenal from where cannonballs were stored and conveyed up to the guns lining the upper ramparts. Marta is happy to broaden the conversation beyond matters historical, and I ask her whether there is an inherent conflict between communism and the dominance of Catholicism in Cuban society. She says that Santeria is common in Cuba. Her mother is a believer. This is a form of Catholicism mixed with ideas brought by slaves from West Africa. Marta says that her personal philosophy is one of self and that she must hold on to the idea of achieving what you want in life.

Our castle tour is coming to an end. As we approach the exit to the castle, Marta points out a stall selling carved figures of voluptuous women. They are in contrast to her elfin shape and we share a joke over the contrast. We say our goodbyes. I give her an avuncular hug of thanks and discreetly pass her a $5 note, expressing the hope that it will be of some value. Since our last visit, the authorities have stamped on the widespread use of the greenback, but she confirms that the offering is more than welcome.

History lesson over, we pile into the Lada for the short journey back to the city. I try unsuccessfully to ask Beche to take the longer but more scenic Carrera Turistica back to the city. He either doesn't understand or has maybe decided that the sooner he can get his hands on the agreed $40 fare, the better, so we return along the same bumpy road.

Next stop is the Moncada Barracks where the "Cuban Revolution" had an inglorious beginning back on the 26th of July 1953. Most of the rebels trying to overthrow the dictator Batista were killed, and Fidel Castro, one of this motley group, was captured. Batista perhaps made his biggest mistake by later granting a pardon, releasing Castro into exile in Mexico some two years later. From here, he plotted his eventual return and after a bitter civil war was ultimately to take power himself following his triumphant re-entry to Santiago de Cuba in January 1959. The barracks now house a school and small museum, but most impressive are the bullet holes in the outer walls, filled in following the 1953 raid but we are assured carefully and accurately "restored" since the "Revolution".

Beche drives us around the Plaza de la Revolucion and soon we are at the point where we have asked to be dropped, Parque Cespedes, in the very heart of the city. There is something of a contretemps as we offer Beche the agreed US $40 fare. We know that the dollar is, officially at least, no longer welcome. Beche points to the bank adjacent to where we are standing, but it is Saturday afternoon and the bank is closed. Reluctantly, and much to Beche's advantage, I pull out a Euro50 note from my wallet. If he was a surgeon, his monthly salary would probably be less than this.

It is time for a drink and we make our way to the verandah of the Hotel Casa Grande to enjoy a strong shot of espresso coffee and a few minutes to absorb the hubbub of the city. The hotel itself has a certain charm; built in classical style, it appears in Graham Greene's *Our Man in Havana* as a haven for the espionage community. Looking around, it is hard to see any of my fellow guests falling into that category, then again what does a spy look like?

We take a stroll around the plaza. An old man sitting on a park bench.

I say old, people here can look older than they do at home, but I guess he is in fact in his seventies and not much older than me. He looks quite distinguished, with square shoulders and a straight back and I am, as it proves totally incorrectly, thinking military. He immediately sees we are strangers:

'Where are you from?' he asks, in a near perfect accent.

'England,' we reply in unison.

'I was an English teacher at the high school. I used to tell my students that you really must practise using a foreign language every day if you want to become really proficient. Perhaps I should follow my own advice.'

I tell him he has nothing to worry about, and that his English is excellent.

Before moving on, Rosie slips him the now customary bar of soap that we know are in short supply and although he readily slips it into his jacket pocket, he says, 'Madam, thank you, but if you really want to help me, I wonder if I can ask you for a pen.'

It is his lucky day. He finishes up with a fine rollerball picked up at some fancy hotel or exhibition. Of no consequence to us but something to cherish for him.

As we turn to leave, I cannot help but wonder if he taught Marta her English. That would make for perfect symmetry; maybe he did but maybe he didn't.

Then for us it is a return to Havana. We are interested in seeing what has changed in the period since our last visit but also to catch some parts of the city we missed first time around. The answer to the former is, very little, except that the renovation has moved on, albeit at a pace that means that it will be ongoing for the foreseeable future, providing funds are still forthcoming from the rest of the world community.

We head for the Plaza Vieja. Almost immediately after entering the square, at one corner we notice a sign indicating a lift to get rooftop views over the city and pay 2 *pesos* to take a ride to the top. It proves money well spent. From the lift, we exit along a narrow corridor before entering a room where two young people are sitting behind a desk selling tickets. For what, we don't know, so we exit onto the rooftop garden from where the views over the square below are brilliant and we can see that apart from one building, the restoration programme in the square below is complete. We begin to take in the wider panoramic views across the city when, from the room we exited, a man silhouetted in the bright sunlight calls across in English,

'Come and see the show. It is a very special way to see the city.' As I walk across, I see that it is not the young man selling tickets but an older man, perhaps in his early fifties, smartly dressed in shirt and trousers, his wavy hair flecked with grey. The older man explains that to enjoy the views costs us 4 *pesos* each, to be paid to the young man at the desk. Once payment has been made, the older man ushers us into a very small and darkened room where we find we are in company with about eight other people.

The man introduces himself. His name is Enrique and he tells the assembled group in both Spanish and English that he is our guide to Havana. We stand around a large inverted contact lens-shape, perhaps 8 feet across, on which through a system of lenses and mirrors we see a projection of the city, enabling Enrique, through manipulating a lever, to scan through 360 degrees, to bring buildings into close-up and to point out the major sights around the city. The presentation lasts only about ten minutes but Enrique is informative and amusing. At the end of the presentation, everyone makes for the exit but Enrique says to us, 'Wait a moment. I have a story to tell you.'

Enrique leads us to a corner of the roof garden and points across to the Castillo del Morro, guarding the entrance to the fine natural harbour. 'The Spanish built this to protect the city. In 1762, 200 British ships gathered in the bay beyond, ready to attack, but the Spanish were ready and pulled a huge chain across the harbour entrance to block their entry. But the British were not to be foiled and instead of attacking the city from the sea, they landed 2,000 troops further up the coast.' He points to somewhere beyond the castle keep. 'They attacked the fortress from the unprotected rear and captured the city. So, for nearly a year, from 1762 to 1763, Cuba was British. If they had stayed, things may have turned out very differently here but then the British got the bargain of the century. They got Florida in exchange for Cuba and the Spanish returned here.'

We ask him about his own background and he says that he has been a manager in the port before taking this job.

Looking down from the roof, we can see a cruise ship in the terminal.

I ask, 'I see that they have renovated part of the port. Do they plan to complete the job?'

'What is the point? Only last week, a cruise ship came in here. This week, we heard that the Americans had bought it, so it will not be coming here again.'

'But what about the present? We heard Fidel was very ill but under his brother Raúl things have begun to change.'

'I don't think so. Same people, same ideas.' He seems pessimistic and downbeat.

His final word on the subject is, 'We are not like our neighbours [referring to the United States]. We all share our poverty here.'

He asks where we come from. 'Do you live near London? My greatest ambition in life is to visit London.'

We wish him well and tell him that it will happen one day.

We say that we plan to stroll through the old city to Centro and he responds, 'You must go to the cigar factory behind the Capitol building. I myself had never been until last week. You will find it fascinating.'

'Do the women still roll the cigars on their thighs?' I enquire.

'Yes,' he replies with a laugh, 'but they are old and fat with heavy thighs,' sensing that I had visualised something altogether more sultry and erotic. I join him with a chuckle, tinged with disappointment.

'And the Capitol.'

'We have seen it on a previous visit.'

'But have you been inside?'

'No, we didn't know that it was possible.'

With that in mind, we take our leave of Enrique and make our way through the square and towards Centro. The streets here have not enjoyed the loving restoration of the main squares. Instead, we make our way cautiously between broken flagstones and rubbish, still able to admire the faded splendour of the buildings with their impressive inner courtyards, despite decades of neglect. We muse that if ever the rest of the world were to offer tangible help to Cuba, it should be in the form of tins of paint.

Following Enrique's advice, we find the cigar factory. We make our way up a dark staircase to the workshop, where a group of generally large and elderly ladies are working away at benches, handmaking the famed Cuban cigar.

Close by is the Capitolio, a smaller version of the building of the same name in Washington DC and outwardly as impressive. Access is not obvious and clearly not via the grand stairway that fronts the building. We wander around and eventually at the rear find an entrance. It looks like it is some ministry or other, with people going in and out in businesslike fashion, and we enter with some reluctance. However, once inside, at the foot of a hugely impressive marbled staircase, a small booth where a young girl is selling entrance tickets. We pay our 4 *pesos* and make our way into the very heart of the building. We wander along wide and empty corridors. We peer through an open door into what, despite the lack of lighting, is clearly a parliament chamber. At this point, a female attendant appears, not to shoo us away as we anticipate but to conspiratorially lead us inside, where she indicates that she will take our photograph. We reward this act of kindness with a few *pesos* and wander off down the corridor. At the office of the Speaker of the Senate there is a repeat performance. An attendant – 'No, you cannot enter' – followed by the furtive glances, the smuggling of us inside and the photograph. We are getting the hang of this. The same happens with the enormous gold-gilded Statue of Liberty, and by the time the attendant wants us to "secretly" visit the library, we are appreciating that far from being a cheap cultural experience, a visit to the Capitolio is in fact becoming, if a little more expensive than it seemed at first, something of an adventure.

After such a busy morning, we take coffee, once again alfresco, in the café part of the Hotel Inglaterra, and from here we take a cab to Vedado. Not in one of the famous '50s American saloons but a modern and well-appointed Renault, a fleet of which seems to have been acquired by the authorities since our last visit. We are headed for the celebrated Coppelia ice cream parlour. There can be few places in the world where it is worth waiting three or four hours in a queue in the hot tropical sun to enjoy a couple of scoops of ice cream, but that is what the Cubans do on a daily basis. We arrive in the early afternoon thinking this might be a quiet time, but already the queues are weaving their way around the adjacent park. Whilst we stand discussing whether to wait in line, a young man stewarding the crowds comes across and recognising immediately that we are tourists addresses us in excellent English with the customary, 'Where are you from?' before shepherding us in the direction of a special area set aside for foreigners where there are no queues. Here, service is immediate and hassle-free, although prices are in convertible *pesos*, ten times the price paid by the locals but still comparable to prices we would pay at home.

From here, we stroll through familiar streets to return to our old haunt, the Nacional Hotel. It has lost none of its charm. Instead of the famed and powerfully strong mojito, another cup of coffee, in its way equally intense, the only way they take it here.

In the evening, we take another walk to find ourselves a café or bar to have a drink and listen to some of the famous rhythms of Cuba. It proves more difficult than we anticipated. The streets are near deserted and most bars are empty. Maybe it is a little early for the nightlife, or perhaps times are now so hard that the locals cannot afford a night out. It is a disappointment, as this was something we missed doing on our earlier visit.

The next day, we are strolling through the old city again and come across Cathedral Square. The renovation is now complete. It is a beautiful location but small and intimate. We stop for a drink, at tourist prices, at El Patio, a café bar housed in what was once a palace. A band is playing for the clientele of the bar. Two old men in pinstripe suits, trilby hats and white patent leather shoes are touting to have their photographs taken with tourists at a dollar a time, or maybe a convertible *peso*. They each have a huge Havana cigar that they pretend to smoke, rather in the manner of Groucho Marx, and we speculate that they probably make more than a doctor or engineer. Ladies in traditional costumes circulate with the same purpose. An old woman who looks at least a hundred, plump middle-aged ladies and young girls with white embroidered blouses worn enticingly off the shoulder. A transvestite in an ill-fitting wig and tight skirt but with no boobs joins the throng dancing to the rhythm of the music.

A few tables away, sitting alone and sipping a mojito from a tall glass, I notice an attractive woman with the classical high-cheekboned features of a Greek goddess. She too is wearing what must be a locally purchased white off-the-shoulder blouse and khaki combat trousers. On her head, a military cap in the style much favoured by Fidel. A lonely tourist fully embracing the revolutionary spirit of the place! Even here she appears oddly eccentric and out of place. She calls across to the waiter to pay. I strain to hear the conversation. She sounds American. I think that she is explaining that although she would like to stay, she has to catch a flight and points to the time on a huge chronograph watch on her wrist. She rises and goes across to the singer in the band, no doubt to thank them for the entertainment, and then she is gone.

The band take a well-earned break and the transvestite begins to circulate around the tables looking for tips and is shooed away by the waiters. I notice three youths, probably in their mid-teens, entering the square from Calle San Ignacio beside the cathedral, and suddenly they are stopped by policemen emerging from the shadows on three sides of the square. The youths are subjected to questioning until a middle-aged man with a large paunch protruding from beneath a pristine white shirt intervenes. An animated conversation ensues. The boys are not cowed and seem to be anxious to make their point, then as quickly as this little fracas has occurred, it subsides. The man continues on his way across the square, the youths make their way, exit left, and the policemen return to the shadows as hurriedly as they emerged.

After our visit to the Moncada Barracks, I am interested in learning more about the Revolution, so we make a visit to the Museo de la Revolucion housed in the former presidential palace. We had simply passed by on our first visit to Havana; now I was intent on exploring the museum more fully. The building has a somewhat rundown air in comparison to the splendour of the Capitolio. In a series of first-floor rooms, it is possible to follow the progress of the Revolution from that initial attack on the barracks in Santiago back in 1953 to the eventual arrival of Fidel into Havana in early 1959 and the ongoing influence of El Comandante in the years since. Apart from a few artefacts, the story is largely told through photographs, with explanatory notes in Spanish and occasionally in English. Outside the building, an extension of the museum contains larger artefacts including *Granma*, the boat that brought Fidel and his compatriots back to the island in 1956 and which we viewed from a distance on our earlier visit to the city.

Given it is nearly half a century that Fidel has been in power, it is perhaps not surprising that we are just some of a handful of visitors. Travelling to Cuba, there cannot be a more appropriate place to end your visit.

Cuba remains as fascinating and alluring as ever. Most share my view. When I exchange notes with people we meet, a minority describe Cuba as dirty, rundown and with terrible food. I don't bother to argue; I just smile inside.

# Seventeen

Colombia: Bolivar and coffee

Colombia: With a population of 50 million, one of the largest countries in South America has a tainted reputation due to years of civil war and a highly developed drug trade. The most infamous drug cartel was that led by Pablo Escobar. Today, the country prefers to be known for its coffee production and burgeoning tourist industry, although its main exports are actually oil and coal. Language – Spanish.

Until recently, it had been an unlikely destination for tourists, but now with the civil war subsided and the drug barons tamed, Colombia has become the must-see place. So here we are enjoying a pre-dinner drink on the verandah outside of our room at the Hacienda Bambusa in the heart of Colombia's Coffee Region or Zona Cafetera.

Periodically, I lift myself from the comfort of the wicker sofa in an attempt to shoot the perfect still frame photograph of one of the many hummingbirds sucking at the honeycomb in the birdfeeder, thoughtfully hung outside our first-floor room by the hotel management. A mission I am determined to pursue, despite the words of derision emanating from Rosie.

The evening air is pleasantly cool and fresh after three days spent at altitude in highly polluted Bogota.

Not that Bogota was without some merit and offered an eclectic mix of sights and sounds, from puffing up to the top of Monserrate, the mountain overlooking the city, to a stroll around La Candelaria, the old city.

In La Candelaria, we first visited the impressive Museo de Oro (Gold Museum). Set in a small square, the entrance area had attracted a noisy array of people. Food stalls, street artists and vendors selling souvenirs. It was here that we saw for the first time evidence that an earlier visitor to the city was Mick Jagger. An ice cream seller having a sign to the effect that Mick had purchased an ice cream from his stall. At the time, apart from mild amusement, we admired his entrepreneurial spirit. Later, we discovered Mick had enjoyed another ice cream, also a hamburger from other stallholders around the old city. Dodging between the crowds, we made our way into the more staid interior of the museum.

As these things go, it has to be said that this is a beautifully presented collection of some of the 50,000 plus gold artefacts and a must for any visitor to the city. Many of the relics are the works of tribes living in the area that we now call Colombia, often dating back hundreds of years. Two displays worthy of special mention are the Poporo Quimbaya and the Balsa Muisca. The *poporo* is a traditional storage vessel. This particular version is of course made of solid gold and has been dated to around AD 300. Stolen from a burial mound, it was later purchased by the museum and became the very first artefact to be displayed when the museum opened in 1939, subsequently becoming a national icon.

The Balsa Muisca has a similarly chequered history. In contrast to the simplicity of the *poporo*, the Muisca raft is an elaborate depiction of a raft with the figure of the tribal chieftain as the centrepiece, surrounded by his guards. It is believed to represent the traditional ceremony of investiture for a new chief. This ritual involved the body of the soon-to-be-anointed king being covered in gold. Then carrying emeralds as tribute to the gods, he dived into the sacred Lake Guatavita. In the museum, the golden raft is presented in a darkened room and with the aid of clever lighting effects appears to float on the surface of the lake. In legend, it is said that when the Spanish invaded, the Muisca raft was hidden by the local people by immersion in the lake. Like the *poporo*, the Balsa Muisca was discovered relatively recently, in 1969, although not in the lake but within a nearby cave complex. Villagers coming across a ceramic pot and discovering, hidden inside, the Muisca raft. The true stuff of legends.

From the Gold Museum, we walk the short distance down to the central square, Plaza de Bolivar. The huge square features a bronze statue of the great man. However, most of the surrounding buildings from the Spanish colonial era have long since gone, so the square itself is something of a disappointment. Noteworthy on our right as we enter the square is the Palace of Justice, scene of one of the bloodiest events in Colombia's long-running civil war. In 1985, members of the leftist M19 guerrilla group took over the building, then occupying the site, taking hostage many judges and in total some 300 people. The Army immediately responded, securing the release of many of the hostages, and the following day it made an attack on the building using some heavy artillery, causing major damage but bringing an end to the siege, sadly leaving a death toll of some one hundred people. The original building being virtually destroyed, today a modern edifice, opened in 2004, stands on the site.

Across from here, only metres away, one building that has stood on the square from the Spanish times, the Catedral Primada, although this particular iteration dates from only 1823, the sixteenth-century building previously on this site having been destroyed by an earthquake. The cavernous cathedral is worth a look, but the main feature of note is that the interior surprisingly lacks ostentation. Perhaps something more interesting about the cathedral we discover later. We are walking up a road at the side when we notice a small door or side entrance. This we learn is the Pauper's Door, an entrance through which the poor were allowed to enter, even then remaining behind a screen erected between them and the upper classes seated in the pews. Whilst all equal before God, some more so than others.

Along from the cathedral at one corner of the square by the Museo Militar, we get a glimpse of the changing of the guard at the nearby Casa de Narino, the presidential palace. We hurry down to get a close-up view but the approach road to the palace is barred and guarded by armed soldiers, presumably awaiting the arrival of some dignitary, or perhaps the imminent departure of the president.

So unable to go in the direction of the palace undaunted, we instead take a left turn into Calle 9 to view the Teatro Colon. Opened in 1892, it has an impressive Italianate-style façade. Next door, set back from the road, is the house once occupied by Bolivar's mistress Dona Manuela Saenz. The story goes that the building on the opposite side of the street is where Bolivar, after returning from his successful military campaigns in Peru and Bolivia, was effectively held under house arrest.

In 1819, Bolivar fought his way through Colombia, winning battles, most significantly at Boyaca, triumphantly arriving in Bogota to be declared President of Gran Colombia, a combination of what is now three separate countries: Colombia, Panama and Venezuela. However, after the initial euphoria of victory, the ruling Congress fragmented into factions; Centralists (later Conservatives), like Bolivar, and Federalists (Liberals) favouring looser links between the newly independent countries of Central and South America.

Although nominally still president of Gran Colombia, Bolivar, hero of South American independence, spends much of the next decade away from home, fighting new causes in countries to the south. In his absence, his deputy, a Federalist, besmirches his reputation. He is a man with contrary views to Bolivar. Bolivar is a staunch Centralist with the vision of an even grander Colombia to match the emerging United States in the north. Thus, in 1830, returning to Bogota, Bolivar finds the political landscape much changed. Fearing that her lover's life was in danger, and with good reason, his longtime mistress, Manuela, goes to the place where he is being held, distracts his captors and facilitates his escape through an open window. A broken man, Bolivar retreats to the coastal town of Santa Marta, where he dies of TB later that year. It is to be a sad end to the man today still revered throughout the Americas.

Moving on, we are in Calle 11. Here, the former buildings of the Banco de la Republica have been turned over to an impressive complex of three museums: art, money and the Museo Botero.

Until we entered the building Fernando Botero was not an artist that we knew, but we are immediately taken by his works after viewing the extensive collection on display here.

Born in Medellin in 1932, Fernando came from a relatively poor background. On leaving school, he is sent by his uncle to train as a matador. With little exposure to the arts, he nevertheless shows a natural talent as a painter and soon leaves his putative career behind, moves to Bogota and in 1952, earns his first exhibition at what for an aspiring artist is a remarkably young age. Within months, he has moved to Europe, initially to Madrid but then to Paris, where he spends much of his time studying works of artists like Picasso in the Louvre. Later, he moves to Italy. Here, he is influenced by the great Renaissance artists.

In the mid-1950s, Botero completes *Still Life with Mandolin*, his first painting in what is to become his unique personal style that is ultimately to prove his trademark. In the '60s, he moves to New York and after a brief flirtation with the New York School of Painters, he returns to what becomes known as "Boterismo", his unique style of inflating portraits of his subjects in a way that has been described as "volumetric stylization of figures" in both paintings and subsequently in sculptures. In my simple terms, his subjects are largely depicted as rotund men and women.

The other essential dimension in Botero's works is the element of political satire. This collection in the Museo Botero is highly representative of both his own work and his influences and was donated by Botero to the nation. It contains not only 123 of his works but also more than eighty works from his personal collection by artists such as Chagall and Picasso, artists that influenced his own artistic development. The Botero collection includes his famous version of the *Mona Lisa,* together with satirical paintings such as *El Presidente*, together with apparently innocuous subject matter with mundane titles, *The Family* and *Man on Horse*. Suffice to say, we liked his material a lot.

For much of our time in Bogota, we used the services of Alexis as our guide. A rather intense young man in his early thirties, quite bookish but suitably knowledgeable and informative. Today, he is taking us on a trip out of the city to the nearby town of Zipaquira. It is famous for its salt cathedral.

This is an odd tourist attraction, because the cathedral is carved within the chambers of a still-operating salt mine. The mine is cavernous. The actual "cathedral" is about a kilometre from the entrance. As you pass through the various chambers, replicated are statues and icons placed every so often and depicting the "stations of the cross" before you eventually reach the area designated as the cathedral. Alexis is the ideal guide, as he previously worked here for five years as a tour guide. There are three naves representing the stages of the birth, life and death of Jesus. Before reaching the cathedral, a small chapel containing a beautifully carved statue made by one of the miners. This became an icon for the miners. They started what has become a ritual of taking it with them as a keepsake when they enter the mine to begin work. The icon is a depiction of the Virgin de Guasa, and she has become the patron saint of miners.

I find it a little bizarre, as this place with its religious overtones also has a commercial element. Occupying nooks and crannies as you walk through the broad passages are an eclectic mix of stallholders selling all manner of goods. One such encounter is when Alexis introduces us to his brother-in-law, who has a stall selling lamps. The mine has attracted not only tourists but also artists. Their works, often utilising the salt, adorn many of the walls with some incredibly elaborate carvings, some with a religious theme, others with random subject matter like birds and flowers, and very much work in progress. An interesting diversion for a morning away from the hustle and bustle of the city.

Afterwards, emerging from the mine, we walk the short distance down to the town square. Although it is Sunday morning, there are plenty of people around and several vendors have set up stalls. The one attracting most attention is an old-fashioned Western movie-style medicine man selling a potion judging by the list of ailments itemised on a large board behind his stall, 'guaranteed to cure all ills'. He is working very hard with his patter and has attracted an interested if not totally convinced group of bystanders.

We spend our last day in Bogota wandering around the downtown area close to our hotel. When we return to our room, we find a complimentary bowl of fruit. I have mentioned before the exotic fruits to be found in South America still not familiar on our supermarket shelves. Today, the hotel has thoughtfully included a little explanatory leaflet. Other than the pineapple, mango and watermelon, none of the fruits are recognisable. I can report the *granadilla* is a large ball coloured orange with a hard outer skin and with flesh akin to that of passion fruit. The *pitahaya,* also a large ball but with nodules. Yellow in colour, it has a soft flesh and pips. The *guanabana* is green, also with a hard knobbly skin. The bitter white flesh can be eaten by scooping it out with a spoon. The *zapote* looks like a plum and can be eaten the same way by removing the stone. The *caimito* is purple and resembles a passion fruit but comes with a warning that its peel can irritate the human skin.

After our few days in Bogota, we take a short plane journey to Armenia, not the country but a small provincial town in Colombia's smallest province, Quindio. This in the heart of the country's coffee region. At Armenia Airport, we are met by one of the unlikeliest-looking tour guides to be accompanying a couple of ageing Brits. Gustavo has a largely shaven head with the semblance of what was once called a Mohican and is heavily tattooed. Despite appearances, we soon relax into his company and we begin a short but delightful relationship, during which there are few discernible gaps between the laughter. I have alluded to this before. A good guide can make your journey memorable. Whilst we prefer to explore large cities on our own, walking or using public transport and maybe with the help of a guidebook, once on the road travelling around a country, the services of a good guide offer quality time learning more about that country. Wherever possible, we like to set off the relationship by saying: *You are the local expert. Tell us what you think is interesting. Our particular interests are in the culture and history of your country; however, if there is any wildlife, birds or animals then don't hesitate to point them out.*

Once on board our vehicle, we are heading the hour or so's drive to Hacienda Bambusa. It isn't long after leaving the town behind that the road deteriorates with increasingly large numbers of ever deeper potholes, and before long we are driving on a rough unmade track. Our accommodation proves to be a little remote, rustic but charming. This is where you find me trying to photograph the elusive hummingbird.

Gustavo has arranged an eclectic mix of activities but in this region it is no surprise when the following morning we find ourselves heading to a coffee plantation. The San Antonio is a family-owned estate set upon a hillside at around 3,000 feet, looking down on the pretty village of Buenavista, itself set upon the top of a hill.

Arriving at San Antonio, we are met by David. A slight figure, quite withdrawn in comparison to the ebullient Gustavo but happy to share a joke whilst describing the cycle of cultivating coffee. It is a stiff climb up into the plantation, where David explains the various stages in growing and ultimately picking the coffee beans. Most of the estate employees live on the site in a communal building. David explains that they include some very old and long-standing employees prepared to work hard in labour-intensive jobs that are increasingly failing to attract the younger generation. We join some of them in the *cantina,* where we exchange pleasantries with the ladies preparing lunch for their fellow workers, before touring the small factory facility where the coffee beans are dried, sorted and bagged.

The tour ends with David testing our coffee knowledge, using not just the sense of taste. There is a blindfold smell and taste test and a set of samples to rank in order of quality. At the end of the exercise, we are declared to be baristas first class.

Gustavo has promised us another interesting itinerary in Quindio. Today, we travel through the provincial capital, Armenia, soon passing a burnt-out ruin of what was clearly once a palatial house. Gustavo explains that it was one of many properties owned by none other than Pablo Escobar, the notorious drug baron. Hard to understand that less than a generation ago such a villainous person could openly hold sway across this substantial and well-developed country.

From here, we are heading into the Andes. Our initial stop is in the town of Finlandia. At first sight, the omens are not good. Gustavo takes us to what the locals have created as a major tourist attraction. In a small but well-laid-out park on the edge of town, they have had constructed Finca el Mirador Finlandia, a tall metal tower with views over the town below and the Cordillera Central part of the Andes chain in the near distance. Today, a fine drizzle hangs over the town, and although we climb up the winding path to the *mirador* and clamber up the seemingly endless staircase to the viewing platform, we can see little beyond our vehicle parked in the road below.

From here, we drive the short distance into the town, park our vehicle and begin to walk towards the central plaza. Already we can appreciate Finlandia's charm, with houses painted in colourful pastel shades and their balconies and doors in stronger hues, offering a cacophony of colour. Typically, a simple front door to a modest house not in red or green or blue but a combination of all three colours.

By the time we have reached the town square, we are blessed. The rain ceases and gradually the skies clear. As ever, it is a square dominated by an impressive church, this painted white with blue trimmings.

However, we do not head for the church. Gustavo is anxious for us to try a local speciality, clearly something of a personal favourite, and he leads us into a small shop. The façade comprises just a door and a tiny window. Inside, it is barely the width of a corridor and to the back of the shop we meet the proprietor, a large, buxom lady wearing a floral apron. We have come to sample her product, fruit-flavoured ice lollies. The lollies are as colourful as the houses and with an infinite variety of hues and flavours on offer. Some of the fruits being used we do not recognise, even after Gustavo attempts to identify them for us, either in Spanish or for that matter English, so we decide to select on the basis of our preferred colour combination. As we soon discover, the unique feature of the lollies is that after every few licks, you actually come across not just another flavour but an actual piece of one of these exotic tropical fruits.

We take a walk around the plaza. This one is so like many of the towns in this part of the world, with the centrepiece; pleasant, well-tended gardens; the church on one side and shops and cafés filling the remaining space around the perimeter. We come across a line of parked Jeeps. Gustavo explains that these are Willys, the same Jeeps used by American forces in World War II and familiar to anyone who has ever watched a movie about the war. The difference is that these jeeps are not painted in military khaki or grey but like their surroundings, they are multi-coloured with various bold embellishments, headlights, klaxons, metal bars, you name it, but all in tip-top condition. Gustavo cannot explain why, but the Jeeps have become a notable feature of the area, both collector's pieces and now also a tourist attraction.

Throughout Colombia, as you might expect, it is easy to find coffee. The most prominent brand is Juan Valdez, incidentally the brand an invention of the fertile mind of some marketeer many moons ago and not an actual person. There is a Juan Valdez coffee shop in the square, but we look for something more local and authentic. It is not difficult and in a side street find a tiny family-run coffee shop where we purchase two coffees, short and mega strong.

Rendezvousing again with Gustavo, we move on to the nearby Los Nevados National Park where we are to take a hike. At the park entrance, Gustavo meets some old friends who are park wardens. Together they chat away and then become quite animated. Pointing to the sky above, not one but several condor gliding on the thermals. Even here in the national park and with professional naturalists, it is obviously a rare sighting, so we regard ourselves as quite privileged.

The plan is to hike up to a viewpoint looking down into a valley below. The terrain is interesting, sloping hills quite bare but for the occasional spindly and extremely tall palm tree. This is the Quindio Wax Palm, the Colombian national tree and a symbol of Colombia. We set off at what we think is a reasonable pace, albeit at altitude quite strenuous, but after about half an hour Gustavo decides that it is time to stop and turn back. He obviously thinks that at our age and level of fitness we are not going to make it to the *mirador* in time to fulfil the rest of our day's itinerary. We feign a degree of disappointment but in practice a sensible decision.

Returning to our vehicle we make our way back down through Cocora Valley, pulling into a resthouse for refreshments. Here, Gustavo introduces us to Roberto, who is running a local eco project. They lead us to a garden plot at the rear. I am to plant a small Quindio wax palm as our contribution to saving the planet. We oblige and it is of course another photo opportunity. We are assured that once the sapling has grown, it will be replanted somewhere on the hillside above.

Our final stop today is in another colourful town, Salento. Amazing to find so much of note in just this small portion of Colombia. Salento boasts the normal plaza, but the main artery of the town is the street that runs from the plaza and at the end of which are steps leading to a *mirador* overlooking the town below. The main street once again has colourful buildings. Today, it seems quite sleepy; a few kids making their way home from school and outside a café, four old men sit around a table playing a board game, which appears to resemble draughts. Rosie is looking to buy some small gifts and we browse in some shops in a tiny arcade off the main street, where she purchases some colourful bracelets.

It has been an extraordinarily productive day for understanding life in this small province in the centre of Colombia, made possible of course thanks to Gustavo's good humour and local knowledge. As I have stated many times, the local guide is an essential ingredient to informed travel, albeit there should always be time to spend exploring without a guide and drawing one's own conclusions. In countries like Colombia, travelling long distances means spending a lot of time on the road; time to get to know your guide and build relationships. Gustavo with his extraordinary hairstyle cuts an unusual figure for a tour guide, but as we discover, he is a pretty normal young man. Quite endearing is his attachment to his grandmother, who he visits most days, although this may in part be due to her home cooking, with Gustavo being particularly partial to her version of the popular local dish *bandeja paisa,* which when described in detail sounds like the equivalent of our mixed grill. The main ingredients according to Gustavo being sausage, beef and rice, together with Granny's personal additions, all topped off with a fried egg.

Gustavo has lived in the United States so his command of English is nuanced, although he is still fascinated by the odd idiosyncratic terminology like "gnat's pee" when we compare American coffee with that we have enjoyed in Colombia. He tells us that he is enjoying our company and we kid him that is what he tells all of his clients, although we know that it is a compliment and that the feeling is mutual. He relates stories about some previous patrons, sometimes the rich and famous, like the Spanish golf club owner whose golf club has something in common with Gustavo's name, a multi-millionaire and a generous tipper. Another not-to-be-named-here client was the head of a famous Parisian fashion house. He treated Gustavo like a slave, demanding this and that on a whim and criticising everything he saw, but relief was at hand. On the third day of a programmed one-week stay, he suddenly demanded, 'Get me a plane out of here. I don't like this place.' He of course was not speaking about a scheduled airline, and Gustavo was mightily relieved when after some frantic organising, the man boarded his executive jet back to Europe.

Today, as I pen these reflections on our time so far in Colombia, I need to bring you up to date. We are taking something of a break from our hectic schedule, hence I have time to watch at close quarters the habits of the hummingbird. This morning, the Hacienda manager organised for us a guided tour of the surrounding estate. It is owned by the Montoya family, the son Pablo being the Formula One racing driver. Gustavo has a problem with the hotel management. They don't approve of him and make things difficult when he collects his clients. No doubt they are influenced by his appearance. Maybe because of this, instead of using him they have found a local guide to show us around. In fairness, he is charming and well informed. His name is Guillermo.

We set off from the hacienda. Making our way through the estate, Guillermo leads us into a field to show us the estate's latest project, producing cacao rather than coffee. Until recently, the powerful coffee growers have ensured that a ban has been in place preventing growing cacao, but now that ban has been lifted, the estate owners have been experimenting. Given the favourable climate, they believe that they can grow a crop in twenty-five days. Cacao has not been successfully grown in Colombia before to a commercial quality, but they are experimenting here, grafting the stronger Ecuadorian variety onto the local plant. We pass a herd of Brahman cattle before coming across an open shed, where the more traditional product coffee beans are drying. Even on one of the wealthiest estates in Colombia, the facilities are rudimentary. Taking us on a circuitous route back to the hacienda, Guillermo leads us towards a bamboo forest. Rosie is reluctant, but entering the forest, a path leads us to a glade where a table has been laid, and we enjoy a picnic of fruit juice and cake.

Our final day in Quindio and after a relaxing morning at the hacienda,

Gustavo arrives to take us to the airport. In Armenia, as befits a location so close to a mountain range, the weather can be changeable. At the airport, we say our farewells to Gustavo in glorious sunshine. Minutes later, a tremendous storm arrives and lightning strikes the roof of the terminal building. As a result, we spend the next two hours waiting for our delayed aircraft to arrive and take us on the short flight back to Bogota. The joys of travel.

# Eighteen

El Salvador: War scars

El Salvador: The smallest and most densely populated country in Central America, tucked away on the Pacific Coast with a population in excess of 6 million. With a gang culture and perpetual drug problems, its largest city, San Salvador, has been dubbed the world's murder capital. Language – Spanish.

El Salvador is a country about which frankly I will confess we know little. A country which rarely receives any press attention in the UK, so it was with some interest when about a month before our visit, I came across, albeit brief, a newspaper article reporting that El Salvador had its first saint.

As our plane taxies across the tarmac to our arrival gate, I can see the sign, the Monsenor Oscar Arnulfo Romero International Airport. Oscar Romero now Saint Oscar, but clearly insufficient time has elapsed for a change of name to Saint Oscar International Airport. It is our first encounter with the country's most famous personage.

Soon, immigration formalities quickly concluded, we are, in the early-evening darkness, taking the two-hour drive from the airport to our accommodation in the small lakeside town of Suchitoto in the company of our driver, Alfredo. The roads are busy; it is a National Holiday, the Day of the Dead, and families are travelling to be with loved ones for a communal supper. Most would have spent the day at the local cemetery, decorating the graves or tombs of deceased relatives.

We pass through the eerily darkened streets in the centre of the capital, San Salvador, before heading north on quieter, even darker and now traffic-free roads towards our destination. Given the length of the drive, Alfredo has time to provide us with a useful introduction to his country and his own story, which proves typical of those we hear later during our journey to this the poorest country in Central America.

Alfredo's mother was a single parent who found herself a husband when Alfredo was six years old. She and her partner wanted to start a new life and emigrated to Canada, leaving Alfredo in the charge of a relative. El Salvador was experiencing a civil war and many Salvadoreans, like Alfredo's mother, fled to North America in search of a better and more peaceful life. Despite the war, Alfredo enjoyed a happy youth, growing up in a loving home with his great-aunt, but when he was sixteen, his mother sent for him to go and live with her in Canada. The reasons were far from altruistic. The Canadian Immigration Service became aware of Alfredo's existence and were asking questions as to why he was not living with his mother. Concerned that this might prejudice her chances of remaining in Canada, his mother exercised her maternal rights. In the event, Alfredo was unhappy in his new home. He was in constant conflict with his stepfather and after two years, when he reached the age of eighteen, he returned to El Salvador.

In Suchitoto, we arrive at a quirky hotel housed in an old hacienda run by a gay couple. One is Pascal, a Frenchman with a background working in the fashion industry; the other, Joaquin, is Salvadorean and a former diplomat. Pascal offers a warm welcome and shows us to our room but firmly advises that, it being after 9 pm, no dinner can be offered. Our room, in keeping with the whole establishment, is also unusual. Entry is through a heavy door off the main courtyard. A small reception room with a set of steep stone stairs leads to the bedroom above, plainly furnished but very large. The only window, at eye level, offers views over the rooftops of the old town.

Next morning, after breakfast, we make our way to the reception area, where we are greeted by our guide, Benjamin, who confirms that he is to accompany us for the rest of our stay in El Salvador. Benjamin is aged around forty, stocky, swarthy, with a low forehead and short, dark wavy hair.

First stop is just a few miles out of Suchitoto, where we are to view the

Tercios Falls. The car park is empty save for a man to whom Benjamin hands a few *pesos* to keep our vehicle safe. From here, Benjamin leads us in a downwards direction, with the rough, uneven path soon disappearing, leaving us to clamber after him over large granite boulders. At one point, legs splayed, fingers trying to grip the rock, I actually turn to Rosie and say, 'I think I'm getting too old for this.' I am thinking maybe I should be taking time out from the travelling to complete this book, particularly as after all the physical effort, when we reach the falls, they are relatively but a dribble. The only saving grace is the interesting rock formation at the face of the waterfall, angular basalt rocks rather like those found at the Giant's Causeway.

After clambering back over the rocks to return to our vehicle, we head for Quintera, which Benjamin explains is a village where during the Civil War guerrillas enjoyed wide support from the local people. Only our second day in the country, but already the lasting impact of the Civil War is becoming apparent. It is noon by the time we reach Quintera and as we are to discover, Benjamin has a voracious appetite and nothing will keep him from his lunch. It explains why he is carrying a few extra pounds around his waistline. He takes us to the community-run *cantina,* deserted but for a few youths using the Wi-Fi connection to play games and the inevitable village dogs roaming aimlessly across the room. Benjamin orders us a local dish, a pancake made from squash and filled with a creamy cheese, washed down with a sweet lemonade.

Afterwards, we make our way down into the centre of the village. There is a small museum dedicated to the Civil War and opposite on the end wall of a building, the names listed of villagers killed in the war. There must have been fifty, maybe more. Next to the list, the stencilled face of a man that Benjamin in response to my enquiry says is the image of Agustin Farabundo Martí Rodriguez, a 1930s revolutionary who lends his name to the guerrilla army in the 1980s' civil war, the FMLN or Farabundo Martí National Liberation Front.

Martí led an unsuccessful peasant revolt in 1932, culminating in a bloody massacre of thousands of his supporters and his own subsequent execution. However, he remains a hero of the Left. The reasons for that revolt and the Civil War half a century later were exactly the same: that of land reform. Benjamin explained that since independence from Spain almost 200 years ago, the country had been ruled by a small number of landowners holding vast estates and employing *campesinos,* or peasant farmers, under appalling working conditions to generate their wealth and extravagant lifestyles. Much of this wealth was derived from the burgeoning coffee industry, fuelled by demand from the US and Europe. To protect their interests, as early as the middle of the nineteenth century, the ruling class created a militia and in 1912 this was formalised by the creation of the Guardia National, an army whose purpose was not defence of the realm but to maintain control within the country. During the twentieth century, this control tightened with a succession of dictatorships, often headed by the military.

A little further along, we come to the village church. Outside, the now unmistakable likeness of Saint Oscar Romero. Time to try and understand a little more about the man and Rome's latest canonisation.

Oscar Romero was born in 1917 and was destined by his father's wishes to become a carpenter, but at the age of thirteen, he decided to enter the priesthood. He later studied at the Vatican before returning home to become a village priest, a role he fulfilled for twenty years. During the 1960s and '70s, he held various largely administrative posts within the church and by the age of sixty had achieved little of note. He was therefore the surprise choice for the role of Archbishop of San Salvador when that position fell vacant in 1977. Seen by the Establishment as socially conservative and low-key, a safe and pliable person at a time of increasing political tensions. His "Road to Damascus" moment came in the same year, when his close friend Rutilio Grande, a Jesuit priest working to help the poor, was assassinated. At this moment, Oscar felt it was his destiny to follow the same path as his friend and to work for the cause of the poor and downtrodden.

Romero became increasingly concerned about attacks both verbal and physical on a group of young, newly ordained and progressive Roman Catholic clergy preaching a more liberal form of Catholicism. He himself began to preach along the same lines through the medium of weekly sermons on a Church-run radio station.

The government saw this as a bad influence on civil society, as signs of organised unrest against the regime were increasing. In March 1980, Oscar Romero delivered a sermon addressed to soldiers asking them to stop following orders repressing the population and violating human rights. Moments later in the doorway of the church, he was shot dead.

Days later, a crowd of some quarter of a million gathered outside the Metropolitan Cathedral in the centre of San Salvador for his funeral ceremony.

Bishops from around the world, including the formal representative of the Pope, were in attendance as the Mass commenced. Partway through the ceremony, a bomb exploded in the square, followed by gunfire. On that day, around fifty deaths occurred, some due to gunshot wounds, others trampled to death in the panic which ensued. The perpetrators were never caught, although it is widely believed that they were soldiers firing from the roof of the nearby National Palace.

Here in Quintera like so many other places in El Salvador, Oscar Romero is remembered, but in the village square there are other more tangible memorials to the Civil War. The remains of two large bombs and the tangled wreckage of a shot-down government helicopter.

Away from the shadow of the Civil War, we drive back to town and down to the lakeside. Lago Suchititlan is actually an artificial lake created in 1976, following the building of a hydro-electric dam further down the Lempa River. The dam has created a lake some 25 miles in length that has a natural beauty in its own right and has become home to countless birds. We take a boat for a ride across the lake on a beautiful, warm, sunny afternoon. We are no birders, but we spot egrets by the thousand, herons, storks, cormorants, yellow flycatchers and many more species. A great way to end a very satisfying day.

Next morning and here we are on what Benjamin has promised will be an easy hike up nearby Volcan Guazapa, although we are wary after the previous day when he had us clambering down that precarious muddy path and then inelegantly scrambling over large boulders to view the Tercios Falls. Today, we have taken the main road out of Suchitoto some 10 miles or so to the village of La Mora. Benjamin has parked our vehicle by the side of the road to rendezvous with a local villager. Alberto appears a little diffident as he greets us. He is in his early forties, wearing a T-shirt, slacks and canvas shoes, which makes me think that perhaps the walk won't actually be too arduous. Alberto is slimly built, in contrast to Benjamin, who carries a few surplus pounds thanks to his predilection for *pupusas*, the local staple, more of which later.

Introductions over, Alberto leads us along the highway for about a quarter of a mile before we cross the road and turn up an unmade track. Initially wide enough for a vehicle, the path soon narrows as it begins winding its way gently upwards on what we later realise are the foothills of the volcano. The path is initially well trodden but gradually becomes less delineated and obviously infrequenty used. We pass the time of day with two men labouring in a field of corn and beyond here the climb becomes steeper.

As our walk unfolds, so will Alberto's story, here at the very place where the guerrilla war began in 1980.

Looking back, the fields as far as the eye can see were once part of a huge estate owned by one of El Salvador's dominant ruling families. Fiefdoms, like Britain in the Middle Ages, with the land tilled by the peasants, generating the huge wealth for the tiny ruling elite.

Successive governments in El Salvador promised land reform, but these promises never became reality. Frustrated, by the mid-1970s, civil society began to show signs of revolution. Initially, this occurred not here in the rural countryside by the disenfranchised but in the capital, San Salvador, particularly amongst intellectuals, like university professors, doctors and lawyers. As intimidation and threats increased, the intelligentsia gradually moved away from peaceful protest, taking up arms and moving from the city into the hills where they found support and willing helpers amongst the rural poor. By 1980, El Salvador was experiencing a full-scale civil war.

At the beginning of the Civil War, Alberto was just four years old. One day, soon after the start of the war, truckloads of soldiers arrived in La Mora. The villagers were gathered together and five women were picked out at random. They were marched off. Later that day, three of the women returned to report the other two had been taken into the forest and shot dead. One was Alberto's mother. Their only crime: they "might" be sympathetic to guerrilla groups that had recently moved into the area. This was the Army's way of warning the villagers not to offer the guerrillas help.

The government's fears were well founded. With proximity of a dense forest on the mountainside for cover and a sympathetic local population, this area was soon to be a guerrilla stronghold. The Army's intimidation of villagers like those in La Mora continued, and as the war intensified, the guerrillas decided that to protect the local people, the village had to be abandoned. With the young men of the village having already left to join the guerrilla army, Alberto, with the remaining inhabitants, some 200 old men, women and children, was spirited away to a life in the jungle.

Alberto was to spend the next four years moving around the forest under the protection of the guerrillas. As we climb, we come across the remains of the old village, now virtually overgrown by the jungle. The village was constantly bombed from the air and large craters are still evident, and here, the remains of the village church. The government tactic was to bomb any building where the roof was visible from the air on the premise that the villagers could not afford to replace them, making habitation difficult. Nature quickly finished the job. The church was no exception.

We reach a clearing, which was the location of the village school. Benjamin explains that to keep the peasants ignorant, the ruling elite provided only three years of schooling for children in the rural villages. Today, all that remains of the school are the foundations.

Further along the path, Alberto points out where he believes his mother was shot. Beyond the village and Alberto disappears up the path ahead of us. When we reach him, we find him at the level of our ankles, his head poking out of an old foxhole dug into the ground. Foxholes acted as the villagers' air raid shelters and are still intact for us to see some thirty years later.

Alberto says that after four years in the forest avoiding the bombs and army patrols, the guerrillas decided it was too dangerous a way of life for their civilian supporters. He, like most of the other village children, was sent to a refugee camp close to the capital. Later, he finished up in an orphanage.

The war was a stalemate and eventually the United Nations persuaded the two sides to sit down to talk peace. The agreement reached included land reform and the return of displaced people to their villages. La Mora, bombed to near destruction, was to be rebuilt on a new site, where it is now located close to the main highway. At this juncture in his story, Alberto was reunited with what was left of his extended family. His two older brothers had joined the guerrilla movement after their mother's death and like him had also survived the war.

Continuing on the path beyond the boundaries of the old village, we reach what was the first guerrilla base here at the start of the war. Nearby, a sign shows that eighteen fighters died here, their remains buried in a simple graveyard. Close to the path, Alberto points out more foxholes and recalls the bombs dropping, he just a small child spending countless hours in one of these crude holes in the ground.

Land reform under the peace agreement at last involved peasant farmers getting land from the large estate owners. The landowners were given the choice of holding their lands or surrendering them to the government in return for generous compensation. The local landowner here around La Mora was one of those agreeing to surrender his estate, which was then apportioned between the villagers. For Alberto, cruel fate. As he was only sixteen at the time, he was not old enough to receive an allocation of land. Today, Alberto rents the small plot he farms.

Sadly, this is not the end of Alberto's story. Alberto is married with a young child. Twice, he has left his family behind and illegally entered the USA, hoping to find work and the chance of a better life. Both attempts have ended in failure, the most recent only a few weeks before our meeting with him. After crossing the US border, he was caught by US Immigration, spent a month in jail and was then repatriated back to El Salvador. Unfortunately for him, this has been a costly mistake. He paid $8,000 to a trafficker to get him over the Mexican border into the United States.

How did he manage to contact a trafficker? It was a person known to him. A harsh lesson in the realities of life here, it was the daughter of the woman killed by the Army at the same time as his mother. He had borrowed the money to pay the trafficker, a loan which now has to be repaid and, irony upon irony, by being away from home, he missed planting his corn crop this year, his main source of income.

In a strange twist for a man wanting to find a better life in the United States, he recalls that after the war, when the La Mora village was being reconstructed in its new location, a *New York Times* journalist arrived in the village, eager to write about reconciliation. Alberto said that the journalist interviewed his brother and said, 'You know, the US spent $8 billion on this war.'

His brother replied, 'Yes, at the cost of 83,000 Salvadorean lives.'

Alberto's story seems pretty typical, and although things have improved for the rural poor since the Civil War, you can appreciate that it leaves behind a sad legacy.

Having reached the end point of our climb, we begin to make our way back down the side of the volcano to where the car is parked. It is an opportunity to chat to Benjamin about his own experiences of the Civil War, given that he is around the same age as Alberto. Living in the city, his story is less harrowing but nevertheless interesting. He recalls little disturbance to his life during his formative years save for the occasional sounds of gunfire and explosions in the distance. I asked if as a teenager he was worried about being conscripted into the Army. He said no, because he was still too young, and even in the war there was no formal conscription. However, he tells us of the experience of his older brother:

'Rather than a formal system of conscription, the Army when short of men would randomly pick up youths on the street or on buses. You were allowed one phone call to let your family know where you were, but as few people had telephones, this meant often young men disappeared for weeks, eventually being allowed to write to their families after they had undergone military training and had been posted to a remote part of the country. It also meant that kids from middle-class families were the ones who tended to be able to make the call and their family were usually able to argue that their son should be exempt from military service. This is exactly what happened to my brother when he was riding a bus in San Salvador. Soldiers boarded the bus and he was randomly selected and taken off to the nearby barracks. Although we did not have a telephone at home, he made his call to his best friend. By chance, his friend's father was an army colonel. My brother came home later that day, much relieved by his good fortune.'

We are back on the highway. It had been an interesting encounter. Benjamin tells us that Alberto will receive a small payment for his morning's work, and he was trying to get him some more assignments telling his story to visitors like ourselves. It will take a lot of storytelling to pay off his debts, but there was clearly empathy between two men of the same age but whose lives seemed destined to take them in different directions.

Benjamin has returned to San Salvador, so we have a day on our own to explore Suchitoto before we too make our way to the capital. When we arrived two days ago, the town plaza was full of the paraphernalia of the festival of the Day of the Dead, but today things are returning to normal, with the last remaining stalls and amusements being dismantled. We are looking for the Museum of Arts and Peace, which we find a couple of blocks away from our lodgings, housed in a former Dominican convent. The buildings look in particularly good order and have clearly received generous funding, we assume from overseas benefactors. This is borne out when we are greeted in the reception area by a young American volunteer worker. She tells us that this being a Monday, the museum is closed, but she kindly finds the key and allows us to wander around. The museum is but a small part of the old convent, and although it contains only a few artefacts, it has a good visual presentation about the indigenous Pipil people and the town's history as the original capital of this region when the Spanish first arrived.

Returning the key, we chat to Amber, the young American. She tells us that she has been here for two years and hopes to remain for a further year.

She says that the complex is more of a cultural centre than just a museum and was established to help the local community return to some form of normality after the horrors and dislocation caused by the Civil War. We remark that there indeed seems to be a normality in local life now that the conflict is becoming a distant memory. She says that El Salvador suffers from serious problems with gang culture, even here in the countryside. She knows a young man from the town who went to a nearby village and was murdered for straying into the territory of a gang active there. This gang culture, even more of an issue in the capital, San Salvador, is sadly another by-product of the Civil War. Many families moved to the United States to escape the war. Being at the lower end of society, they found themselves in the poorer areas of cities like Los Angeles, with problems of poverty, crime and drugs and notorious for the prevalence of gangs. Young men fell into this lifestyle. For some, life in the United States was tough, so after the end of the Civil War, many families returned home to El Salvador bringing the worst aspects of their life in the US with them.

We say our goodbyes to Amber and she says we must go next door to the old chapel, where there is an exhibition that will interest us, being dedicated to the Day of the Dead. It proves thought-provoking, as she has suggested. Local people have been invited to make exhibits showing what that festival means to them. The exhibits vary in size and complexity. Quite often, they feature photos of the deceased, often young relatives who perished in the Civil War. Some have personal effects and others provide reminders of the deceased persons' professions, like fishing and carpentry, or interests, like sport. It is quite poignant and interesting how death is managed within this culture in contrast to our own.

After three days in Suchitoto, we head for the capital, San Salvador. On our first morning, reunited with Benjamin, we drive out of the city and take the winding road up to El Boqueron, the volcano and national park which towers above the city. El Boqueron is "Big mouth" in Spanish, which in this case refers to the *caldera* of the volcano with its steep sides. We walk through the park to a lookout to view the bottom of the *caldera* far below. It is a pleasant walk through the wooded area up to the lookout, with lots of bird-spotting opportunities. By the time we drive back towards the city centre, it is approaching noon and Benjamin is ready for lunch. He wants us to try the local dish, the *pupusa*.

He enquires, 'Café or street food?' 'Café,' we reply in unison.

The *pupusa* is a corn dough (or rice) pancake with the choice of many and varied fillings. The café that Benjamin has selected is a large establishment that can seat dozens of people at busy times. Many *pupusa* outlets, and there are very many, can be found everywhere in El Salvador, most commonly street stalls or small family premises with just a few tables. This establishment though is producing on an industrial scale and although only midday is already busy with a queue of people placing orders and a small army of women in the kitchen preparing the food. We place an order for two *pupusas* each and move along the counter with a little chit in hand to where a cashier is taking the money. The man on the till has a distinctive accent that we immediately identify as Welsh, and in a short conversation, we discover he hails from a valley village near Swansea. The conversation is short because our order is already ready for us to collect further along the counter. We have selected *pupusas* with a variety of fillings. Rosemary, being vegetarian, has chosen cheese and beans, whilst I have one with pork and another with a vegetable filling, the main ingredient I determine being squash. The *pupusa* is traditionally also served with a pickled cabbage slaw called *curtido*. At a dollar a time on the street, one can certainly eat cheaply here. Even here in a café, our bill comes to just ten dollars.

Later, we drive downtown to the centre of the city. It might not be one of the great capital cities of the world but there is plenty to see here. The Centro Historico is contained within a relatively small area comprising three plazas.

First, we find ourselves in Plaza Morazan, named after General Francisco Morazan. Whilst Bolivar was freeing South America from Spanish rule and seeking to form a Federation of States of the Greater Colombia, much the same was happening in Central America. The chief architect was Morazan, a military strategist, liberal thinker, secularist and all-round political giant in his time, although he is little known outside of the Central American countries. In the decade of the 1830s, he was variously head of state in Honduras, the country of his birth, Costa Rica and El Salvador and also President of the short-lived Federal Republic of Central America. After the Federation collapsed, he went into exile in Peru but later returned to Central America where not unlike Bolivar his reputation was being derided by his conservative enemies. The main reason for his desire to return from his exile was that the British were showing what he regarded as an unwelcome interest in the region. Another imperialist state getting involved in the affairs of the Central American countries so soon after they had thrown off the yoke of Spanish colonialism.

His return was not welcomed by all, even those once loyal to him, and ultimately in 1842 he met an untimely death in front of a firing squad in Costa Rica. The general's statue is the centrepiece of the square bearing his name. The plaza itself is an unpretentious place save for the National Theatre building along one side. Built in 1911 in French Renaissance style, it is suitably impressive as the cultural centre of the city.

A short walk finds us in Plaza Libertad. It is a large open area dotted with trees to offer shade, yet with ample space for social gatherings. A favourite spot it seems for musicians to gather to chat and play. Dozens of mainly middle-aged and elderly men, most with a guitar, sit around, some strumming, most happy to be in male company chewing the cud. In the centre of the plaza, a statue celebrating independence from Spain in 1811 and suitably called Monument to the Heroes. Its pinnacle, the Angel of Liberty.

At the far end of the plaza, a surprisingly modern-looking edifice. Benjamin is anxious to show us and we find the unobtrusive entrance in a side street; this is Iglesia El Rosario. A controversially modern construction in the heart of the historical centre of the city, it is nevertheless impressive. It has been compared with an aircraft hangar rather than a church, and certainly it has an unusually huge uncluttered air, being without supporting pillars. A very contemporary feel, the church building was opened in 1971; the main feature is not those modern building materials used in its construction but the stained glass windows that offer incredible visual challenges to the visitor.

From here, we beat a retreat back across the square past the musicians and head towards the nearby Plaza Barrios. The centrepiece is the statue of a man on horseback, former President General Gerardo Barrios. He actually fought with Morazan and had similar liberal views when twenty years later he too became president. Benjamin wants to take us to the cathedral but first I want to take a look inside another building lining the square, the Palacio Nacional. No longer used as a presidential palace, it houses the National Archive, although as we discover, most of the larger first-floor rooms are empty save for occasional pieces of old furniture. My particular interest is in viewing its proximity to the Catedral Metropolitana. From a first-floor window I can see that the cathedral is a small matter of yards away across the street. Reputedly, it was from here at Archbishop Romero's funeral in 1980 that police marksmen shot dead twenty-four mourners, whilst another forty-four people died when they were trampled by the fleeing crowd running from the mayhem. It is eerily quiet away from the street noise, and being the only visitors on this hot afternoon, I take the opportunity to contemplate those events.

To complete this particular story, we leave the Palacio National and walk across the street to the cathedral. A suitably impressive structure in its own right, in the crypt lay the mortal remains of Saint Oscar. It is a grand yet simple elegant bronze sculpture that depicts Romero as if he were sleeping, guarded by the four evangelists, a red jewel representing his heart.

We are leaving San Salvador behind and heading west out of the city. Benjamin is keen to show us how being on a fault line influences life here, so we take a slight detour to a *mirador* with views over a large lava field below. He explains that El Salvador is the victim of frequent earthquakes. Twenty-three of its many volcanoes are active, the most recent violent activity occurring as recently as 2013. Two days later, this conversation takes on a new significance.

Next stop is Joya de Ceran. I have mentioned our burgeoning interest in Mayan culture as we have travelled through Central America, and once again, far distant from the epicentre of Mayan civilisation, we come across remains of a Mayan village. Sometimes called the "Pompeii of the Americas" because around AD 600, this site became the victim of a volcanic explosion from the nearby Loma Caldera, leading to the village being engulfed in ash. This was a village of farmers and it seems likely that the residents had some warning of the impending disaster and were able to evacuate the village, given that no human remains have been found on the site.

Benjamin explains that the site has been discovered relatively recently, in 1976, when a bulldozer driver clearing the site for a new grain storage facility uncovered artefacts. The name is not that of the village, as no record remains of what it was called, but it is "Jewel of Ceran", Ceran being the family name of the modern-day landowner. The important element of Joya de Ceran is that the volcanic ash preserved intact many signs of the day-to-day lives of simple farmers living and working here over 1,000 years ago. As a consequence, we know what they grew in their fields and gardens and the implements they used. Excavation continues, but under rough canvas covers, we are able to view the twelve structures that have been uncovered to date. Although this is a UNESCO World Heritage site, today we are the only visitors apart from a group of noisy Spanish students on a study tour.

Time to move on. This is to be a long and exhausting day.

With lunchtime approaching, it is no surprise when Benjamin takes a turn off the main highway and shortly we find ourselves parked outside a local restaurant. In fairness, the food is generously portioned and we have stunning views down to Lake Coatepeque below. Having eaten my fill, I spot a colourful gecko popping its head above a nearby parapet and spend the remainder of the lunch break hanging precariously over the edge in order to obtain the perfect photograph. Meanwhile, Benjamin, undeterred, demolishes another pile of tacos.

Next stop is the Cerro Verde, also known as the Volcanoes National Park, where there are more stunning views to be had; this time across to three volcanoes: Santa Ana, Izalco and Cerro Verde. Given we have met few tourists during our time in El Salvador, the car park is surprisingly full with groups of school kids and assorted other hikers and tourists. Benjamin has arranged for us to take a walk through the forest and we are escorted by two teenage boys from the local village. The idea is to encourage local people to embrace tourism by offering these kids some employment, albeit limited. They don't speak any English, but one of them seems quite knowledgeable, pointing out trees and plants, although disappointingly there are no birds to be seen. The walk takes us around the escarpment of the Cerro Verde *caldera*. By the time we get back to the car park, things have quietened down, as it is late afternoon, and we still have miles ahead to travel.

Benjamin is anxious for us to make one further stop, in the town of Sonsonate. The town has little of note and our travel guide says as much, adding that it is on a drug-running route and has an abnormally high murder rate, even by Salvadorian standards, due to the activity of organised gangs. However, Benjamin must have noted our interest in Farabundo Martí, so he wants to show us something that he thinks will interest us.

By the early twentieth century, El Salvador became known as the Coffee Republic and on the back of this, just fourteen families had become hugely rich, whilst the vast majority of the population were peasants fed by the patron on a breakfast of two tortillas and two spoonfuls of beans before they began their long working day in the fields and paid not a wage but in scrip tokens, only redeemable in stores owned by the landowner.

In the 1920s, the peasantry began to try and improve their working conditions, but they were largely unorganised until the formation of a Communist party led by Farabundo Martí. Unfortunately for the protagonists, this coincided with the global economic depression and a fall in coffee prices, making the landowners even more resistant to change. This culminated in an organised uprising in January 1932. The peasants lacked weaponry and although they briefly took control of towns in this region, the insurrection was treated harshly by government forces. Some 25,000 mainly indigenous people were believed to have been killed. Rebel leaders were subject to public hangings in town centres, with local women and children forced to watch. Here, in Sonsonate, Benjamin shows us a memorial stone in the place where several hundred were mown down by machine gunfire.

Darkness has fallen by the time we reach our next destination, Conception de Ataco. We check into our accommodation, a large and solid hacienda in the centre of the town.

Benjamin is staying locally with a friend, so given the late hour he leaves us to find his overnight accommodation whilst we go in search of food. Our lodging, the Casa de Graciela, is situated adjacent to the central plaza. The daily activity around the square is ending, stallholders packing up their wares. A quick recce establishes that apart from the inevitable large church, the square is lined with several bars and small restaurants, and we choose an eatery on one corner of the square, noticeable only after we have entered the front door by the lack of other punters. We are just backing gingerly out of the door when the proprietor, a middle-aged lady, appears. She doesn't speak any English and our once reasonably fluent Spanish has deserted us, but we take a seat at a small table and manage to order some food with views alfresco, overlooking the now empty and dimly lit square.

It has been a hectic day, but back at our lodgings hopes of a restful night are soon shattered. Our room with metre-thick walls seems immune from external distractions, but the only window, set high on a wall facing out to the road, is ill-fitting and as we discover, inaccessible. We are soon aware that the clock of the church just across the street chimes loudly on the hour and half hour, day and night. If that is not enough disturbance, as dawn breaks the next morning, the priest, on an amplifier set at full volume, summons the locals to early-morning mass. To add to the irritation, shortly after 7am, a loudspeaker van tours the square blasting out what we assume to be political propaganda. We later discover that it is in fact the daily purveyor of local news: births, deaths and any other local items of news and impending events.

The hacienda is a typical L-shape, set around two sides of a garden courtyard, and with the sun shining brightly, we take breakfast here, al fresco. After breakfast, whilst we are still bleary-eyed from our interrupted night, Benjamin arrives to take us on a tour along the Ruta de las Flores. As the name implies, these 20 miles of road linking a series of small towns have hedgerows festooned with flowers. However, as we soon discover, not at the time of our visit. A little disappointed, it has to be said, we nevertheless enjoy calling at each of the towns along the route.

Our first stop is Apaneca. A quiet place, with adobe houses and a neat whitewashed church. We find ourselves in a small craft shop. The proprietor clearly has a cat fixation, a trait shared with our daughter-in-law for whom we purchase a stuffed moggy toy and a number of colourful purses also by way of presents for various loved ones at home.

Onward to Juayua. More typical of towns around Central America, with everything of note in or around the central plaza. In this case, the centre is a pleasant, well-tended park, but the feature of the town is to be found in the church. Here we find a sculpture of the Black Jesus.

The odd thing is that this icon, found behind the church altar and dating back to colonial times, is unlikely to represent the indigenous population yet was created when few if any of African descent had reached this area. A statue by the same sixteenth-century artist is believed to exist in Guatemala.

The next town along the route is Nahuizalco. Here is a very lively market, and Benjamin decides it is time to do some shopping. His purchases include plentiful amounts of fruit and vegetables, plus strange-looking shellfish resembling oysters that he intends to take home for his supper when he leaves us in two days' time. We look at each other rather quizzically, wondering about the pervading smell in the vehicle in the meantime.

On to Salcoatitan. The town is notable for its mosaics; however, the first thing of note on entering the town is the giant *ceiba* tree. Subject of local legend and reckoned to be some 400 years old. In the town, mosaics decorate the walls of the park, which we stroll across on our way to view what Benjamin tells us is the oldest surviving still occupied house in the whole of El Salvador.

Finally, by late afternoon, we are back in Ataco, where Benjamin takes us on a walking tour. Highlight is the town's famous murals. Although there is a local tradition of painting murals, these are more contemporary. I am told that they are an early twenty-first century phenomenon. A local lady opened an artisan shop in the town and to attract customers painted the external wall of her shop. This proved an inspiration for other locals and ultimately attracted artists from far and wide. One notable mural is *Memita,* painted by two local brothers without any previous experience as artists. The striking painting is of an old lady drinking coffee. Many Salvadoreans believe it captures the true essence of the mother figure in Salvador society. Themes vary; political subjects are discouraged but some are evident. Overall, the murals make this humble rural town very appealing.

Next day and the morning begins in spectacular fashion. We are in our room completing our morning ablutions when everything moves. We rush from the room into the courtyard, where the staff have already gathered. It is an earthquake. Later that morning, tuning into the car radio, Benjamin confirms that it was a modest 4.2 on the Richter scale. Sufficient though for us to appreciate how life is on the San Andreas Fault, where this is a regular occurrence and often with much more serious consequences.

Given our interest in the Maya, Benjamin has amended our planned itinerary and we head to Tazumal, first passing through Ahuachapan, a large provincial town of little note. Tazumal proves to be modest in size compared, say, with Copan or Chichén Itzá, although it does appear to have had direct links with these great Mayan cities. An interesting side story is that the site was excavated in the 1940s by Stanley Harding Boggs, an American archaeologist. Boggs, a Harvard graduate, had an unusual background, being a close relative of not only one but two US presidents, Harding and Ford, through his maternal lineage.

The site at Tazumal itself comprises two large pyramid structures, suggesting this was a largely ceremonial site. It may well have been surrounded by a town, but further excavation beyond the confines of the existing site looks unlikely, as a modern town now stands, surrounding right up to the very boundaries of the historic site.

We move on to Santa Ana, the second city of El Salvador. We don't have much luck viewing the two major buildings located in the central plaza. The impressive Catedral de Santa Ana with its white façade and twin spires is thought to be the only building in the whole of Central America in the Gothic style. Our viewing however is limited by the Mass taking place, providing us with only a brief glimpse of the interior.

Just along the street is another impressive building, the Santa Ana National Theatre, a building seeming too grand for such a modest provincial city built in the early twentieth century, when Santa Ana was hailed as the "Coffee Capital of the World". Not our lucky day, as our efforts to view inside are thwarted by virtue of a rehearsal taking place on stage. We encourage Benjamin to get us access with promises that we will be quiet and not disturb the performers, but the bulky security man on the door remains unmoved by our pleading. After we have strolled in the plaza and taken our photographs, Benjamin decides that it is time to drive back towards Ataco and find what will be for him an extraordinarily late lunch.

It will be our second visit to the El Jardin de Celeste. Maybe rustic by European standards, it is a large restaurant but very busy on both of our visits, no doubt due to an extensive menu and excellent cuisine. On both of our visits, we are served by Luis, a young man around thirty years of age, and despite his limited English and our very limited Spanish we have struck up a conversation with him when ordering and between courses. Replete but with no time for a rest, we are heading for our final visit of the day to the El Carmen Coffee Estate.

It is late afternoon by the time we reach El Carmen, and it seems like we have arrived on the wrong day or maybe because of the late hour just too late, as the site appears deserted. Nobody in sight, Benjamin wanders off to see if he can rouse anyone in the factory, leaving us at the gate. He returns, suggesting that we take a walk around. There are coffee beans everywhere, large open pens covered in beans of various hues drying in the sun. It seems like he is playing for time, but suddenly things begin to happen. Despite the hour, an old open-backed truck arrives and two men alight and begin to unload. They look scrawny but belie their stature, heaving 50-kilo sacks of beans onto their backs and depositing the contents into a large hopper. Then next to our vantage point watching the unloading, ancient machinery revs up and a production line begins on its noisy motion, carrying beans on their way into the factory proper. On the drying beds, workers appear with rakes, beginning the tortuous and nightly process of creating piles of beans and covering them in a tarpaulin until the same process is reversed the following morning. We follow the production process, essentially one of washing, drying and grading through to the packing into sacks for export, the beans still green, not roasted until they reach the customer, the main customer we learn being Starbucks.

At the end of the mill tour, we meet José, a rather charming and stunningly handsome barista. He is going to prepare some samples of the Ataco Gourmet coffee produced for the domestic market. José uses the traditional *chorreador* dripper process, which he says is better than any of the more modern methods. This simple method involves hanging a small cloth bag or *bolsita* on a wooden frame. The coffee grains are placed in the bag and hot water slowly poured into the bag, seeping through to the cup placed below. The result, it has to be said, is an excellent brew. José offers several different blends for our delectation, explaining the merits of each, including the nose, as with a fine wine. This is a fourth-generation family business and they clearly know all about producing a good coffee.

Tomorrow is our last day in El Salvador with a late-evening flight. The travel company have arranged for a driver to transfer us to the airport but we, as a special favour, ask Benjamin if he can take us, better utilising our last day with a guided tour, taking a significantly more circuitous route to the airport. An opportunity to see more of the country before we depart. Benjamin is amenable, and this arrangement is subsequently agreed with his boss. However, Benjamin asks us for a favour in return. Can he bring his son, Benjamin Junior, with him? We readily agree.

The plan is for us to spend the morning in Ataco. Benjamin has travelled back to San Salvador to collect his son and will meet us at noon. We will then take a trip down to the coast and eventually back to the airport.

Ataco on a Saturday morning is transformed. The square is full of vendors with their market stalls, and people from the surrounding villages are disgorging from the colourful buses and the pick-up trucks so prevalent in Central America. Our attention is drawn to a large crowd on the steps of the church. By chance, here we spot Luis, the young waiter that we chatted with at the El Jardin de Celeste restaurant. He explains that this is a graduation ceremony for children leaving primary school. He introduces us to his wife, Jennifer, and younger daughter who although too young to be participating is also dressed up in her best party frock. When the children emerge from the church, the boys and girls have been put together, emerging in pairs hand in hand. The boys all have smart dark suits, white shirts and ties; the girls of course are in pretty dresses. The crowd are mainly proud parents and some onlookers like ourselves. When Luis' son emerges, he looks suitably embarrassed as would any self-respecting ten-year-old boy holding a girl's hand, and that embarrassment is only to be prolonged whilst photographs are taken, before the chance to escape into the welcoming arms of his father. The charm of Ataco is that although we must stand out in the crowd as strangers, no one bothers or pesters us as we spend the morning strolling in the streets, making some last-minute purchases from Tierra Madre, one of the many artisan shops.

Around noon, Benjamin arrives and introduces us to Benjamin Junior, his thirteen-year-old and very well-behaved son. We take the road south, heading down to the Pacific Coast at the town of Acajutla. From here, we follow the coastline, stopping along the way to enjoy the views from some high cliffs, looking down on the ocean far below. At the town of La Libertad, we stop and take a walk on the pier, past fishermen selling their freshly caught catch of the day. Beyond the town, we stop for late lunch at an upscale restaurant, again with magnificent views over the ocean. From here to the airport and farewells.

El Salvador has been our final call on this particular trip and one that does not disappoint. It has been an epic journey with a fitting end. Before arriving in El Salvador, Rosie and I had travelled from London to Fiji via Abu Dhabi and Sydney. After a few days' rest, we had embarked upon a small expedition ship, taking a month crossing the Pacific Ocean, calling at some rarely visited islands like Wallis and Futuna, the Cook Islands, Tahiti, the Tuamotus, Pitcairn of *Mutiny on the Bounty* fame and land of the Moais, Easter Island. We had eventually reached South America, taking time out in Valparaíso, Chile, before catching a plane from Santiago to Bogota in Colombia. We have now visited every country on the American continents, but our travels are not over.

At the airport, we say our goodbyes to Benjamin and Benjamin Junior with genuine heavy hearts.

Epilogue

It is a year since our visit to Colombia and here we are again. Once again following in the footsteps of Bolivar. Travelling in a small cruise ship, we have reached the coastal town of Santa Marta. After that narrow escape in Bogota assisted by his mistress, Bolivar eventually arrives in Santa Marta, where he seeks sanctuary. By now, he is very sick, it is said with tuberculosis, although some claim as a result of poisoning by his enemies in Bogota.

We are in Bolivar Plaza with the customary statue of the great man astride his horse. On arriving in Santa Marta, Bolivar is given shelter in the old Customs House, a fine building we discover nearby in the centre of the town, he having declined the invitation of wealthy local merchant Joaquim de Mier to spend time at his hacienda. However, the Customs House with its central location proves uncomfortably noisy for a sick man, and Bolivar gracefully reconsiders and accepts that offer of sanctuary at Quinta de San Pedro Alejandrino.

After a stroll around the old town, visiting the cathedral and the Parque de los Novios, we travel a short distance from the city to Quinta de San Pedro Alejandrino, which is now a museum and gardens. The huge surrounding sugarcane estate from Bolivar's time no longer exists. However, the hacienda and many of the estate buildings are still standing and well preserved. It is here that after a few days enjoying the grounds, Bolivar takes to his bed and on 17th December 1830, he dies. Knowing the end is close, he dictates an address to the people of Colombia: 'My wishes are for the happiness of the people. If my death should unite them I will go to my tomb content.' The museum features many artefacts from this time, including his deathbed and on an outside wall an inscription with the full text of that final declaration to his people.

Today in the beautifully maintained gardens, a mausoleum dedicated to The Liberator, although his body is not here. Briefly interred in the cathedral back in Santa Marta, his mortal remains were later transferred to his home city of Caracas in Venezuela.

Next day and our ship has taken us along the coast to our final stop in Colombia, to one of the best-preserved colonial cities in the New World, Cartagena de Indias. Having meandered through the streets of the old city on previous visits, we decide to join an organised walking tour with a guide.

We begin in Getsemani. A former working-class area adjacent to but outside the city walls, it has to a degree become gentrified. Refurbished buildings formerly occupied by artisan workers are now boutique hotels, cafés and restaurants. The eclectic mix of old and new, however, means the area still maintains the vibrancy of its former days. The largely modest but colourfully painted *casas bajas*, single-storey buildings, narrow alleyways opening into small plazas dotted with bars and cafés make this an attractive addition to the sights of the old city that we have seen on previous visits to Cartagena.

From here, we enter the old city and pass the Teatro Heredia, shop in Plaza Merced, walk through the Plaza Santo Domingo with its Botero sculpture *La Gorda Gertrudis,* the reclining figure in bronze of a fat lady, and at the main entrance to the city the Plaza de los Coches, site of the one-time slave market, we admire the statue of the city founder Pedro de Heredia.

We find ourselves in the Plaza San Pedro, named in tribute to the seventeenth-century monk who devoted his life to helping the oppressed black slaves. A feature of the plaza is the series of elaborate metal sculptures depicting local life. The chess players, the barber, lady carrying a basket of fruit and more.

It is the end of our walking tour of Cartagena and from here we make our way through one of the city gates to our awaiting bus. I see one final photo opportunity. Photo taken, I look up and see that I am the last one to board the bus. In my haste, I overlook a low chain fence. I fall headlong. I lie there face down. I open my eyes, not wanting to move until I have come to my senses. All I can see is a pool of blood growing by the second from wounds to my nose and chin. I am quickly lifted up and taken to the bus. In minutes, a paramedic arrives and patches up my abrasions.

I am sitting in the waiting room of a local private medical clinic. Things have moved along quickly. The facial injuries are covered by dressings but more seriously, X-rays confirm something not immediately apparent at the time of my fall: a broken arm. I am waiting for the doctor to confirm that I am fit to travel home. I look around. All the other patients in the waiting area are heavily pregnant women. This is absurd, laughable. I literally have to pinch myself.

I am led into the treatment room where the doctor confers via an app with the orthopaedic surgeon in a nearby hospital and confirms that I can travel home. The nurse begins to bandage my arm. Rosie, who is in the room, is alarmed and through our interpreter, determines they intend to put my arm in plaster. With a plaster, I will not be able to fly. We manage to express our concern and it is agreed that the arm will merely be bandaged and supported with a sling. Panic over.

It is fifteen years since I retired and I am now seventy-five years old. Over those years, without ever setting out to achieve this as a goal, Rosie and I have visited every country in Central and South America as well as the United States, Canada and most of the islands of the Caribbean, the Americas.

In this moment, a decision: I am going to make this the last page of my book, although hopefully not my last chapter.

As in life, it is left to Rosie to have the final word: 'Maybe one trip too many!'

For exclusive discounts on Matador titles,
sign up to our occasional newsletter at
troubador.co.uk/bookshop